RUNAWAYS

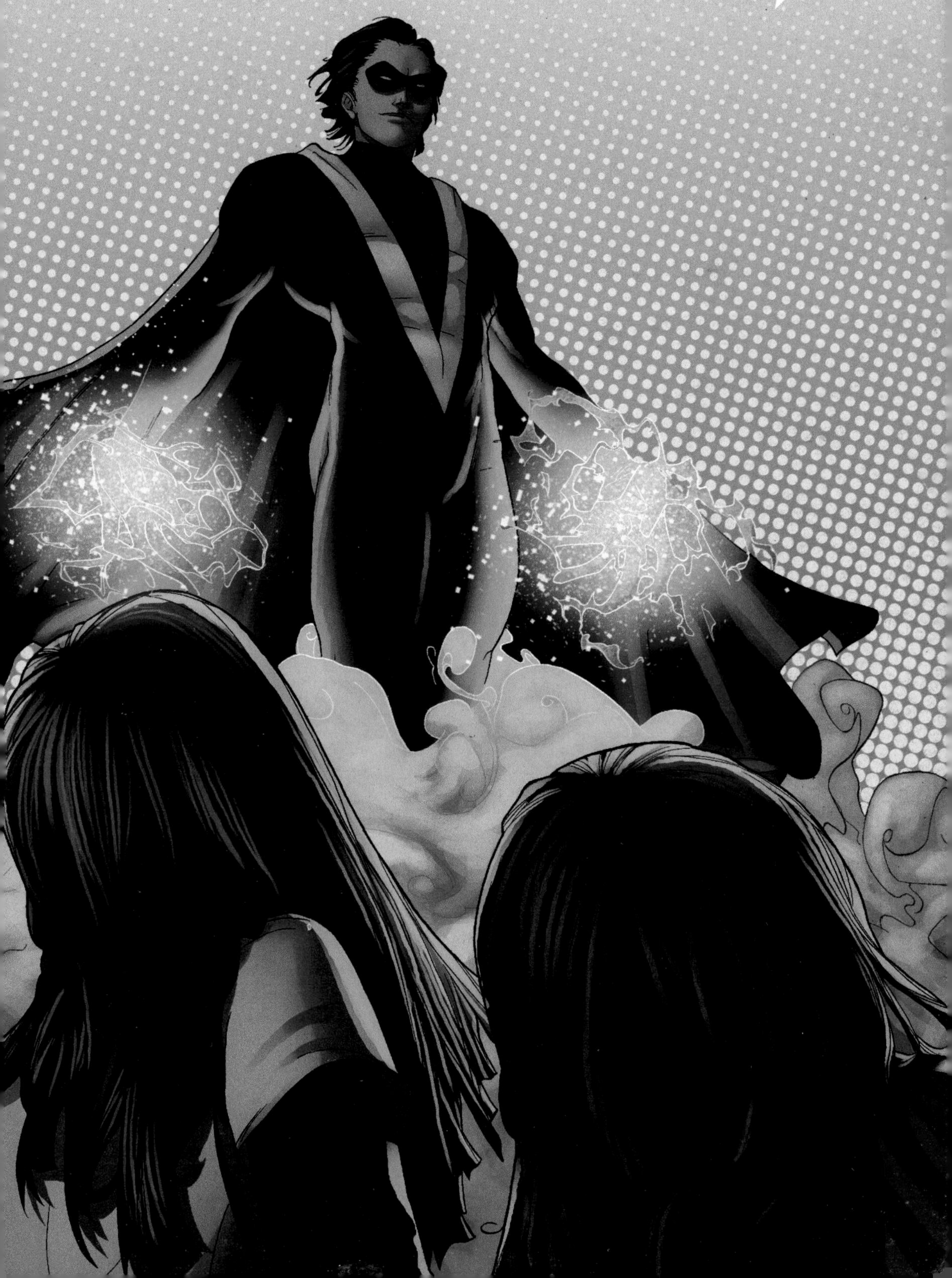

RUNAWAYS

WRITER: **BRIAN K. VAUGHAN**

PENCILS: **ADRIAN ALPHONA**

INKS: **CRAIG YEUNG**

COLORS: **CHRISTINA STRAIN**

LETTERS: **VC's RANDY GENTILE** & **DAVE SHARPE**

COVER ART: **JO CHEN**

EDITORS: **MACKENZIE CADENHEAD** & **C.B. CEBULSKI**

RUNAWAYS CREATED BY **BRIAN K. VAUGHAN** & **ADRIAN ALPHONA**

RUNAWAYS VOL. 4: TRUE BELIEVERS. Contains material originally published in magazine form as RUNAWAYS #1-6. Second edition. First printing 2017. ISBN# 978-1-302-90869-0. Published by MARVEL WORLDWIDE, INC., a subsidiary of MARVEL ENTERTAINMENT, LLC. OFFICE OF PUBLICATION: 135 West 50th Street, New York, NY 10020. Copyright © 2017 MARVEL No similarity between any of the names, characters, persons, and/or institutions in this magazine with those of any living or dead person or institution is intended, and any such similarity which may exist is purely coincidental. **Printed in the U.S.A.** DAN BUCKLEY, President, Marvel Entertainment; JOE QUESADA, Chief Creative Officer; TOM BREVOORT, SVP of Publishing; DAVID BOGART, SVP of Business Affairs & Operations, Publishing & Partnership; C.B. CEBULSKI, VP of Brand Management & Development, Asia; DAVID GABRIEL, SVP of Sales & Marketing, Publishing; JEFF YOUNGQUIST, VP of Production & Special Projects; DAN CARR, Executive Director of Publishing Technology; ALEX MORALES, Director of Publishing Operations; SUSAN CRESPI, Production Manager; STAN LEE, Chairman Emeritus. For information regarding advertising in Marvel Comics or on Marvel.com, please contact Vit DeBellis, Integrated Sales Manager, at vdebellis@marvel.com. For Marvel subscription inquiries, please call 888-511-5480. **Manufactured between 4/7/2017 and 5/8/2017 by QUAD/GRAPHICS WASECA, WASECA, MN, USA.**

10 9 8 7 6 5 4 3 2 1

COLLECTION EDITOR: JENNIFER GRÜNWALD
ASSISTANT EDITOR: CAITLIN O'CONNELL
ASSOCIATE MANAGING EDITOR: KATERI WOODY
EDITOR, SPECIAL PROJECTS: MARK D. BEAZLEY
VP PRODUCTION & SPECIAL PROJECTS: JEFF YOUNGQUIST
SVP PRINT, SALES & MARKETING: DAVID GABRIEL

EDITOR IN CHIEF: AXEL ALONSO
CHIEF CREATIVE OFFICER: JOE QUESADA
PRESIDENT: DAN BUCKLEY
EXECUTIVE PRODUCER: ALAN FINE

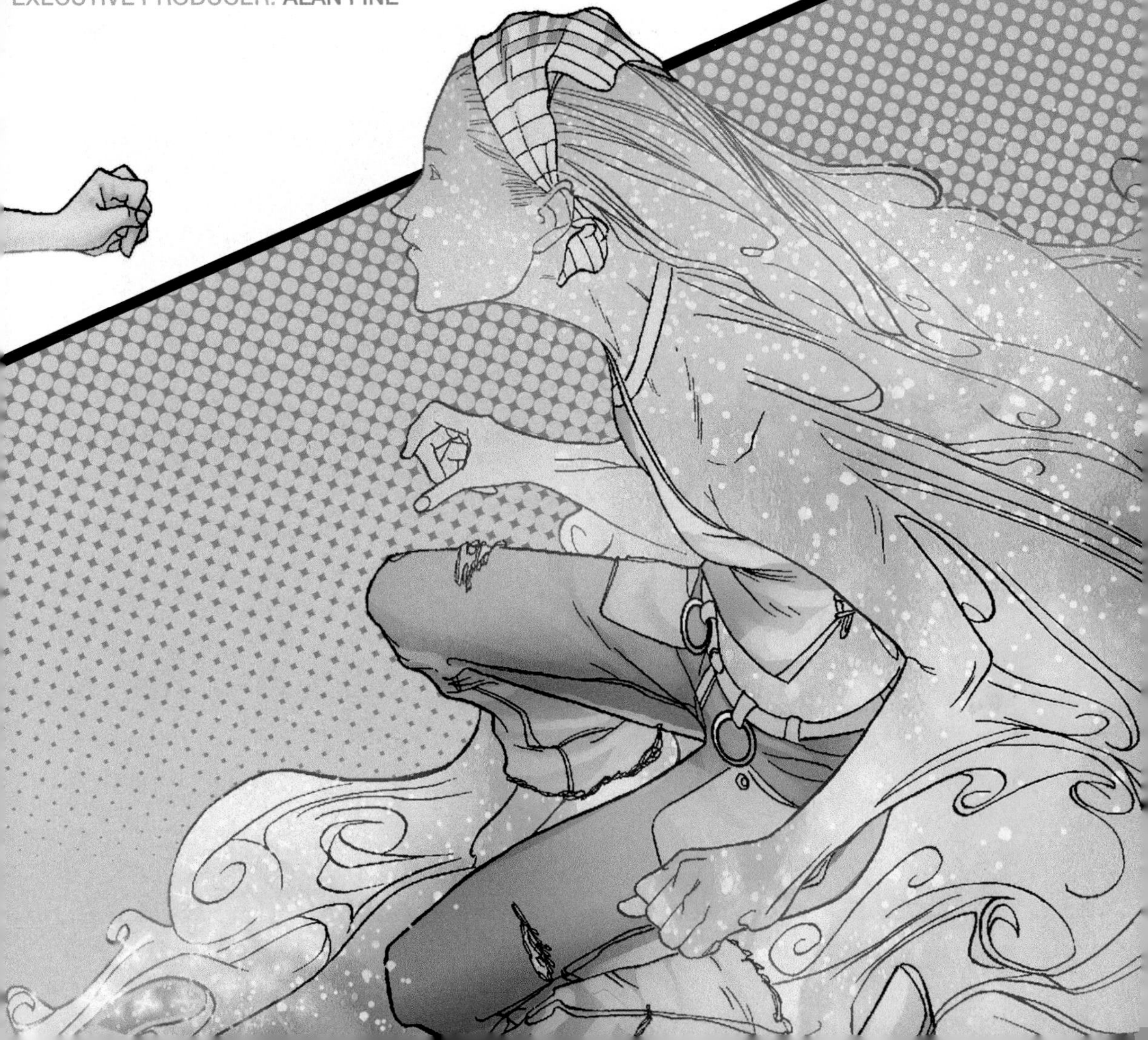

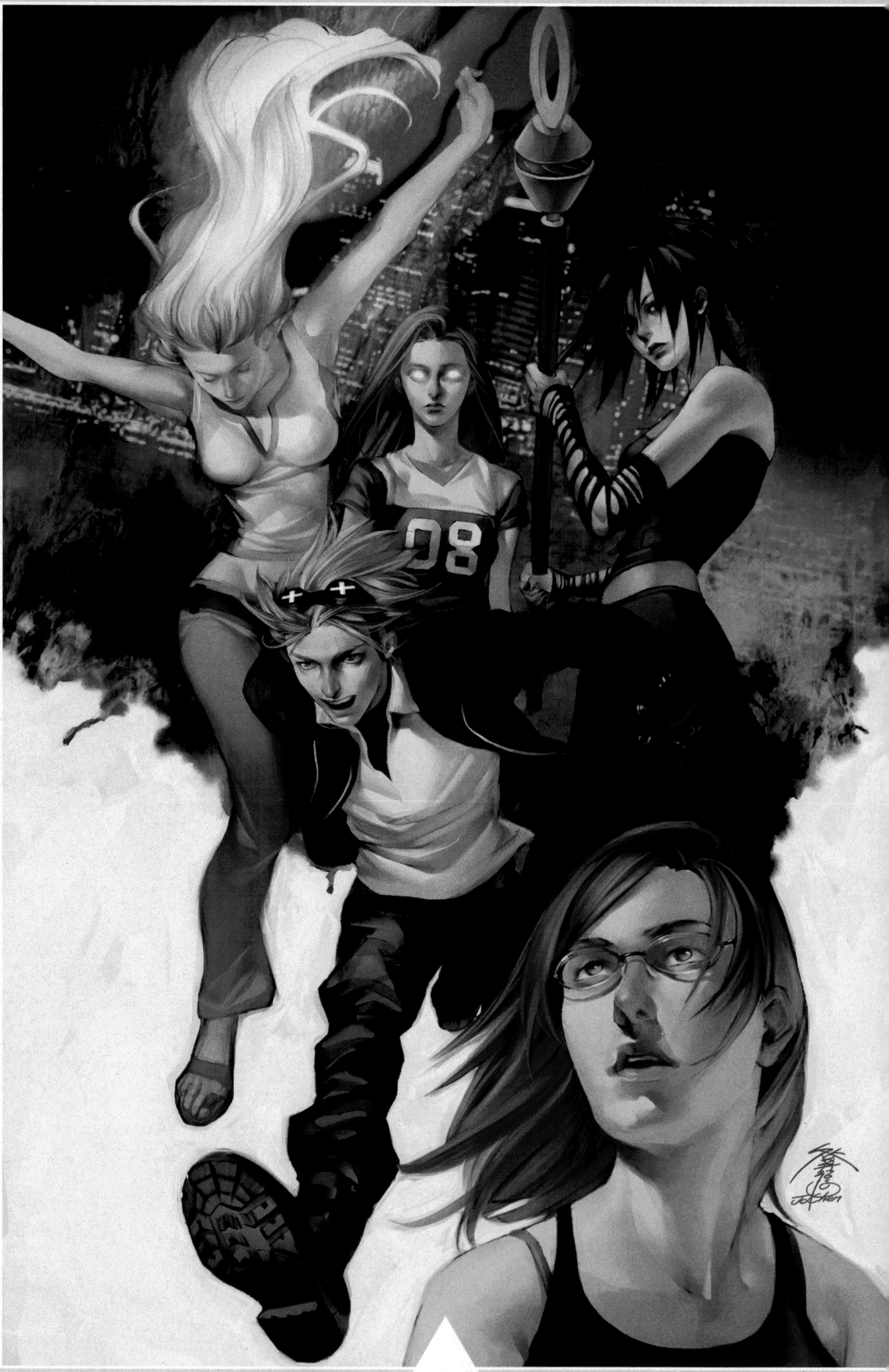
08

1

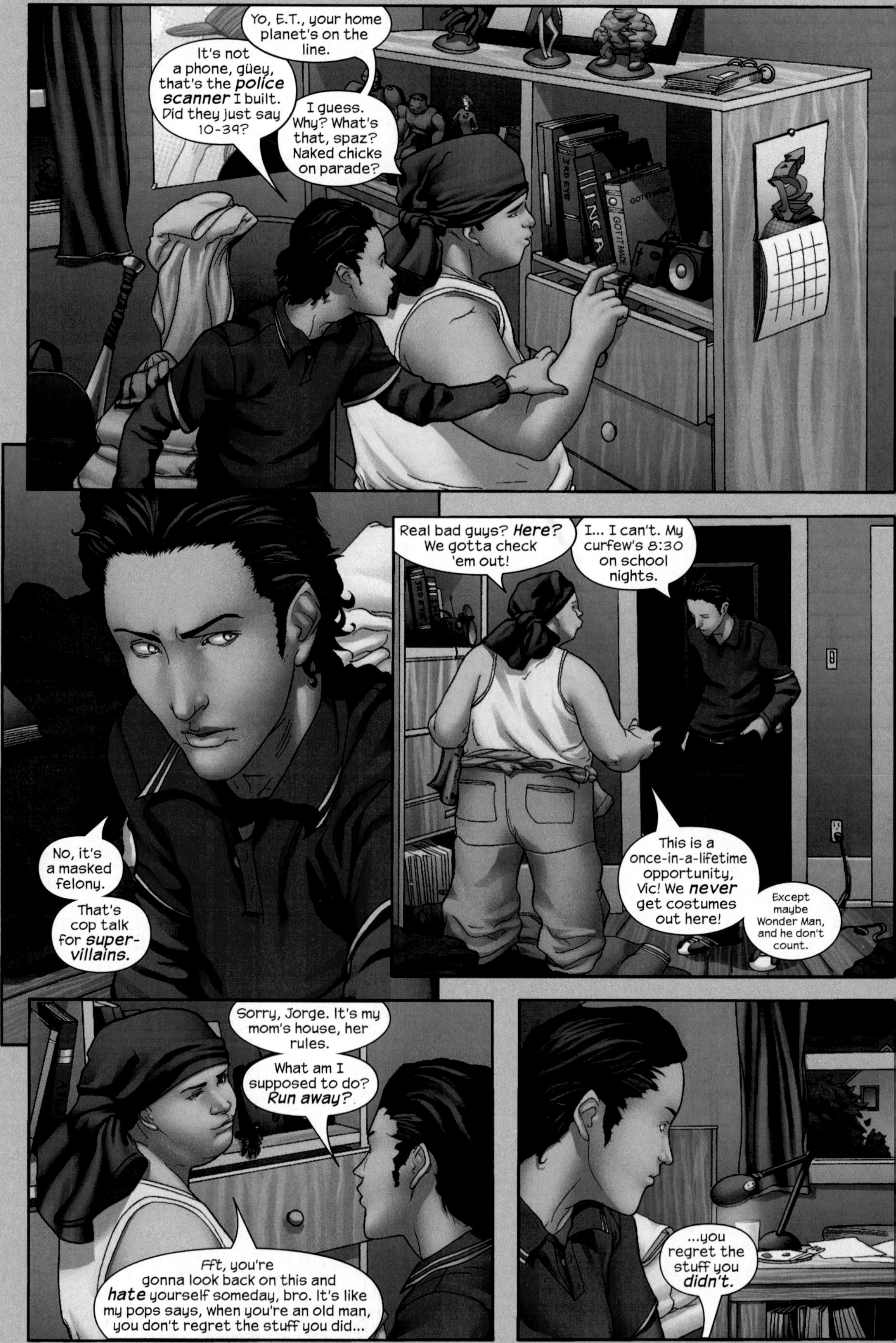
Yo, E.T., your home planet's on the line.
It's not a phone, güey, that's the police scanner I built. Did they just say 10-39?
I guess. Why? What's that, spaz? Naked chicks on parade?
No, it's a masked felony.
That's cop talk for super-villains.
Real bad guys? Here? We gotta check 'em out!
I... I can't. My curfew's 8:30 on school nights.
This is a once-in-a-lifetime opportunity, Vic! We never get costumes out here!
Except maybe Wonder Man, and he don't count.
Sorry, Jorge. It's my mom's house, her rules.
What am I supposed to do? Run away?
Fft, you're gonna look back on this and hate yourself someday, bro. It's like my pops says, when you're an old man, you don't regret the stuff you did...
...you regret the stuff you didn't.

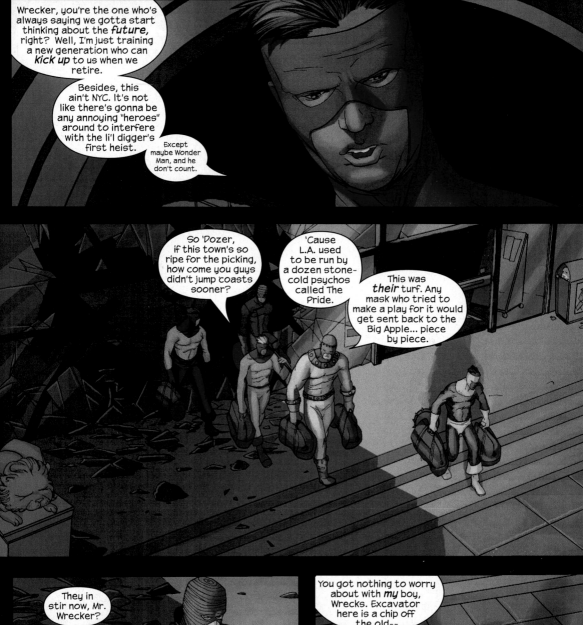

Wrecker, you're the one who's always saying we gotta start thinking about the *future*, right? Well, I'm just training a new generation who can *kick up* to us when we retire.

Besides, this ain't NYC. It's not like there's gonna be any annoying "heroes" around to interfere with the li'l digger's first heist.

Except maybe Wonder Man, and he don't count.

So 'Dozer, if this town's so ripe for the picking, how come you guys didn't jump coasts sooner?

'Cause L.A. used to be run by a dozen stone-cold psychos called The Pride.

This was *their* turf. Any mask who tried to make a play for it would get sent back to the Big Apple... piece by piece.

They in stir now, Mr. Wrecker?

No, they're not "in stir", you annoying piece of...

The Pride is *dead*, okay? They were betrayed by their spoiled children, in what should have been a valuable *lesson* to every hood who's got an "accident" or two out there.

You got nothing to worry about with *my* boy, Wrecks. Excavator here is a chip off the old--

Hey, Village People!

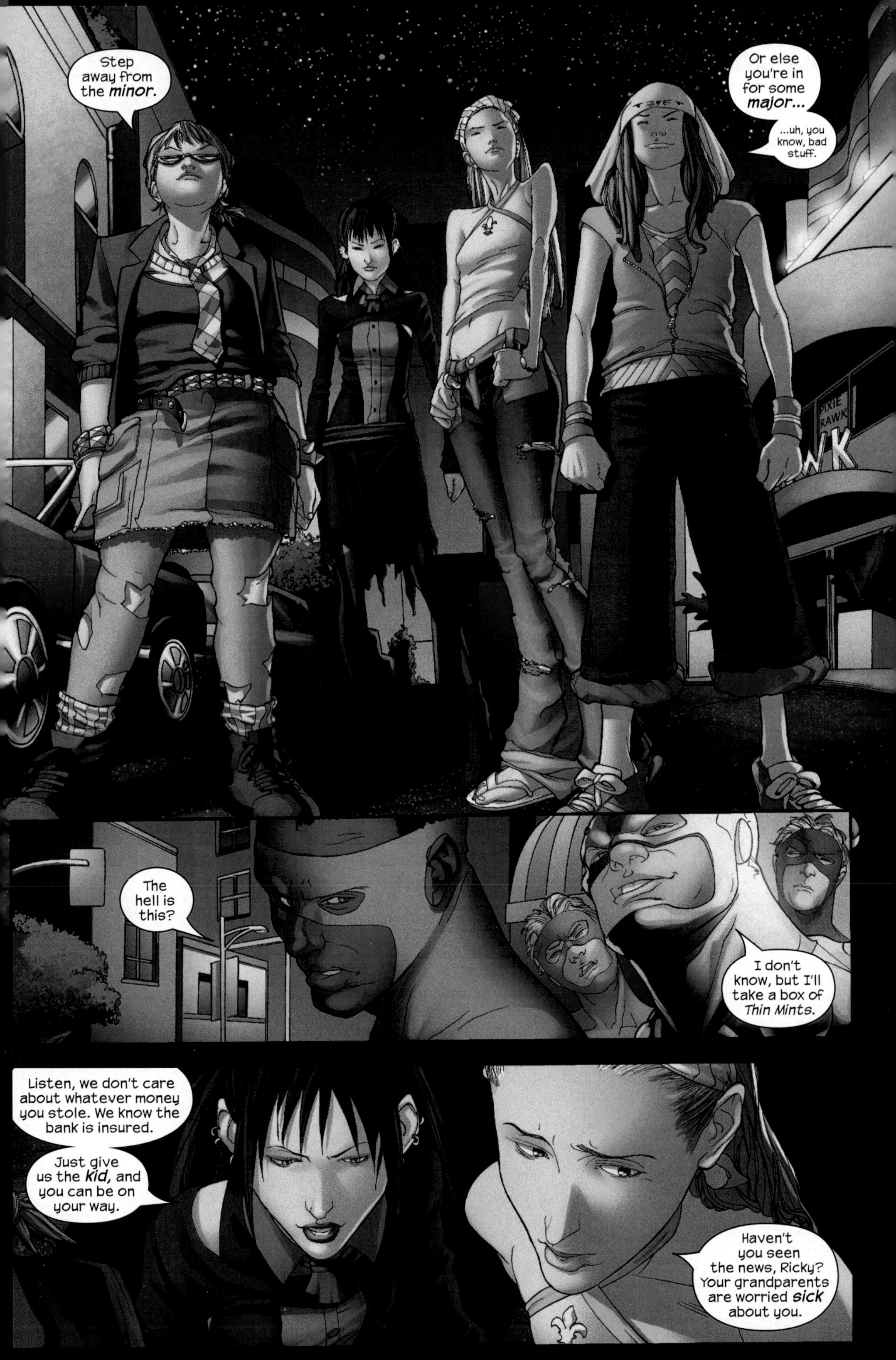
Step away from the *minor.*
Or else you're in for some *major...*
...uh, you know, bad stuff.
PIXIE RAWK
WK
The hell is this?
I don't know, but I'll take a box of *Thin Mints.*
Listen, we don't care about whatever money you stole. We know the bank is insured.
Just give us the *kid,* and you can be on your way.
Haven't you seen the news, Ricky? Your grandparents are worried *sick* about you.

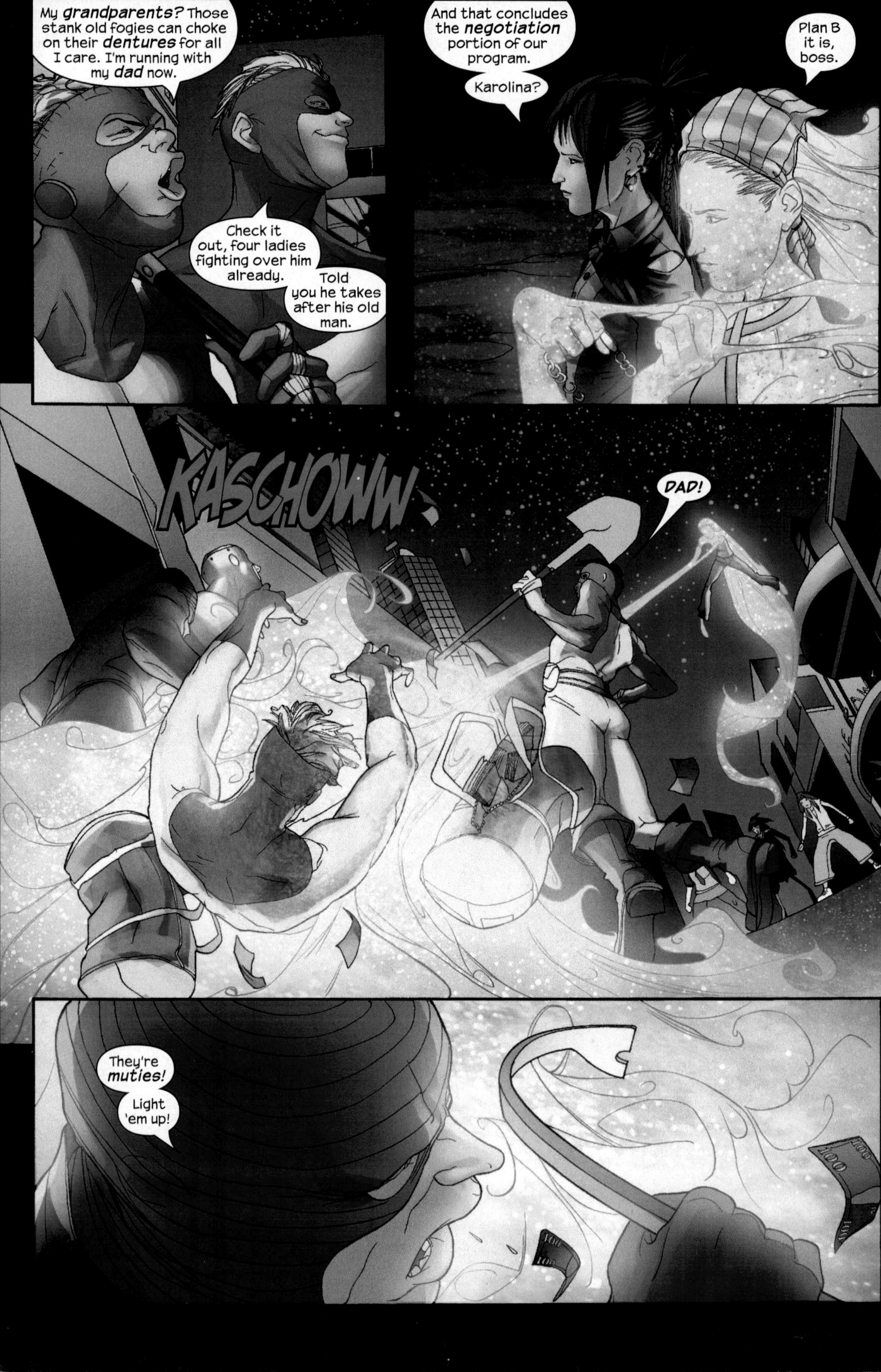
My grandparents? Those stank old fogies can choke on their dentures for all I care. I'm running with my dad now.
Check it out, four ladies fighting over him already.
Told you he takes after his old man.
And that concludes the negotiation portion of our program.
Karolina?
Plan B it is, boss.
KASCHOWW
DAD!
They're muties!
Light 'em up!

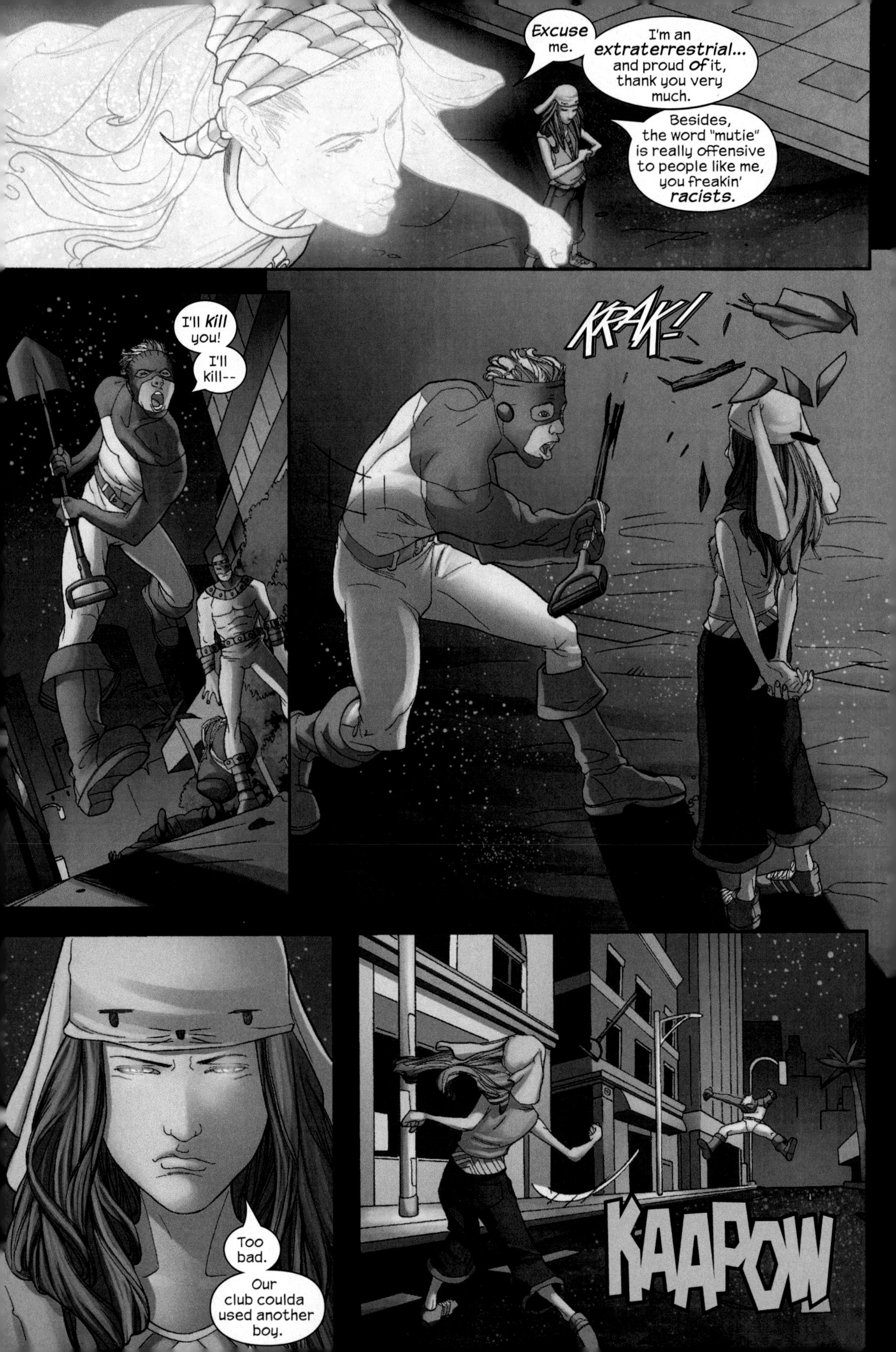
Excuse me.
I'm an extraterrestrial... and proud of it, thank you very much.
Besides, the word "mutie" is really offensive to people like me, you freakin' racists.
I'll kill you!
I'll kill--
KRAK-!
Too bad.
Our club coulda used another boy.
KAAPOW

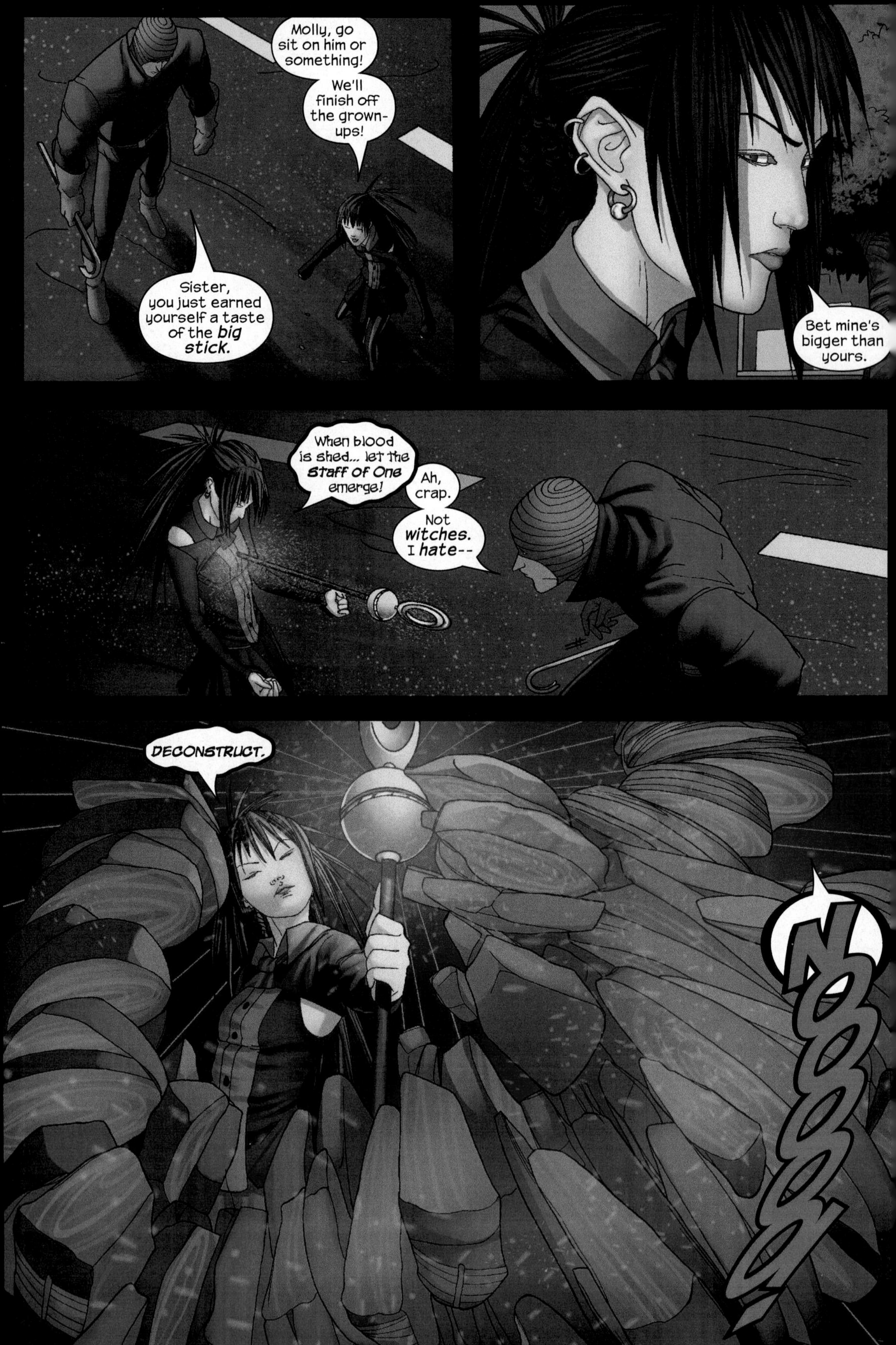
Molly, go sit on him or something!
We'll finish off the grown-ups!
Sister, you just earned yourself a taste of the *big stick.*
Bet mine's bigger than yours.
When blood is shed... let the *Staff Of One* emerge!
Ah, crap.
Not *witches.* I *hate*--
DECONSTRUCT.
NOOOOO

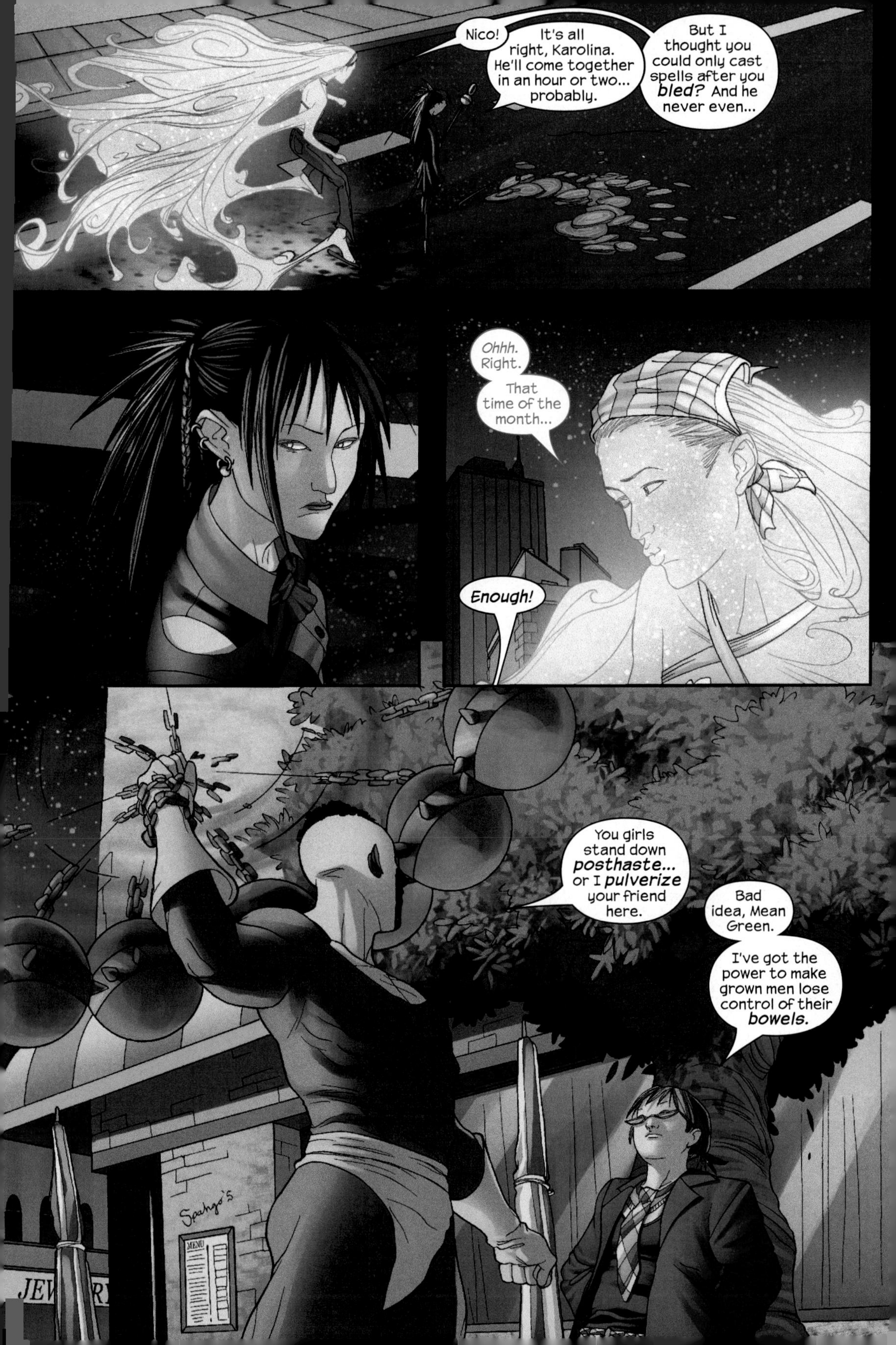

Nico!
It's all right, Karolina. He'll come together in an hour or two... probably.
But I thought you could only cast spells after you bled? And he never even...
Ohhh. Right.
That time of the month...
Enough!
You girls stand down posthaste... or I pulverize your friend here.
Bad idea, Mean Green.
I've got the power to make grown men lose control of their bowels.
Spahgo's
MENU
JEWELRY

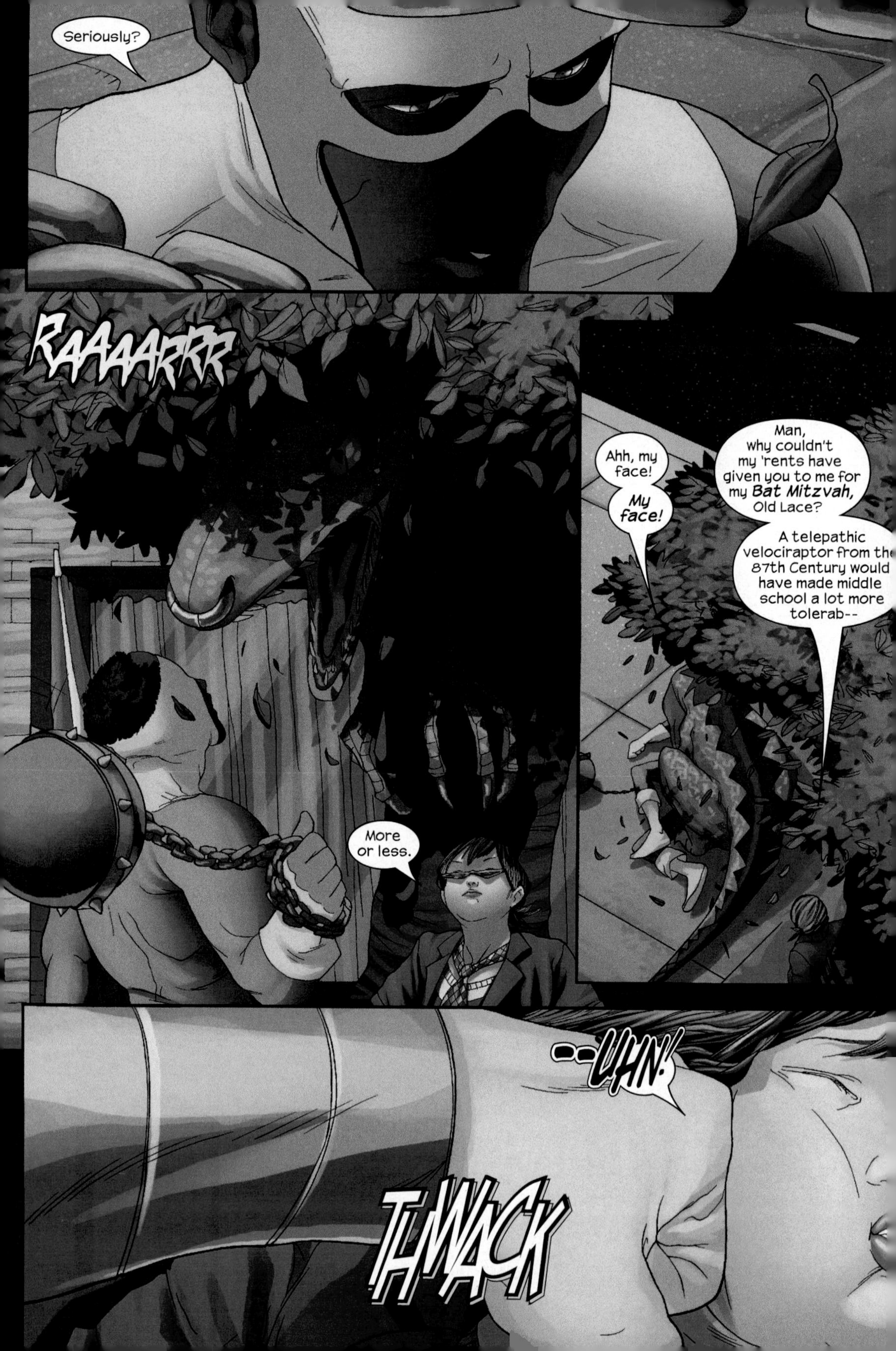
Seriously?
RAAAARRR
More or less.
Ahh, my face!
My face!
Man, why couldn't my 'rents have given you to me for my Bat Mitzvah, Old Lace?
A telepathic velociraptor from the 87th Century would have made middle school a lot more tolerab--
--UHN!
THWACK

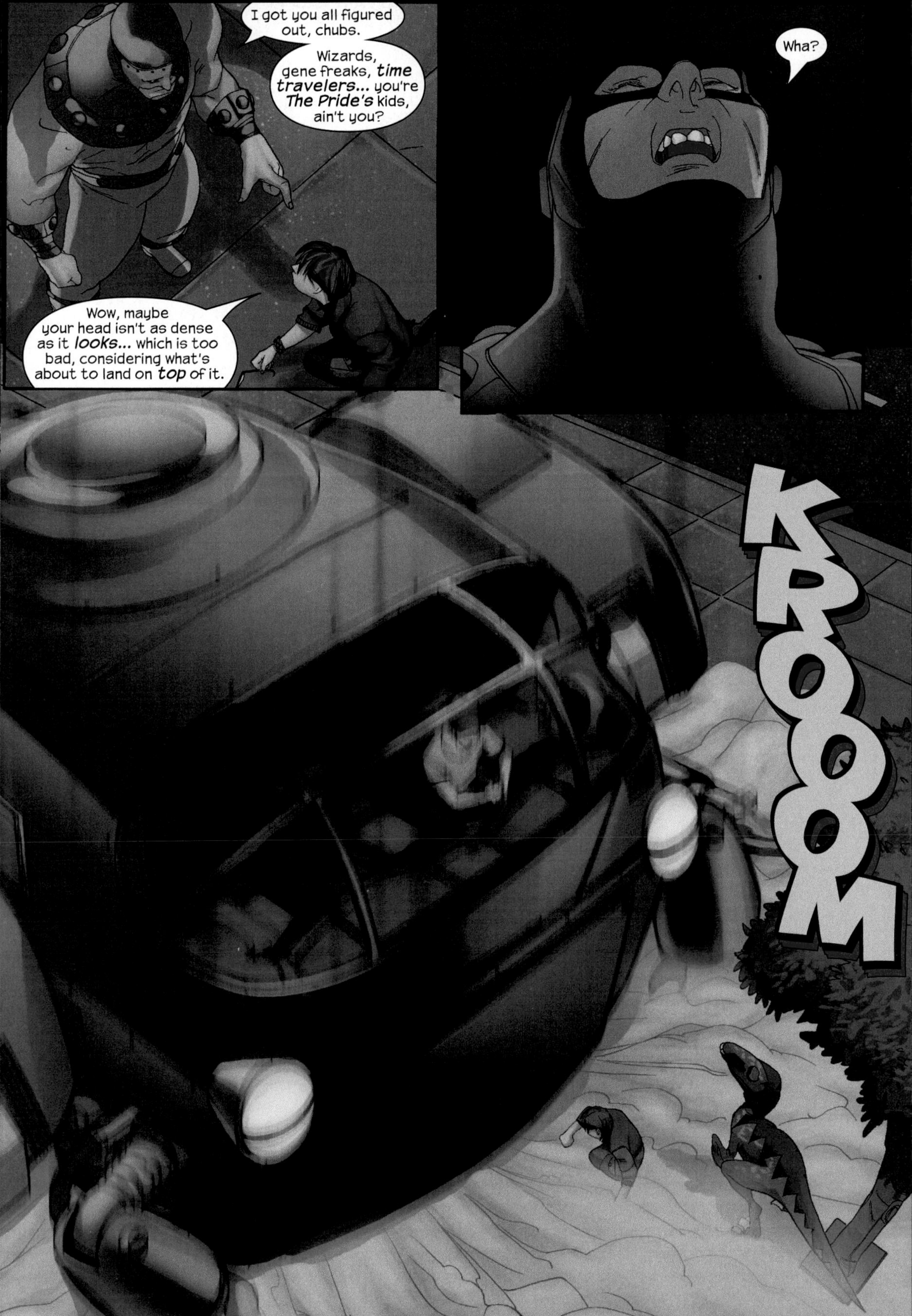
I got you all figured out, chubs.
Wizards, gene freaks, *time travelers...* you're *The Pride's* kids, ain't you?
Wow, maybe your head isn't as dense as it *looks...* which is too bad, considering what's about to land on *top* of it.
Wha?
KROOOM

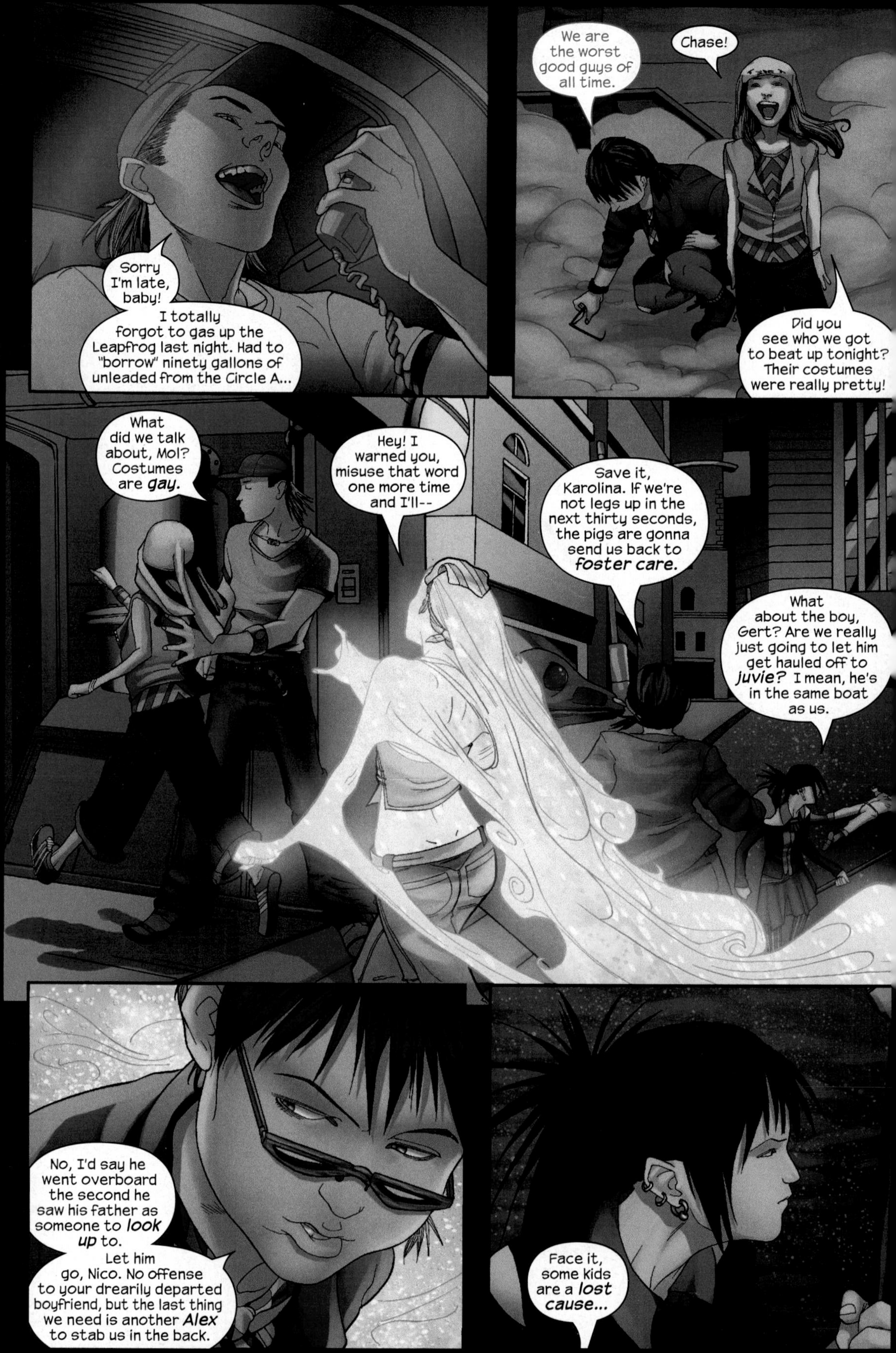
Sorry I'm late, baby!
I totally forgot to gas up the Leapfrog last night. Had to "borrow" ninety gallons of unleaded from the Circle A...
We are the worst good guys of all time.
Chase!
Did you see who we got to beat up tonight? Their costumes were really pretty!
What did we talk about, Mol? Costumes are *gay.*
Hey! I warned you, misuse that word one more time and I'll--
Save it, Karolina. If we're not legs up in the next thirty seconds, the pigs are gonna send us back to *foster care.*
What about the boy, Gert? Are we really just going to let him get hauled off to *juvie?* I mean, he's in the same boat as us.
No, I'd say he went overboard the second he saw his father as someone to *look up* to.
Let him go, Nico. No offense to your drearily departed boyfriend, but the last thing we need is another *Alex* to stab us in the back.
Face it, some kids are a *lost cause...*

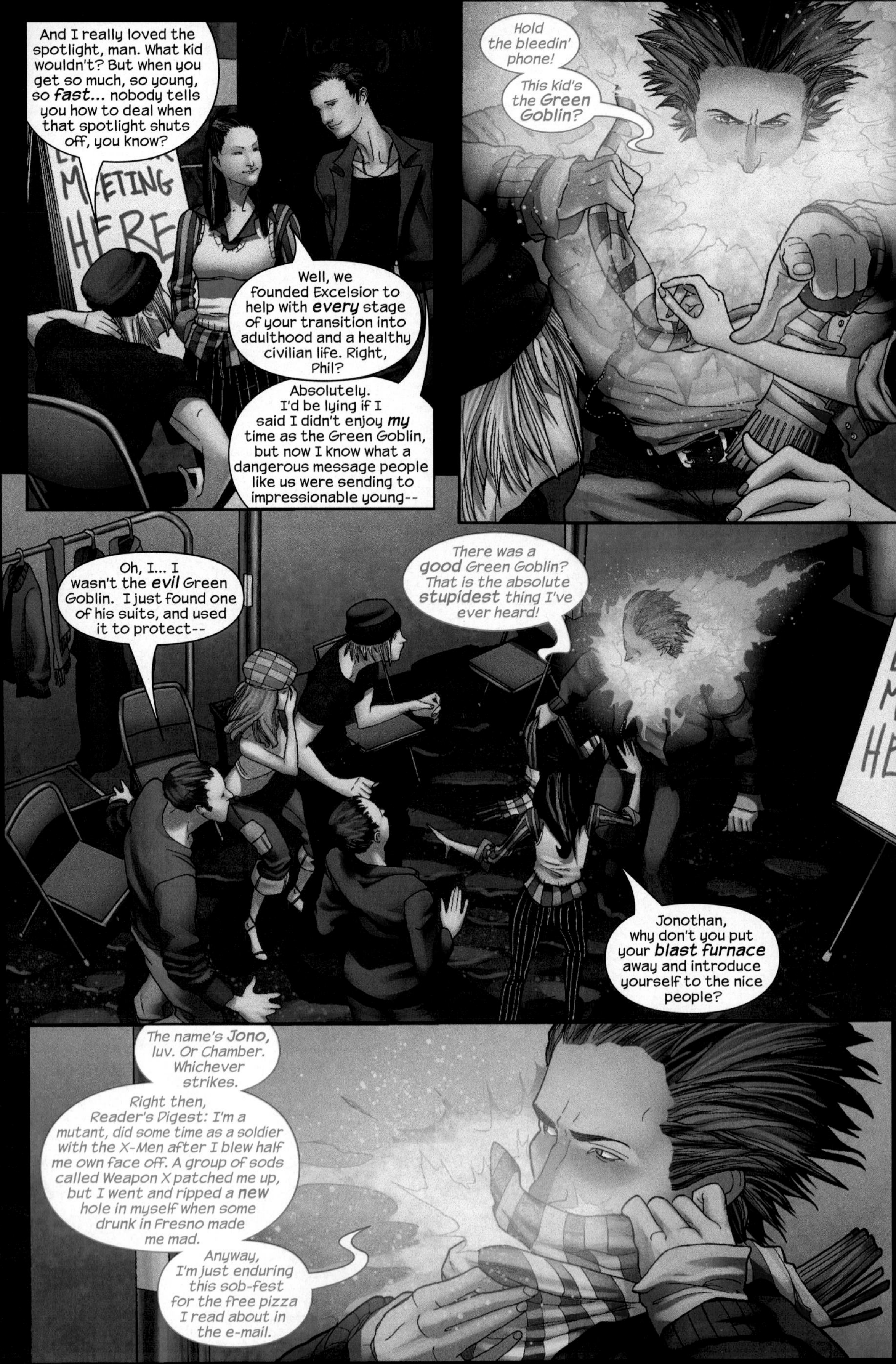
And I really loved the spotlight, man. What kid wouldn't? But when you get so much, so young, so *fast*... nobody tells you how to deal when that spotlight shuts off, you know?
MEETING HERE
Well, we founded Excelsior to help with *every* stage of your transition into adulthood and a healthy civilian life. Right, Phil?
Absolutely. I'd be lying if I said I didn't enjoy *my* time as the Green Goblin, but now I know what a dangerous message people like us were sending to impressionable young--
Hold the bleedin' phone!
This kid's the *Green Goblin*?
Oh, I... I wasn't the *evil* Green Goblin. I just found one of his suits, and used it to protect--
There was a *good* Green Goblin? That is the absolute *stupidest* thing I've ever heard!
Jonothan, why don't you put your *blast furnace* away and introduce yourself to the nice people?
The name's *Jono*, luv. Or Chamber. Whichever strikes.
Right then, Reader's Digest: I'm a mutant, did some time as a soldier with the X-Men after I blew half me own face off. A group of sods called Weapon X patched me up, but I went and ripped a *new* hole in myself when some drunk in Fresno made me mad.
Anyway, I'm just enduring this sob-fest for the free pizza I read about in the e-mail.

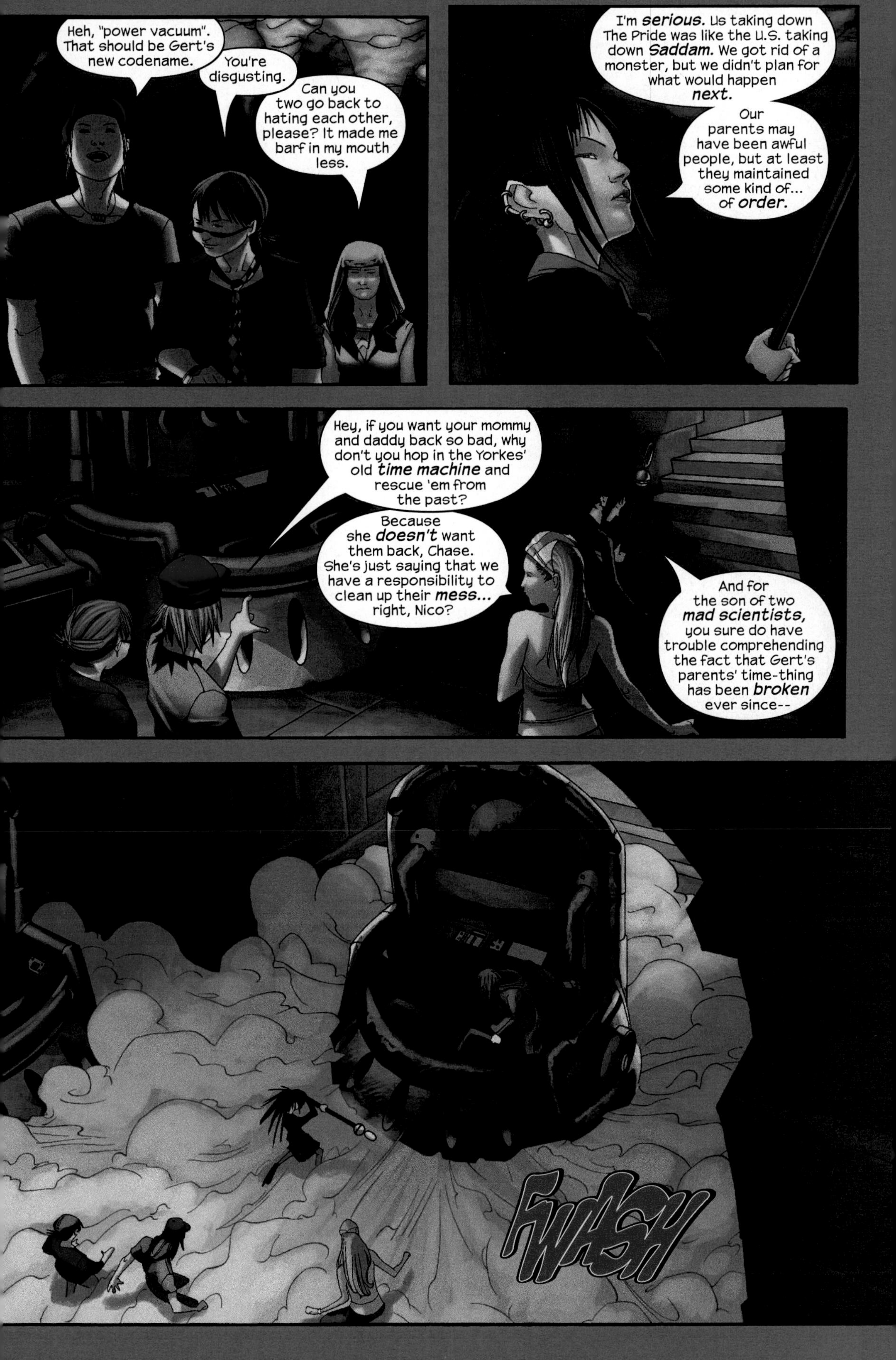
Heh, "power vacuum". That should be Gert's new codename.
You're disgusting.
Can you two go back to hating each other, please? It made me barf in my mouth less.
I'm serious. Us taking down The Pride was like the U.S. taking down Saddam. We got rid of a monster, but we didn't plan for what would happen next.
Our parents may have been awful people, but at least they maintained some kind of... of order.
Hey, if you want your mommy and daddy back so bad, why don't you hop in the Yorkes' old time machine and rescue 'em from the past?
Because she doesn't want them back, Chase. She's just saying that we have a responsibility to clean up their mess... right, Nico?
And for the son of two mad scientists, you sure do have trouble comprehending the fact that Gert's parents' time-thing has been broken ever since--
FWASH

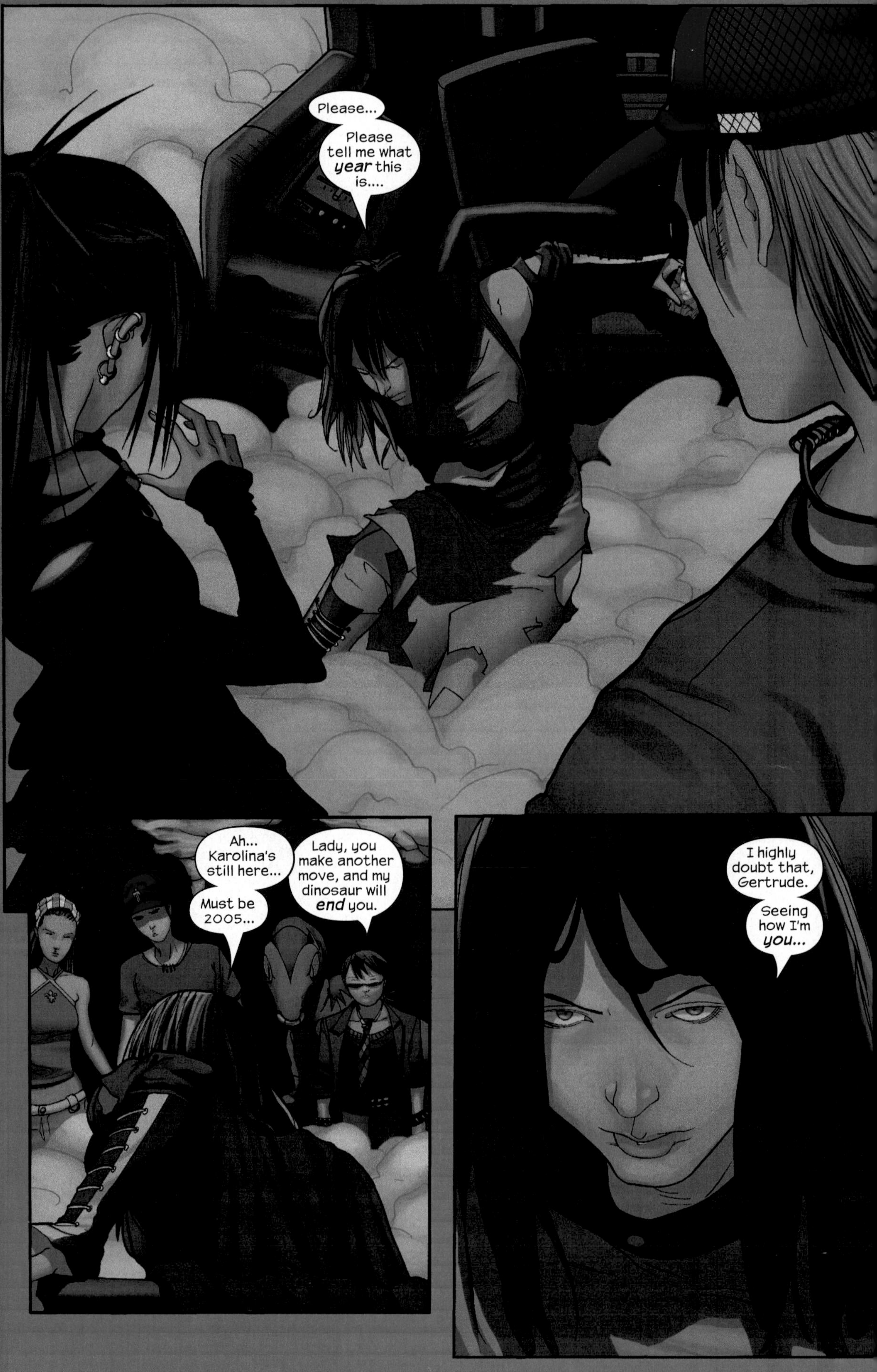
Please...
Please tell me what year this is....
Ah... Karolina's still here...
Must be 2005...
Lady, you make another move, and my dinosaur will end you.
I highly doubt that, Gertrude.
Seeing how I'm you...

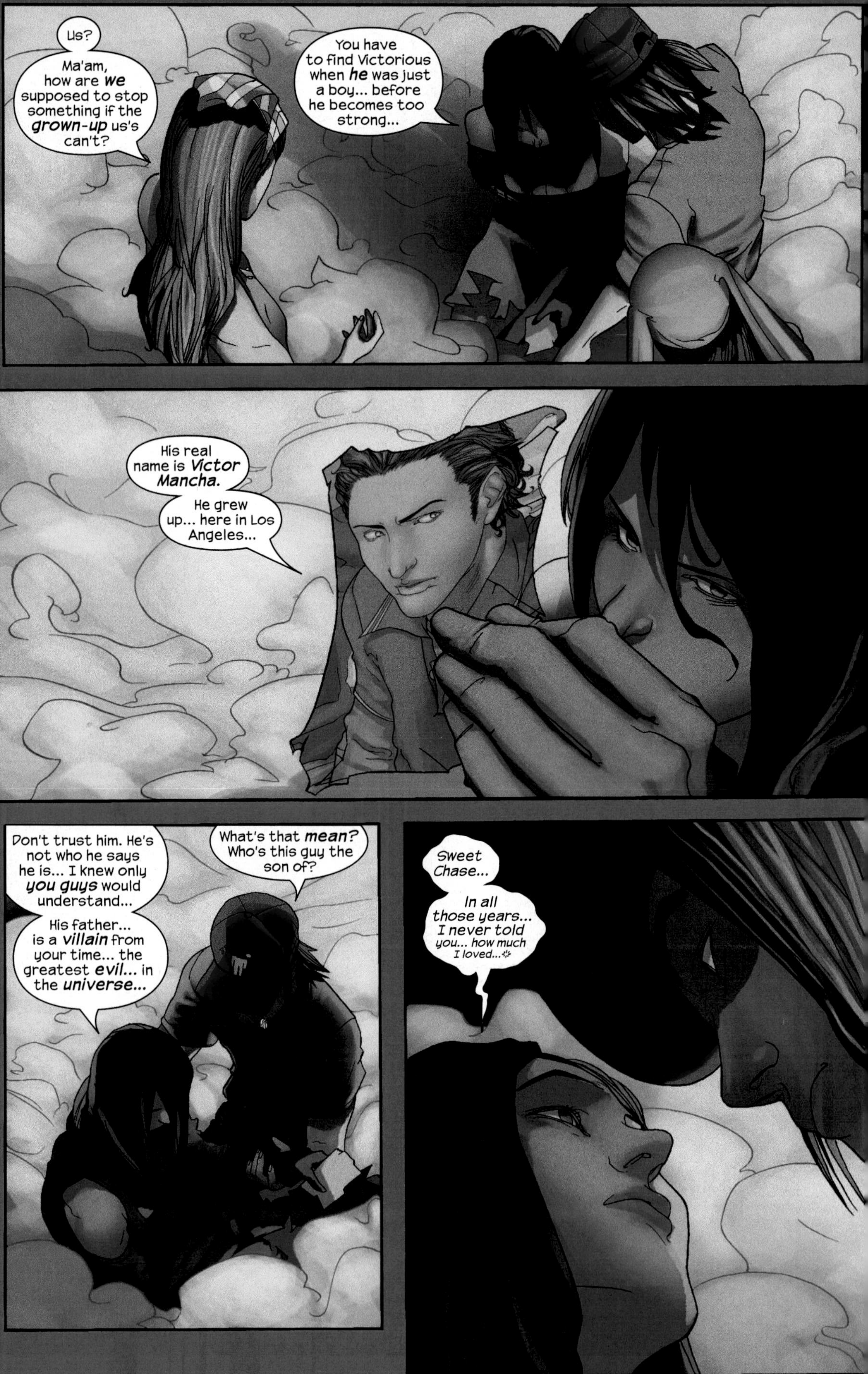

Us?
Ma'am, how are we supposed to stop something if the grown-up us's can't?
You have to find Victorious when he was just a boy... before he becomes too strong...
His real name is Victor Mancha.
He grew up... here in Los Angeles...
Don't trust him. He's not who he says he is... I knew only you guys would understand...
His father... is a villain from your time... the greatest evil... in the universe...
What's that mean? Who's this guy the son of?
Sweet Chase...
In all those years... I never told you... how much I loved...

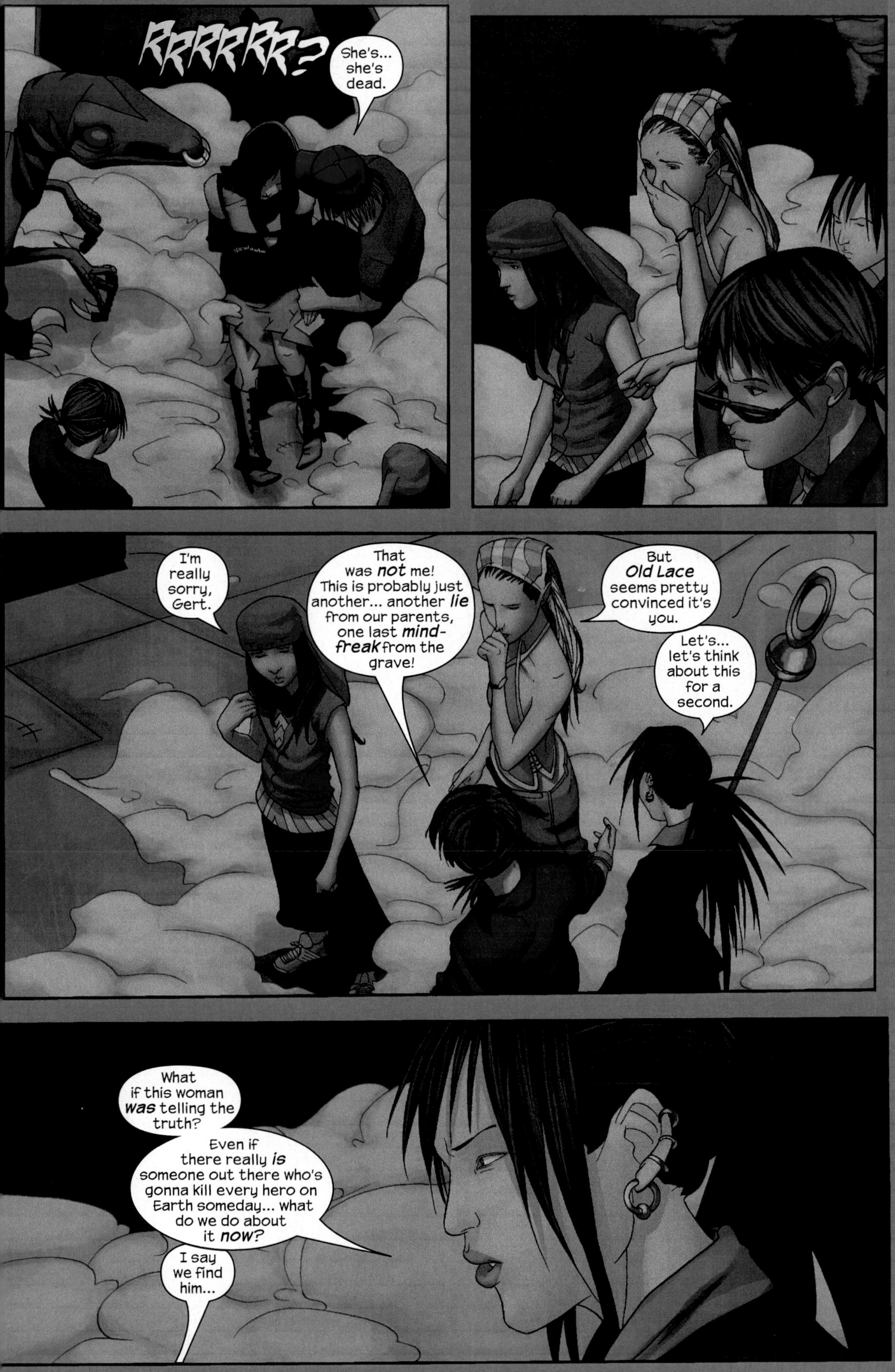

RRRRRR?
She's... she's dead.
I'm really sorry, Gert.
That was not me! This is probably just another... another lie from our parents, one last mind-freak from the grave!
But Old Lace seems pretty convinced it's you.
Let's... let's think about this for a second.
What if this woman was telling the truth?
Even if there really is someone out there who's gonna kill every hero on Earth someday... what do we do about it now?
I say we find him...

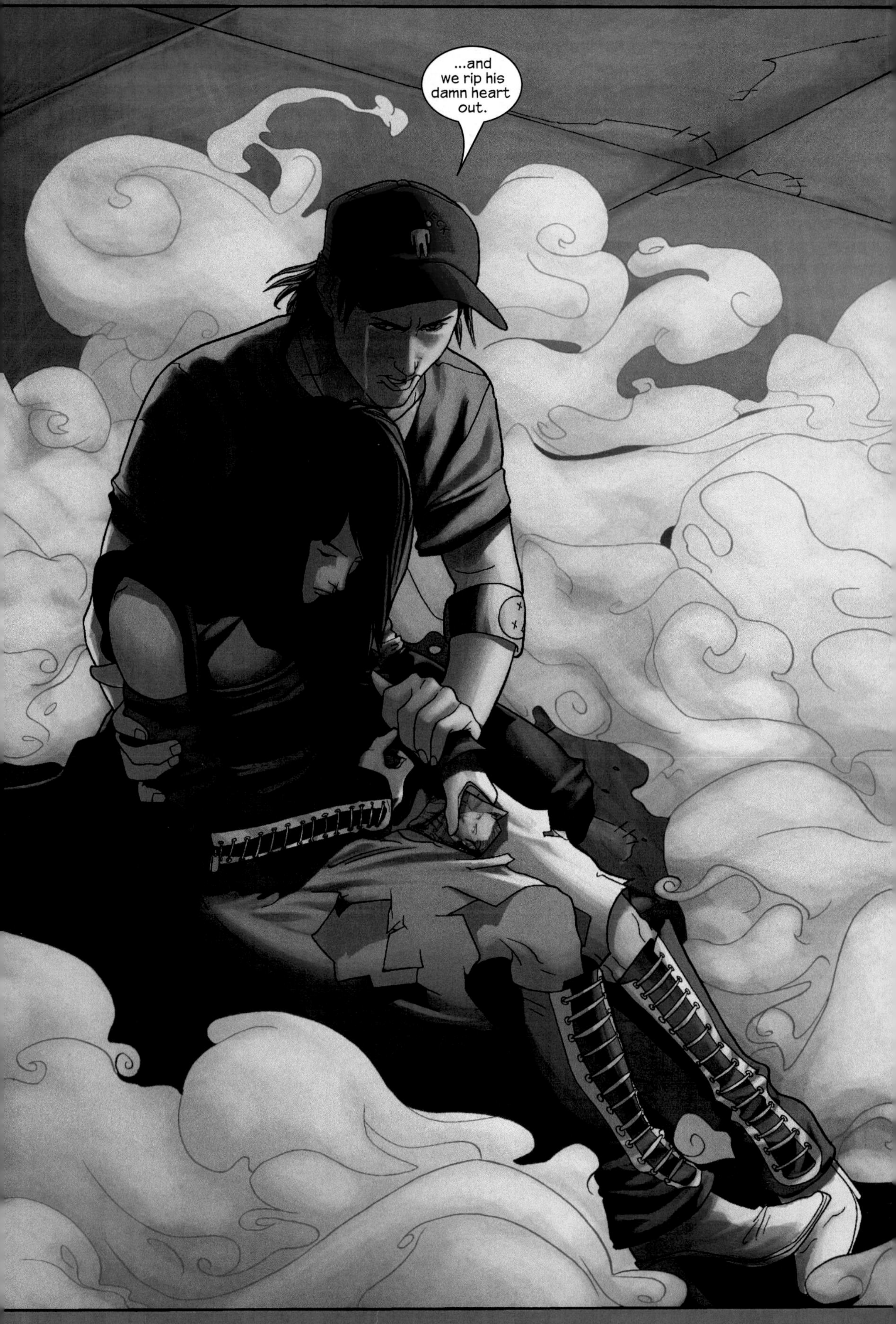
...and we rip his damn heart out.

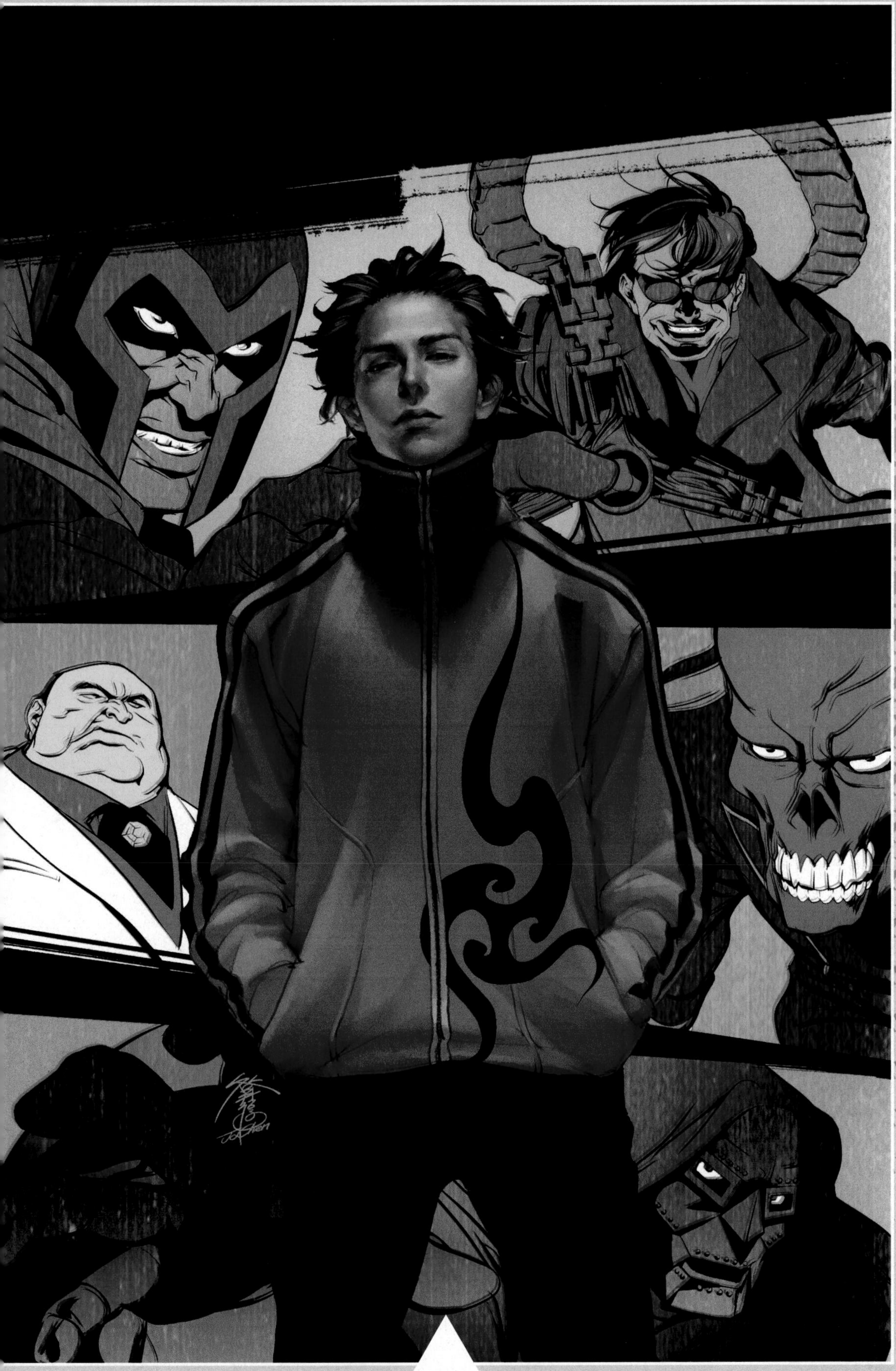

2

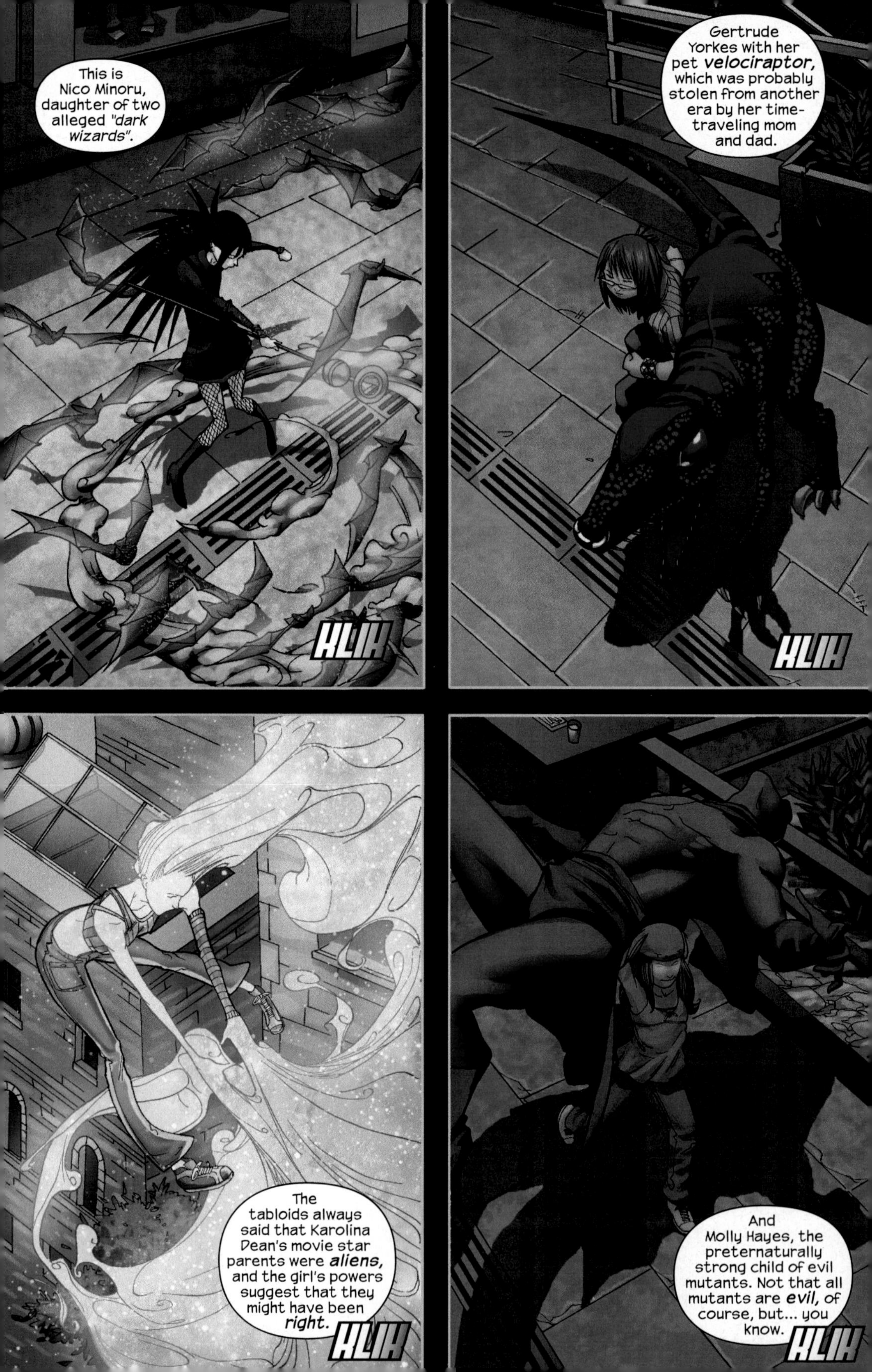

This is Nico Minoru, daughter of two alleged "dark wizards".
KLIK
Gertrude Yorkes with her pet velociraptor, which was probably stolen from another era by her time-traveling mom and dad.
KLIK
The tabloids always said that Karolina Dean's movie star parents were aliens, and the girl's powers suggest that they might have been right.
KLIK
And Molly Hayes, the preternaturally strong child of evil mutants. Not that all mutants are evil, of course, but... you know.
KLIK

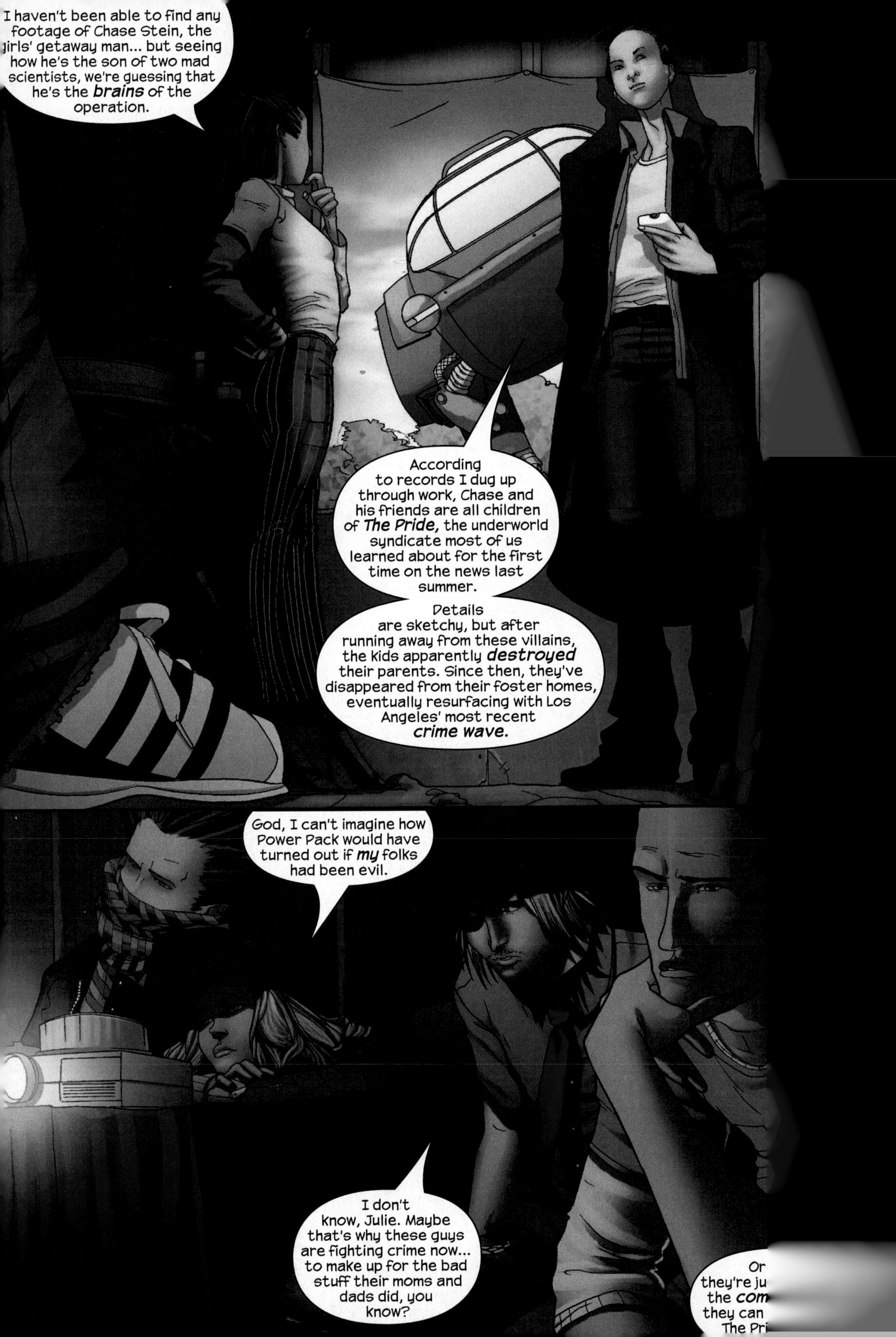

I haven't been able to find any footage of Chase Stein, the girls' getaway man... but seeing how he's the son of two mad scientists, we're guessing that he's the *brains* of the operation.
According to records I dug up through work, Chase and his friends are all children of *The Pride,* the underworld syndicate most of us learned about for the first time on the news last summer.
Details are sketchy, but after running away from these villains, the kids apparently *destroyed* their parents. Since then, they've disappeared from their foster homes, eventually resurfacing with Los Angeles' most recent *crime wave.*
God, I can't imagine how Power Pack would have turned out if *my* folks had been evil.
I don't know, Julie. Maybe that's why these guys are fighting crime now... to make up for the bad stuff their moms and dads did, you know?

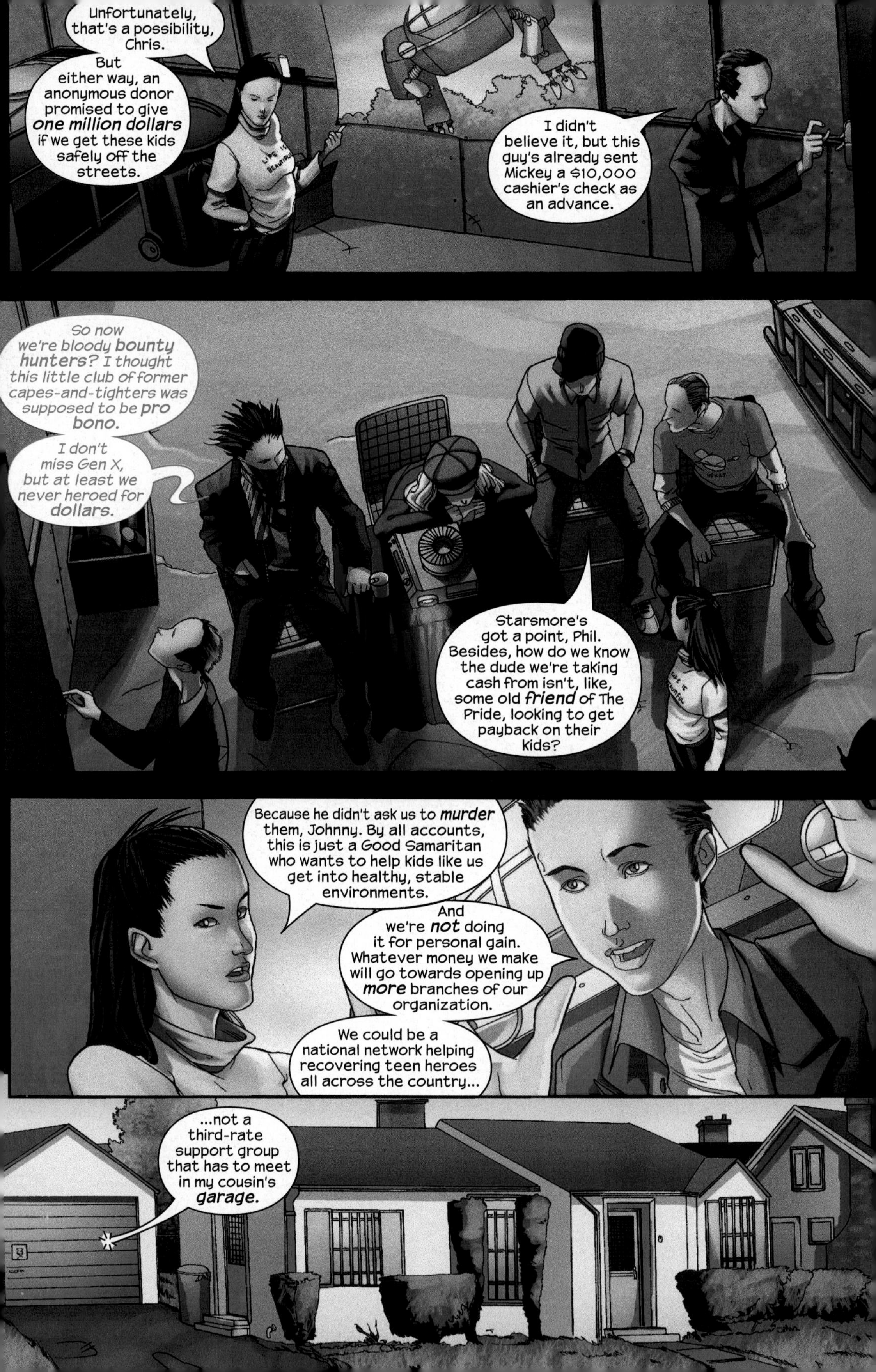
Unfortunately, that's a possibility, Chris.
But either way, an anonymous donor promised to give **one million dollars** if we get these kids safely off the streets.
I didn't believe it, but this guy's already sent Mickey a $10,000 cashier's check as an advance.
So now we're bloody **bounty hunters?** I thought this little club of former capes-and-tighters was supposed to be **pro bono**.
I don't miss Gen X, but at least we never heroed for **dollars**.
Starsmore's got a point, Phil. Besides, how do we know the dude we're taking cash from isn't, like, some old *friend* of The Pride, looking to get payback on their kids?
Because he didn't ask us to *murder* them, Johnny. By all accounts, this is just a Good Samaritan who wants to help kids like us get into healthy, stable environments.
And we're *not* doing it for personal gain. Whatever money we make will go towards opening up *more* branches of our organization.
We could be a national network helping recovering teen heroes all across the country...
...not a third-rate support group that has to meet in my cousin's *garage*.

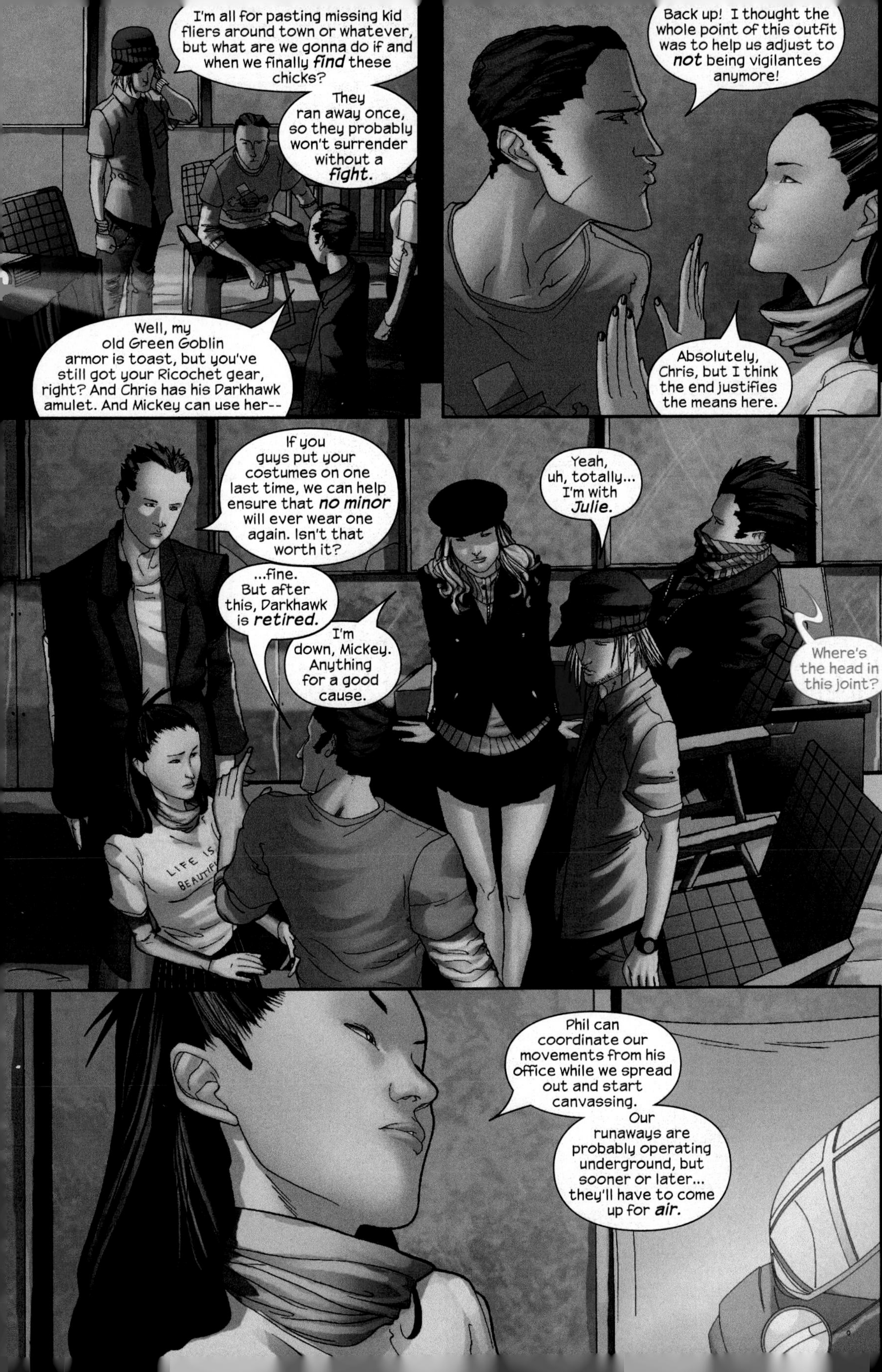
I'm all for pasting missing kid fliers around town or whatever, but what are we gonna do if and when we finally *find* these chicks?
They ran away once, so they probably won't surrender without a *fight.*
Well, my old Green Goblin armor is toast, but you've still got your Ricochet gear, right? And Chris has his Darkhawk amulet. And Mickey can use her--
Back up! I thought the whole point of this outfit was to help us adjust to *not* being vigilantes anymore!
Absolutely, Chris, but I think the end justifies the means here.
If you guys put your costumes on one last time, we can help ensure that *no minor* will ever wear one again. Isn't that worth it?
...fine. But after this, Darkhawk is *retired.*
I'm down, Mickey. Anything for a good cause.
Yeah, uh, totally... I'm with *Julie.*
Where's the head in this joint?
LIFE IS BEAUTIFUL
Phil can coordinate our movements from his office while we spread out and start canvassing.
Our runaways are probably operating underground, but sooner or later... they'll have to come up for *air.*

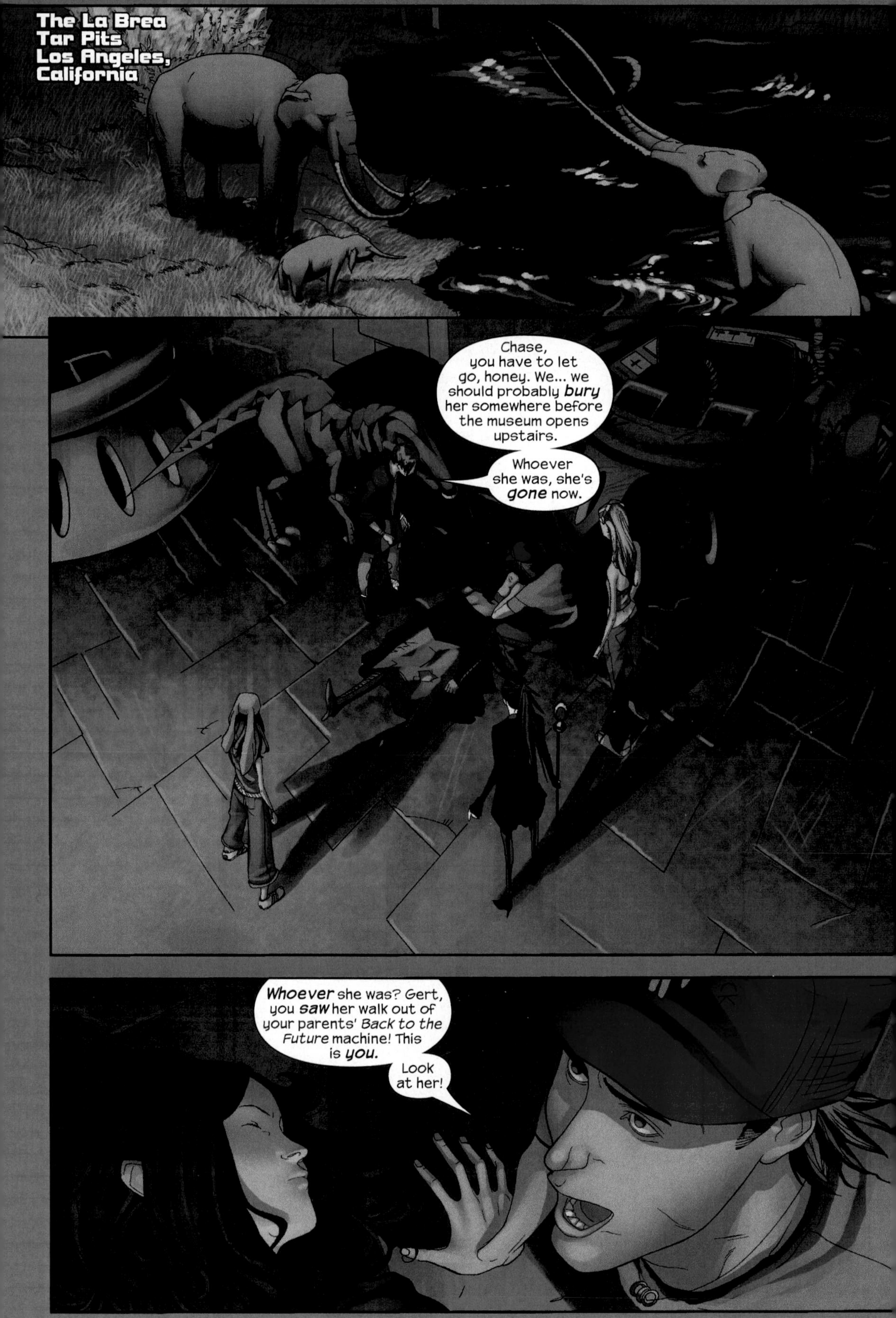
The La Brea Tar Pits Los Angeles, California
Chase, you have to let go, honey. We... we should probably bury her somewhere before the museum opens upstairs.
Whoever she was, she's gone now.
Whoever she was? Gert, you saw her walk out of your parents' Back to the Future machine! This is you.
Look at her!

I told you, this is probably some *trap* our parents left for us before they died.

That could be a clone, or... or a magic trick, or a--

That's it!

Nico, use a *spell*! Bring her back to life!

I *can't*, Chase. I can only cast the same spell once, and I already tried a resurrection enchantment.

You tried to raise the dead? When? *Who?*

It was right after we defeated The Pride.

I... I tried to save *Alex*.

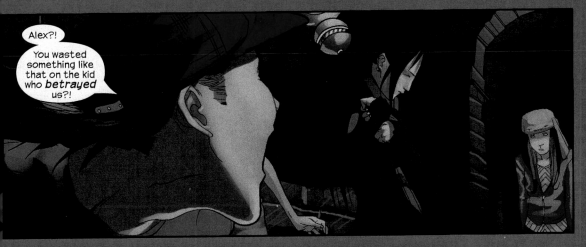

Alex?!

You wasted something like that on the kid who *betrayed* us?!

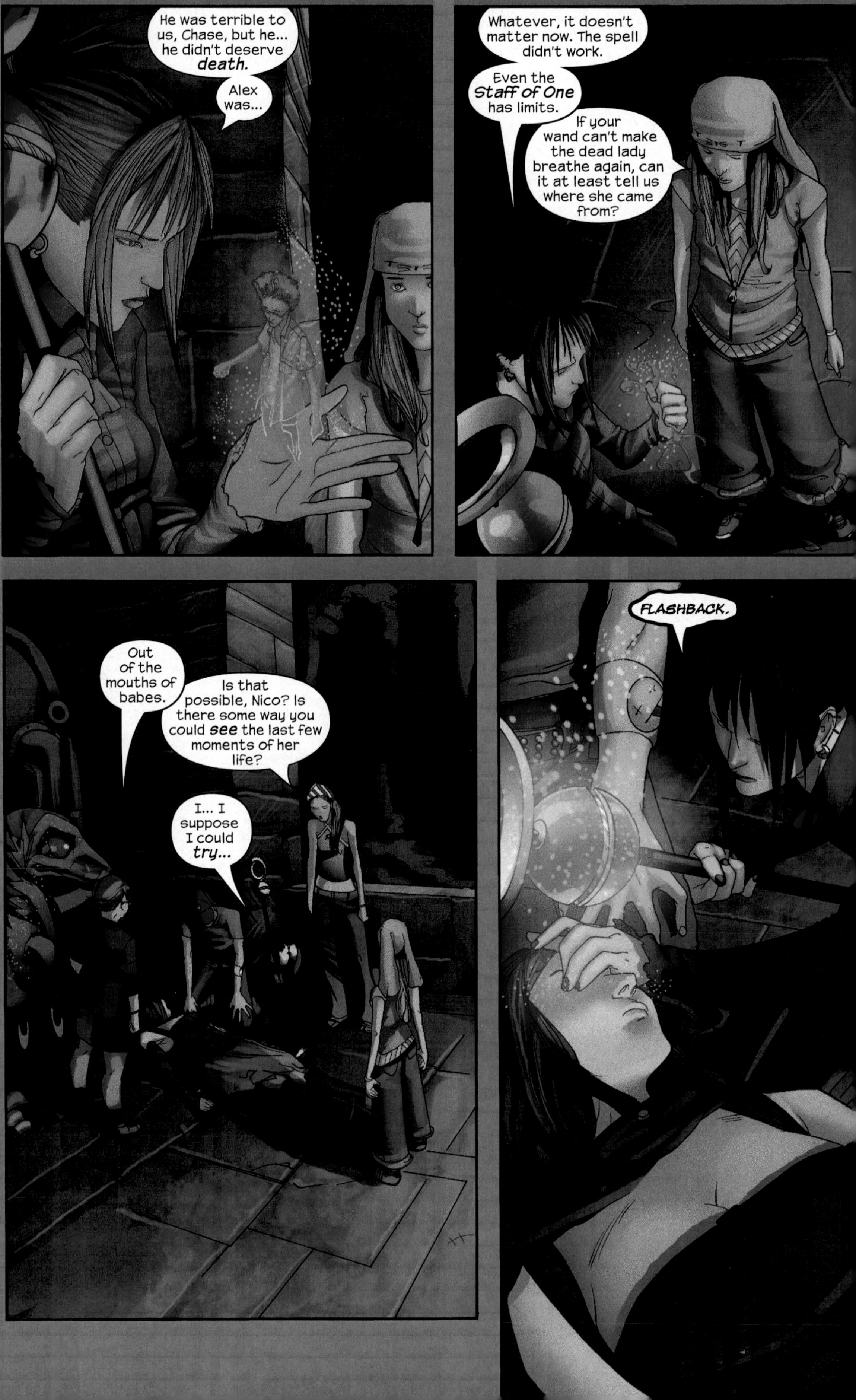

He was terrible to us, Chase, but he... he didn't deserve *death.*
Alex was...
Whatever, it doesn't matter now. The spell didn't work.
Even the *Staff of One* has limits.
If your wand can't make the dead lady breathe again, can it at least tell us where she came from?
Out of the mouths of babes.
Is that possible, Nico? Is there some way you could *see* the last few moments of her life?
I... I suppose I could *try...*
FLASHBACK.

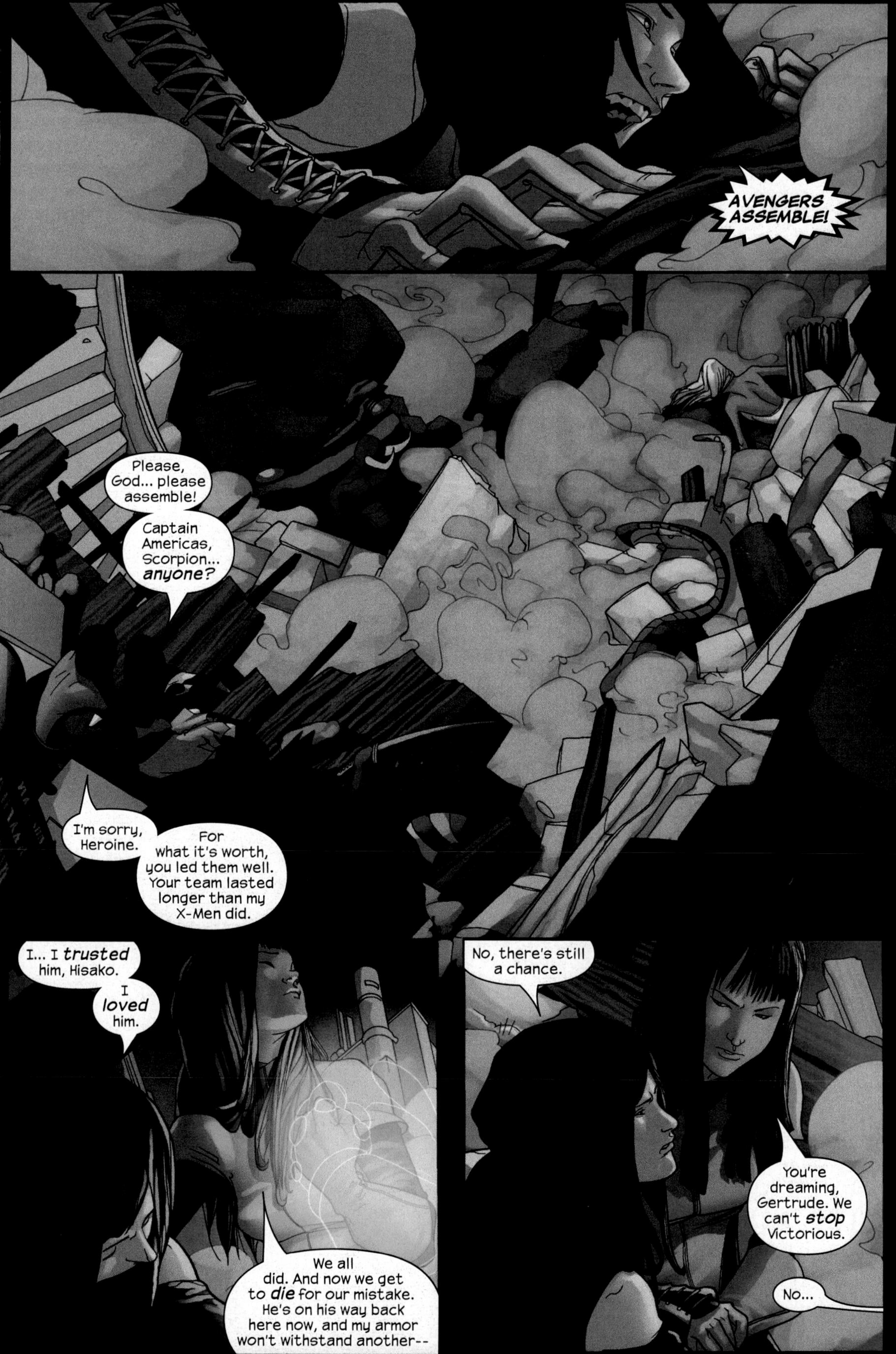
AVENGERS ASSEMBLE!
Please, God... please assemble!
Captain Americas, Scorpion... *anyone*?
I'm sorry, Heroine.
For what it's worth, you led them well. Your team lasted longer than my X-Men did.
I... I *trusted* him, Hisako.
I *loved* him.
We all did. And now we get to *die* for our mistake. He's on his way back here now, and my armor won't withstand another--
No, there's still a chance.
You're dreaming, Gertrude. We can't *stop* Victorious.
No...

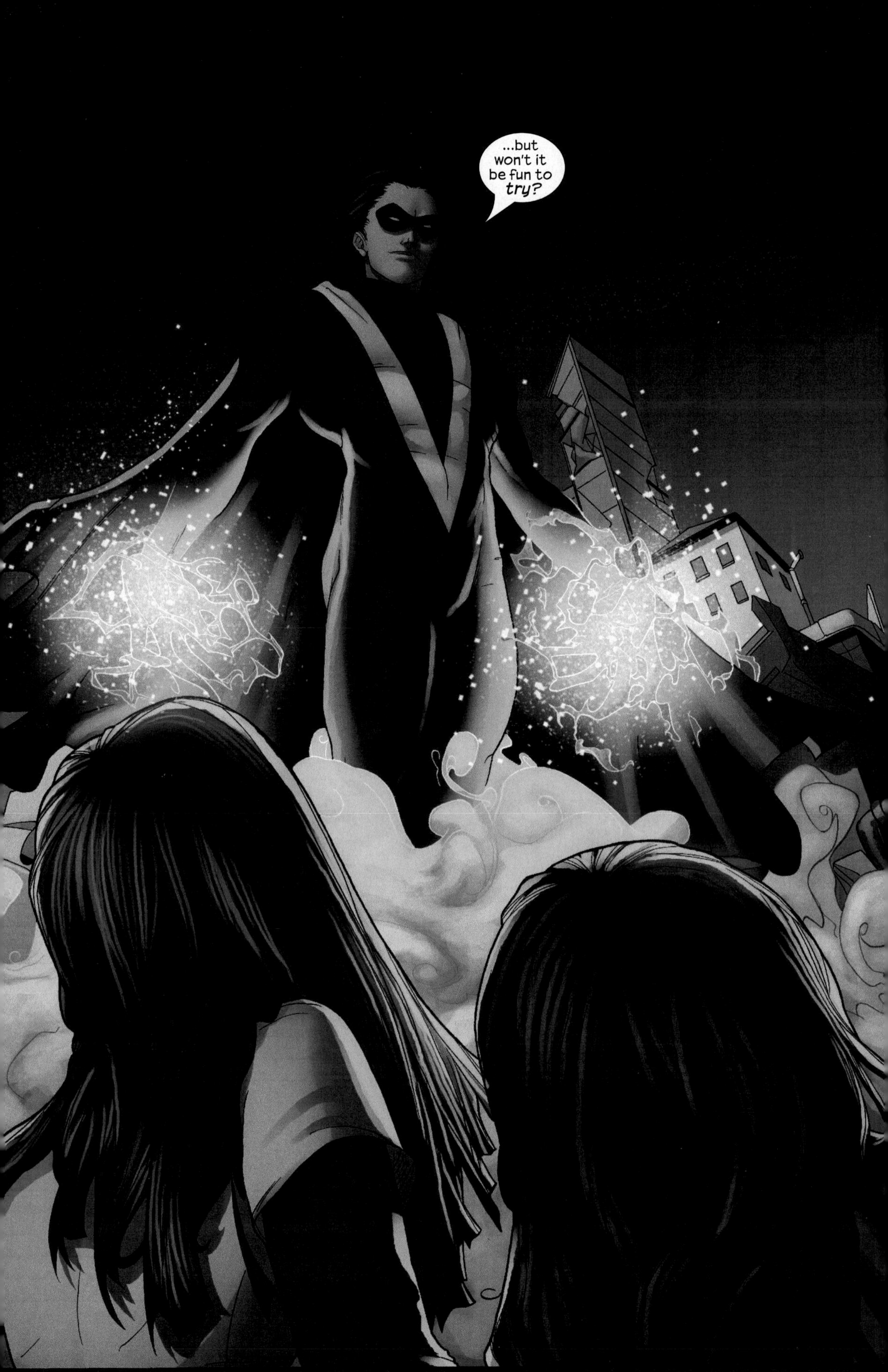
...but won't it be fun to *try?*

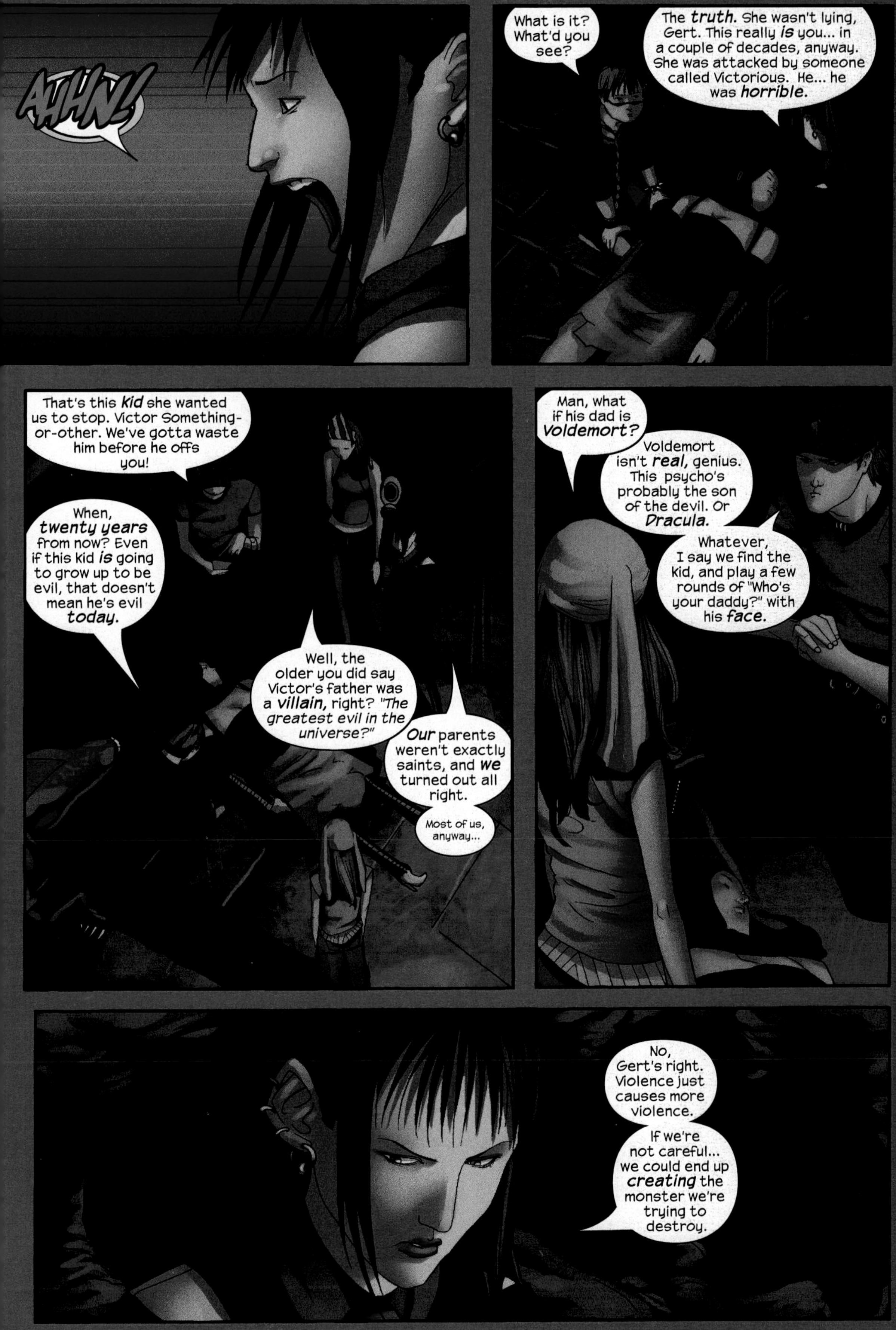
AUHN!
What is it? What'd you see?
The truth. She wasn't lying, Gert. This really is you... in a couple of decades, anyway. She was attacked by someone called Victorious. He... he was horrible.
That's this kid she wanted us to stop. Victor Something-or-other. We've gotta waste him before he offs you!
When, twenty years from now? Even if this kid is going to grow up to be evil, that doesn't mean he's evil today.
Well, the older you did say Victor's father was a villain, right? "The greatest evil in the universe?"
Our parents weren't exactly saints, and we turned out all right.
Most of us, anyway...
Man, what if his dad is Voldemort?
Voldemort isn't real, genius. This psycho's probably the son of the devil. Or Dracula.
Whatever, I say we find the kid, and play a few rounds of "Who's your daddy?" with his face.
No, Gert's right. Violence just causes more violence.
If we're not careful... we could end up creating the monster we're trying to destroy.

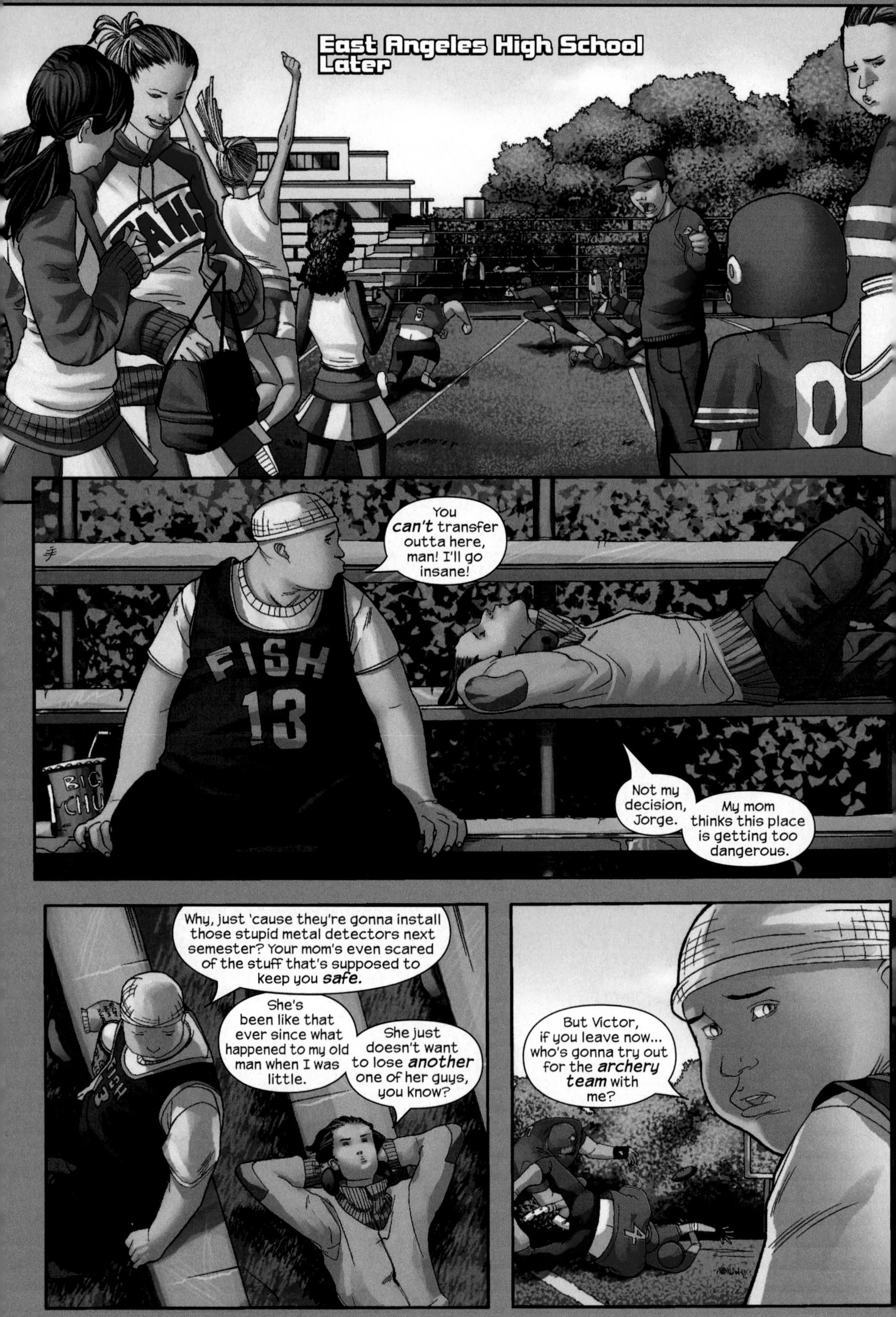
East Angeles High School
Later
EAHS
You can't transfer outta here, man! I'll go insane!
FISH 13
BIG CHU
Not my decision, Jorge.
My mom thinks this place is getting too dangerous.
Why, just 'cause they're gonna install those stupid metal detectors next semester? Your mom's even scared of the stuff that's supposed to keep you safe.
She's been like that ever since what happened to my old man when I was little.
She just doesn't want to lose another one of her guys, you know?
But Victor, if you leave now... who's gonna try out for the archery team with me?

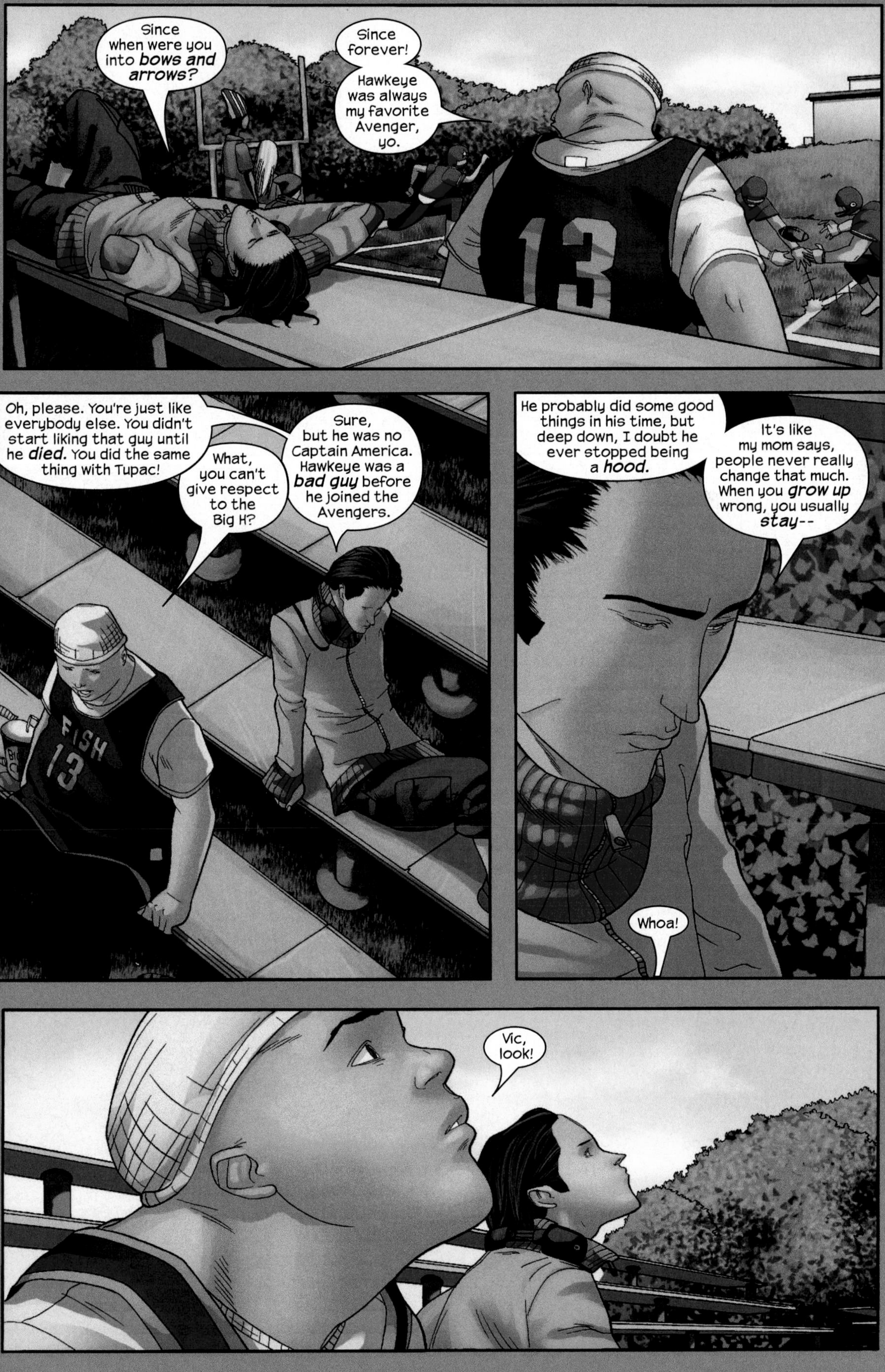

Since when were you into **bows and arrows**?
Since forever!
Hawkeye was always my favorite Avenger, yo.
Oh, please. You're just like everybody else. You didn't start liking that guy until he **died.** You did the same thing with Tupac!
What, you can't give respect to the Big H?
Sure, but he was no Captain America. Hawkeye was a **bad guy** before he joined the Avengers.
He probably did some good things in his time, but deep down, I doubt he ever stopped being a **hood.**
It's like my mom says, people never really change that much. When you **grow up** wrong, you usually **stay--**
Whoa!
Vic, look!

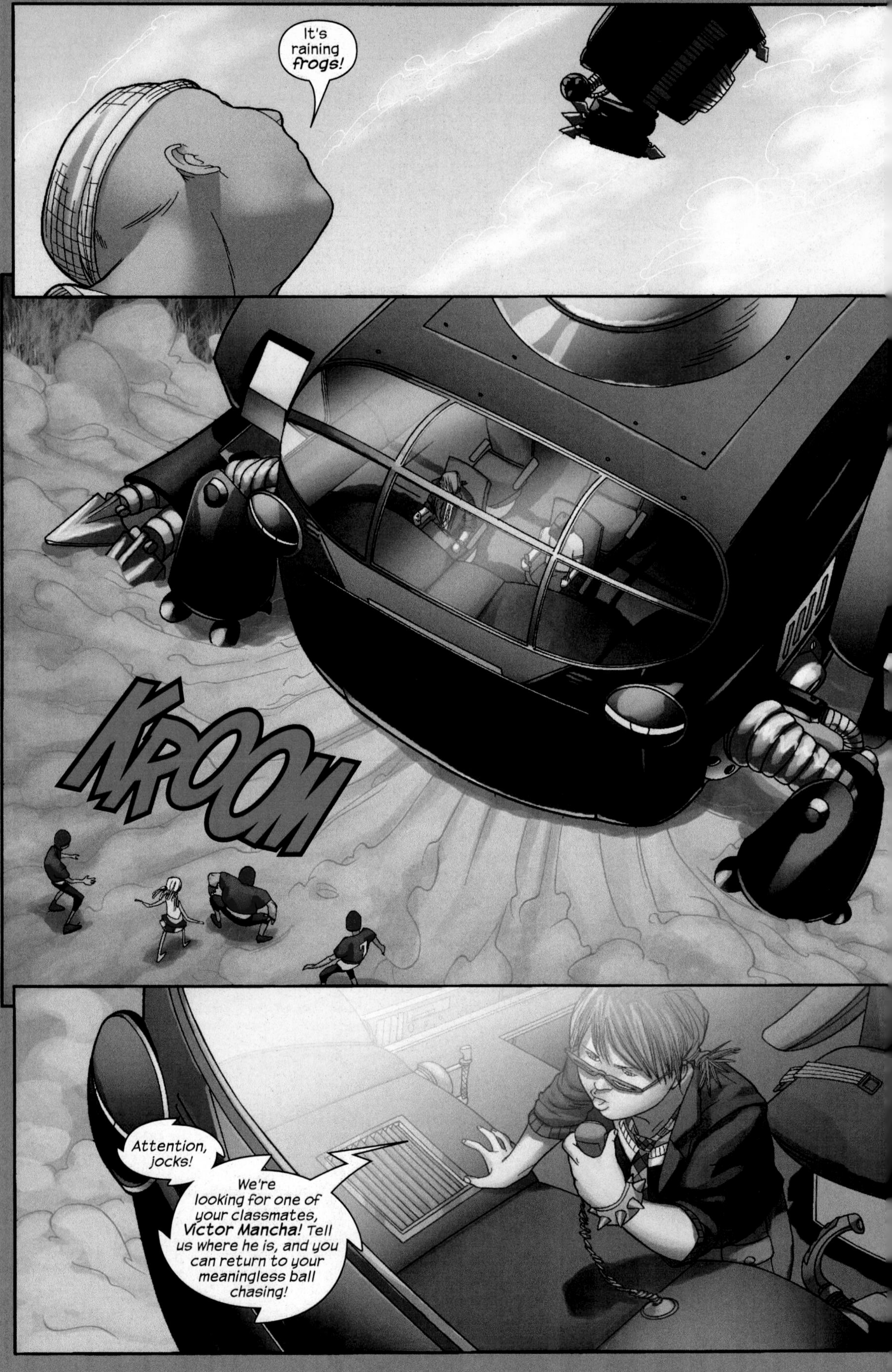
It's raining frogs!
KROOM
Attention, jocks!
We're looking for one of your classmates, Victor Mancha! Tell us where he is, and you can return to your meaningless ball chasing!

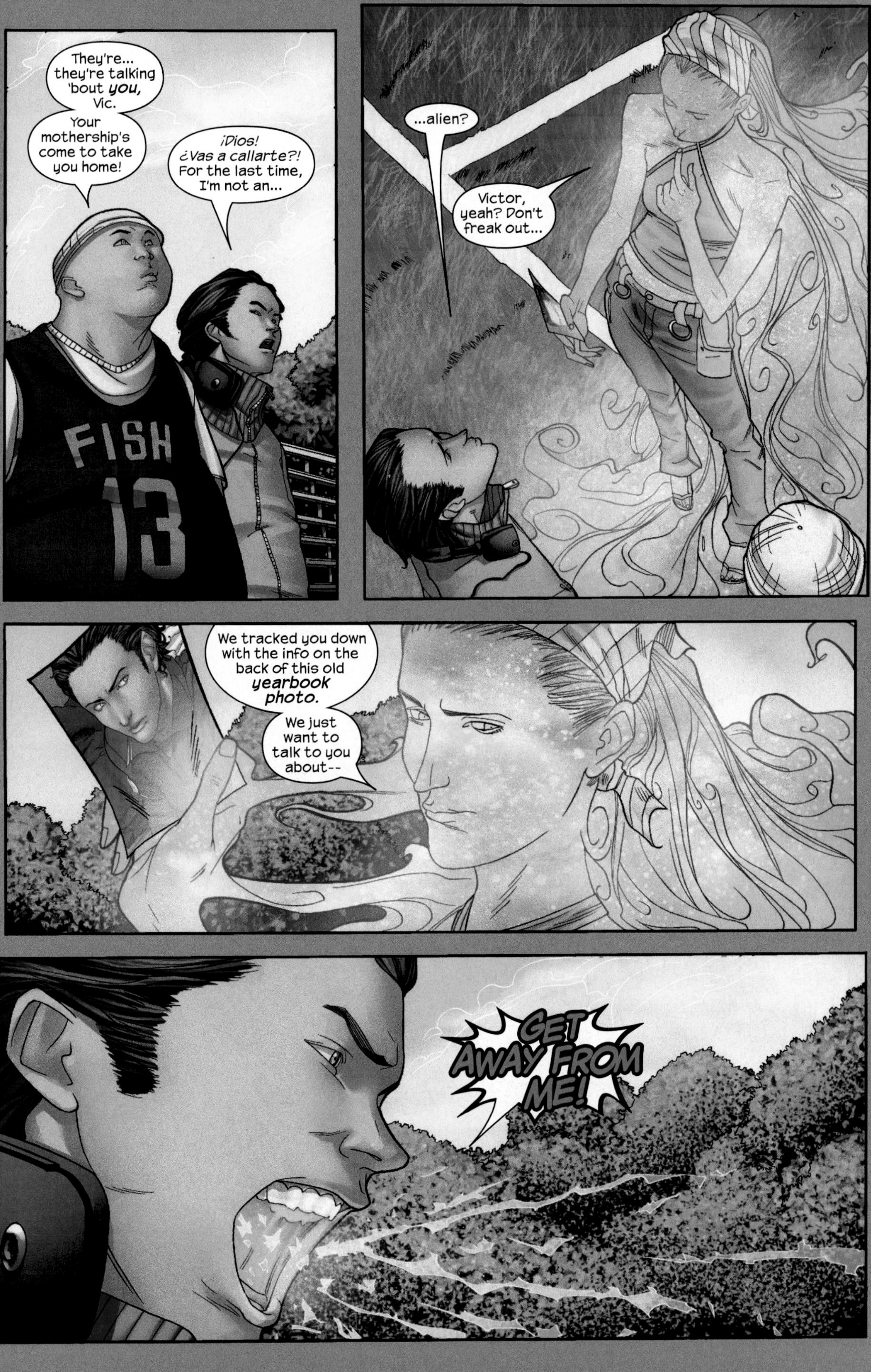
They're... they're talking 'bout *you,* Vic.
Your mothership's come to take you home!
¡Dios! ¿Vas a callarte?! For the last time, I'm not an...
...alien?
Victor, yeah? Don't freak out...
We tracked you down with the info on the back of this old *yearbook photo.*
We just want to talk to you about--
GET AWAY FROM ME!

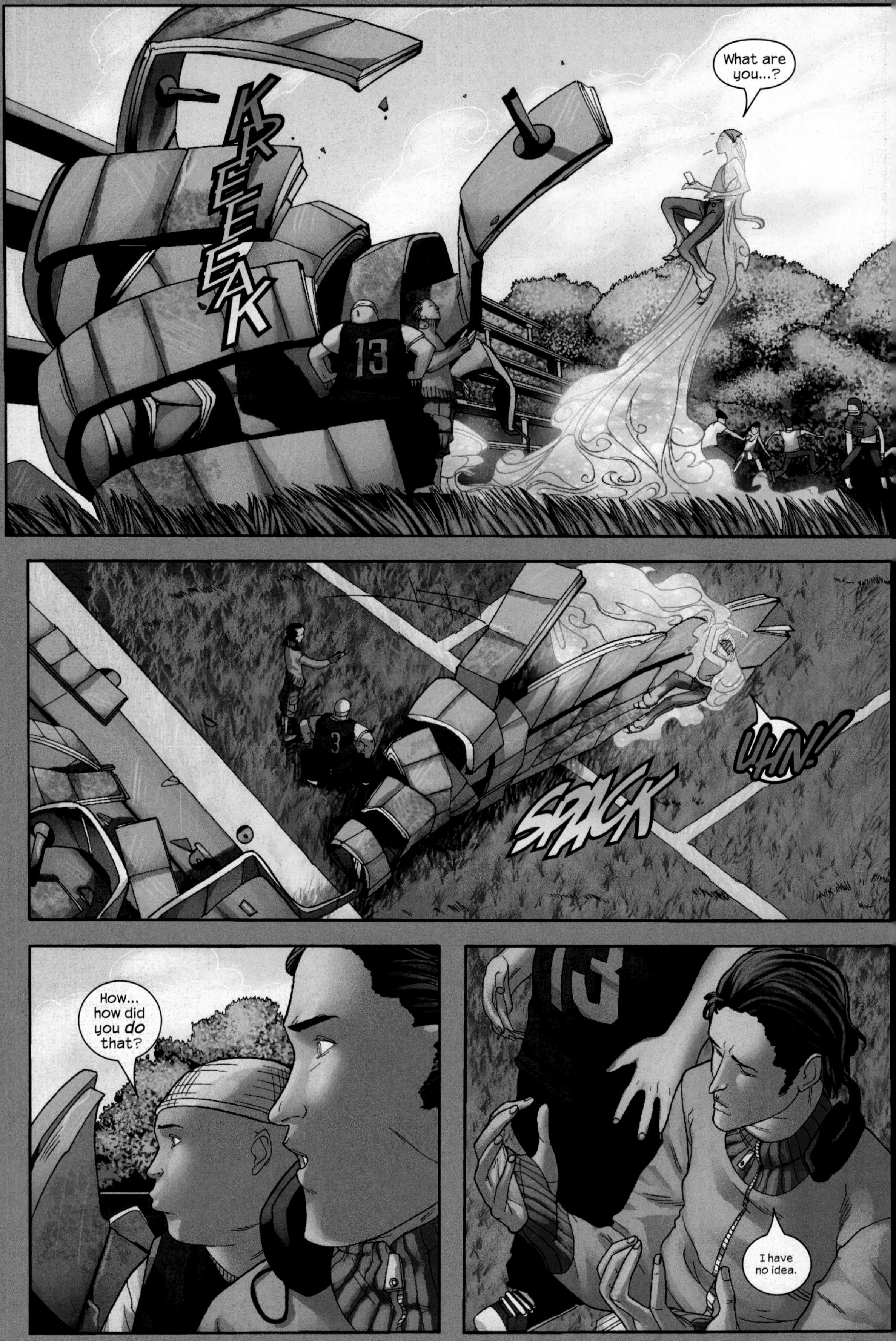

What are you...?
KREEEAK
SPACK
UHN!
How... how did you *do* that?
I have no idea.

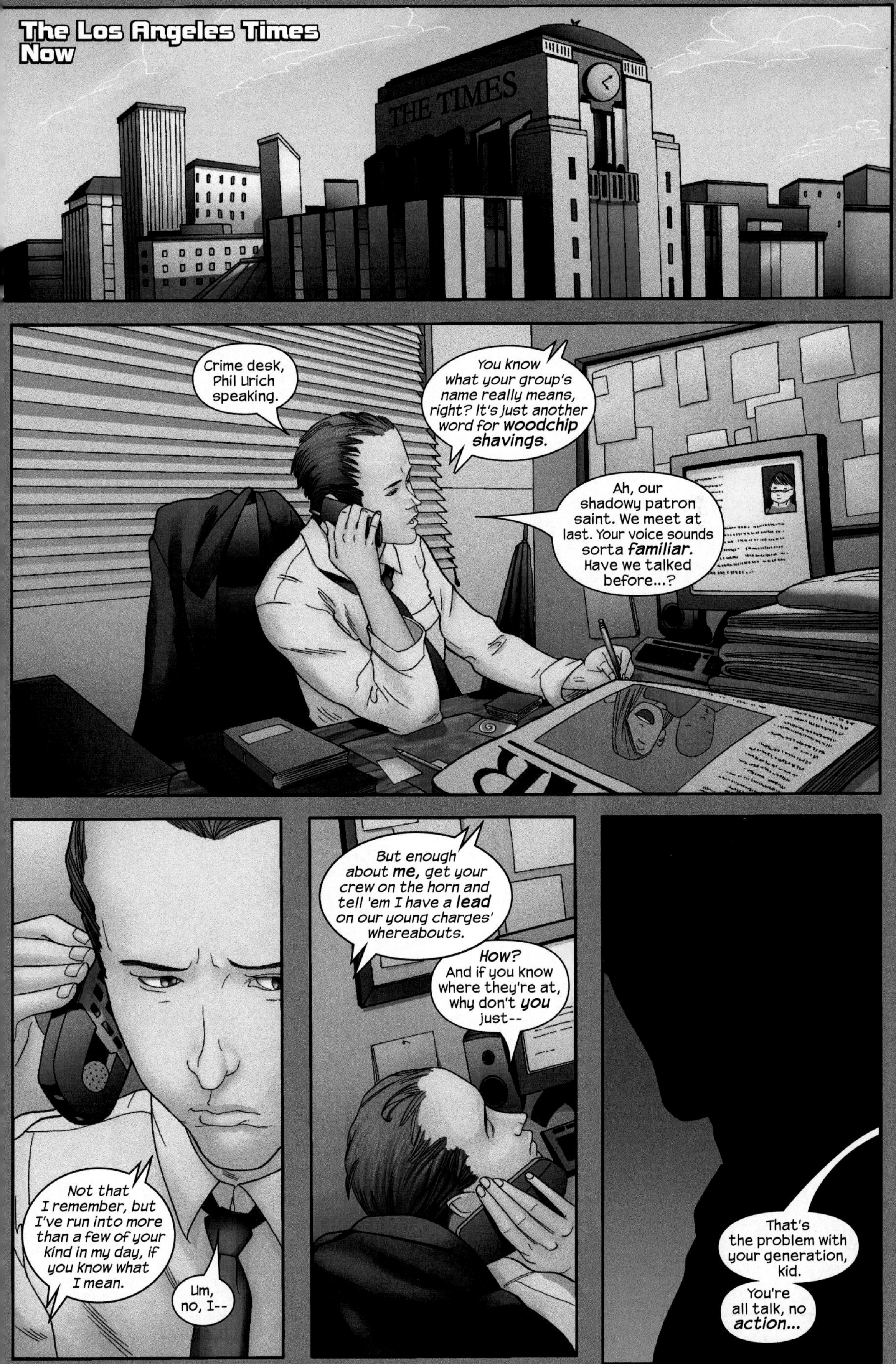

The Los Angeles Times
Now
THE TIMES
Crime desk, Phil Urich speaking.
You know what your group's name really means, right? It's just another word for woodchip shavings.
Ah, our shadowy patron saint. We meet at last. Your voice sounds sorta familiar. Have we talked before...?
Not that I remember, but I've run into more than a few of your kind in my day, if you know what I mean.
Um, no, I--
But enough about me, get your crew on the horn and tell 'em I have a lead on our young charges' whereabouts.
How? And if you know where they're at, why don't you just--
That's the problem with your generation, kid.
You're all talk, no action...

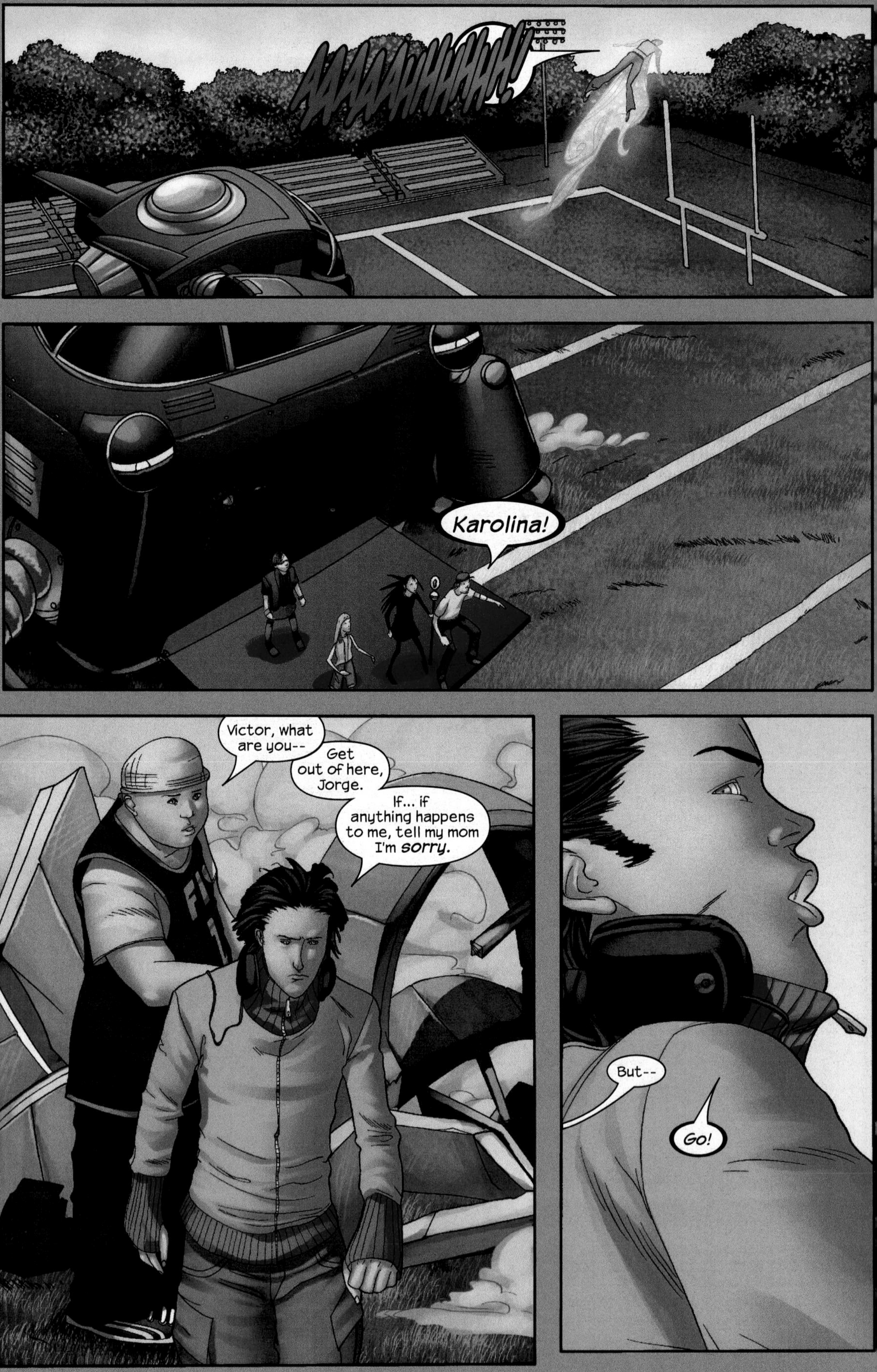
AAAAAHHHHH!
Karolina!
Victor, what are you--
Get out of here, Jorge.
If... if anything happens to me, tell my mom I'm sorry.
But--
Go!

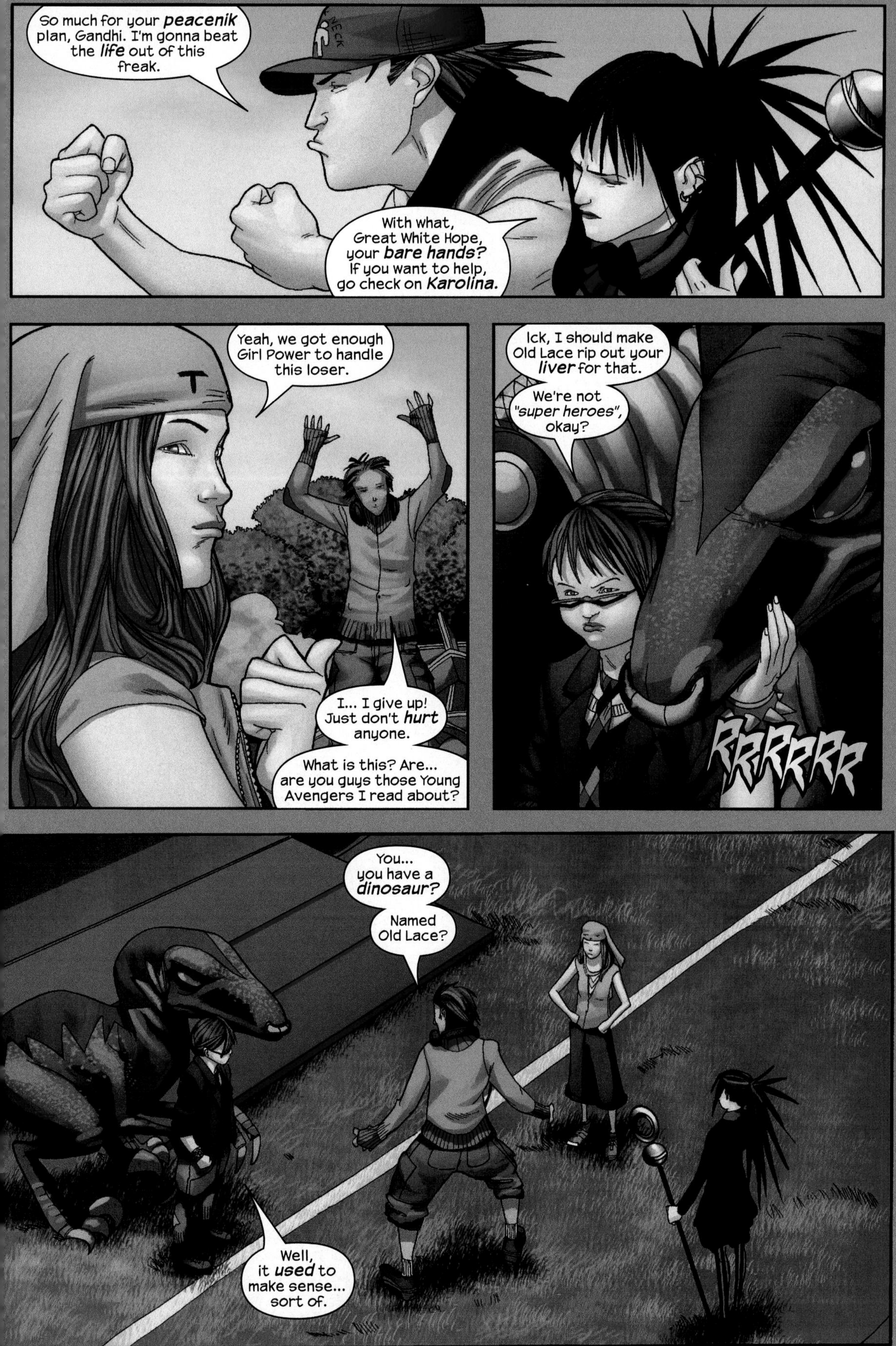
So much for your *peacenik* plan, Gandhi. I'm gonna beat the *life* out of this freak.
With what, Great White Hope, your *bare hands?* If you want to help, go check on *Karolina.*
Yeah, we got enough Girl Power to handle this loser.
I... I give up! Just don't *hurt* anyone.
What is this? Are... are you guys those Young Avengers I read about?
Ick, I should make Old Lace rip out your *liver* for that.
We're not *"super heroes"*, okay?
RRRRRR
You... you have a *dinosaur?*
Named Old Lace?
Well, it *used* to make sense... sort of.

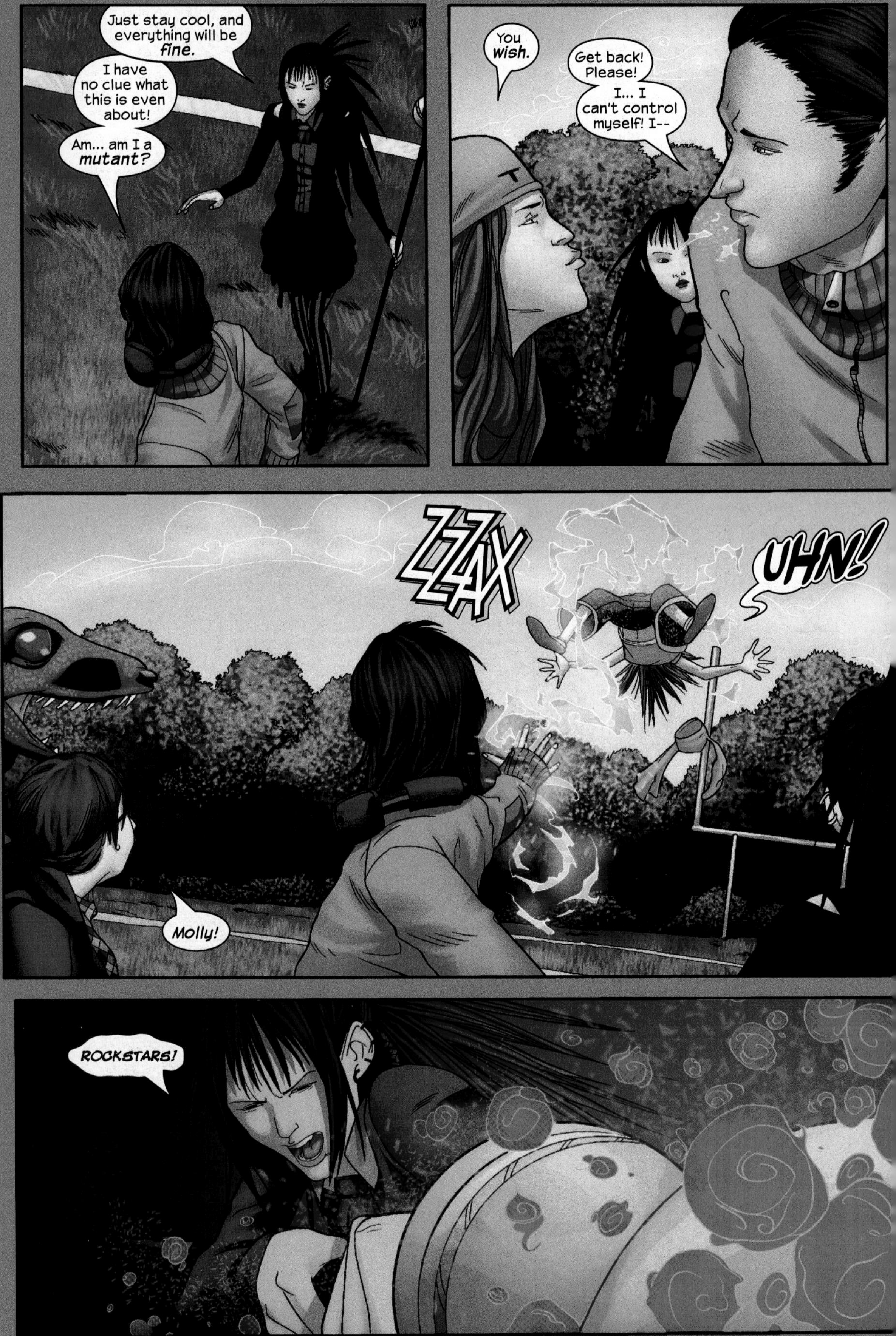
Just stay cool, and everything will be *fine.*
I have no clue what this is even about!
Am... am I a *mutant?*
You *wish.*
Get back! Please!
I... I can't control myself! I--
ZZZAX
UHN!
Molly!
ROCKSTARS!

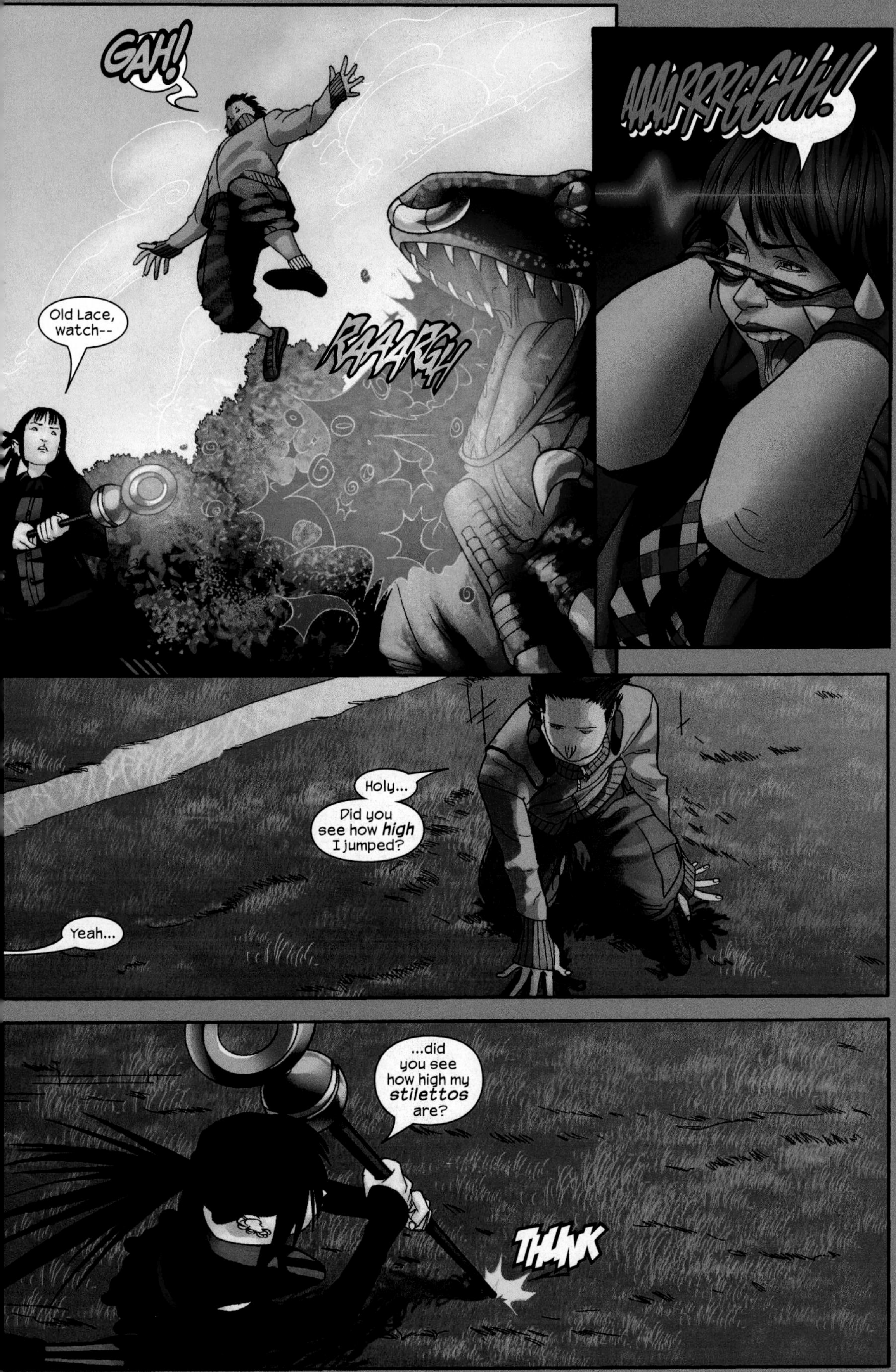
GAH!
Old Lace, watch--
RAAARGH
AAAARRRGGHH!!
Holy...
Did you see how *high* I jumped?
Yeah...
...did you see how high my *stilettos* are?
THUNK

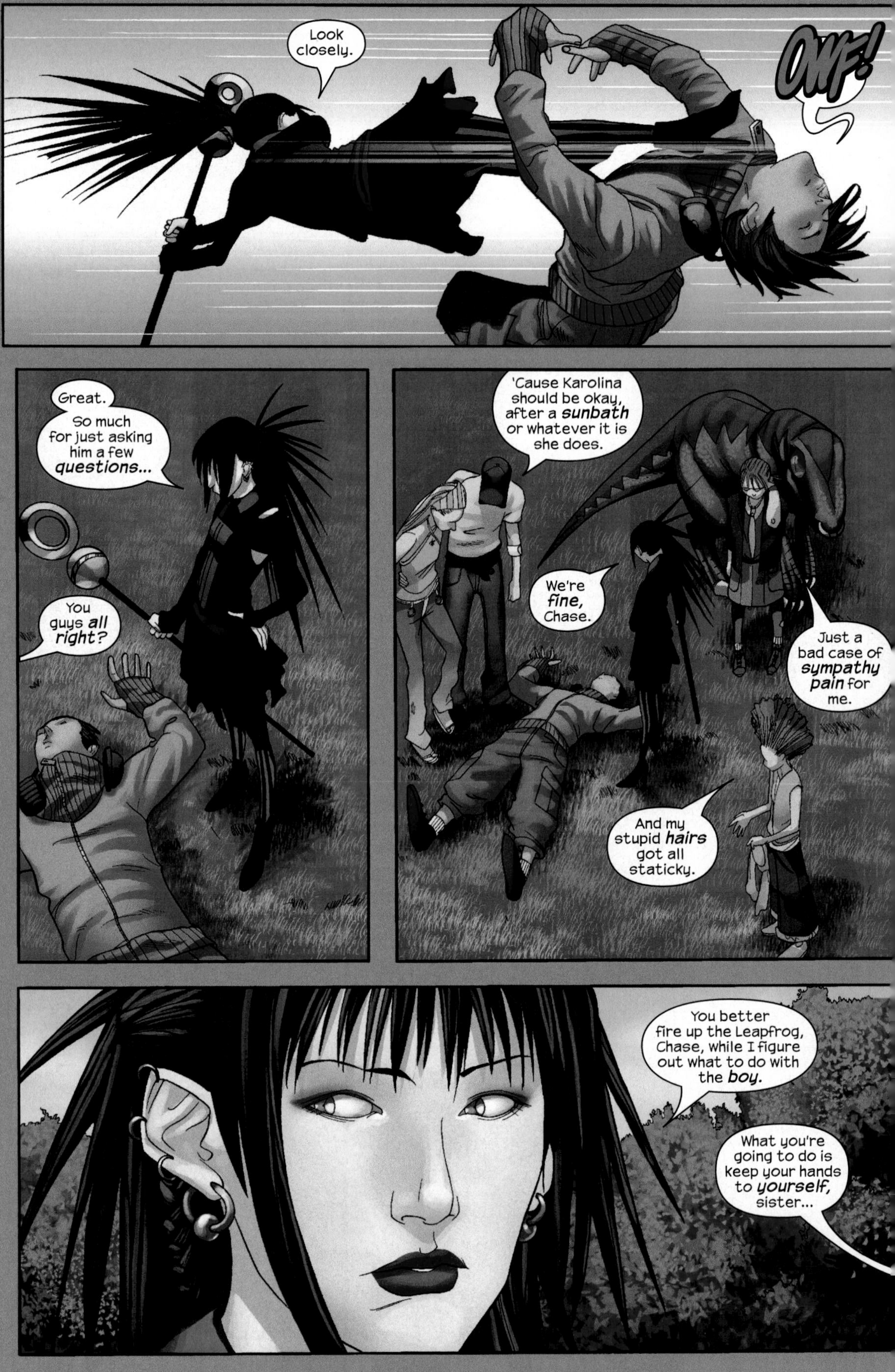
Look closely.
OWF!
Great. So much for just asking him a few questions...
You guys all right?
'Cause Karolina should be okay, after a sunbath or whatever it is she does.
We're fine, Chase.
Just a bad case of sympathy pain for me.
And my stupid hairs got all staticky.
You better fire up the Leapfrog, Chase, while I figure out what to do with the boy.
What you're going to do is keep your hands to yourself, sister...

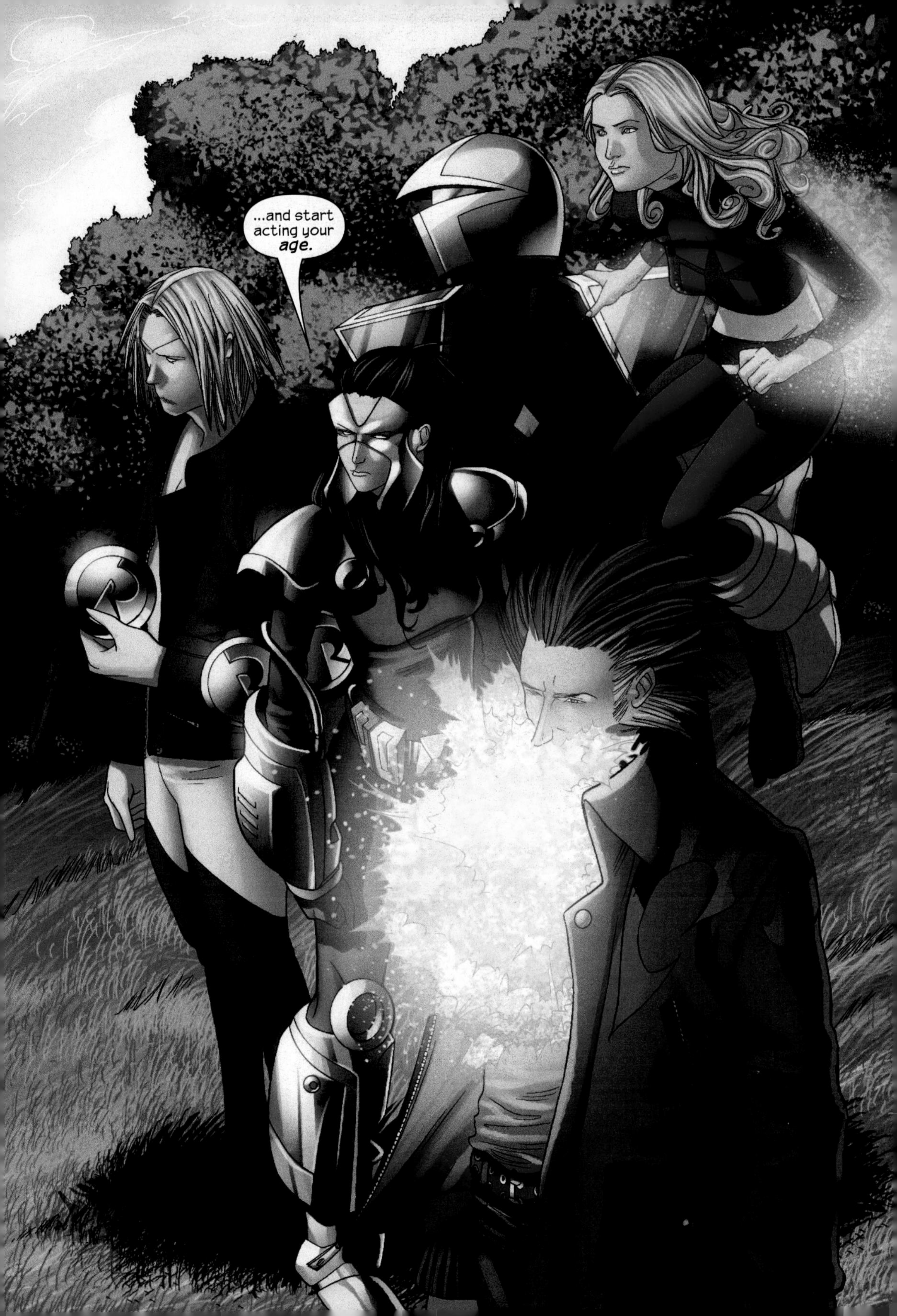
...and start acting your age.

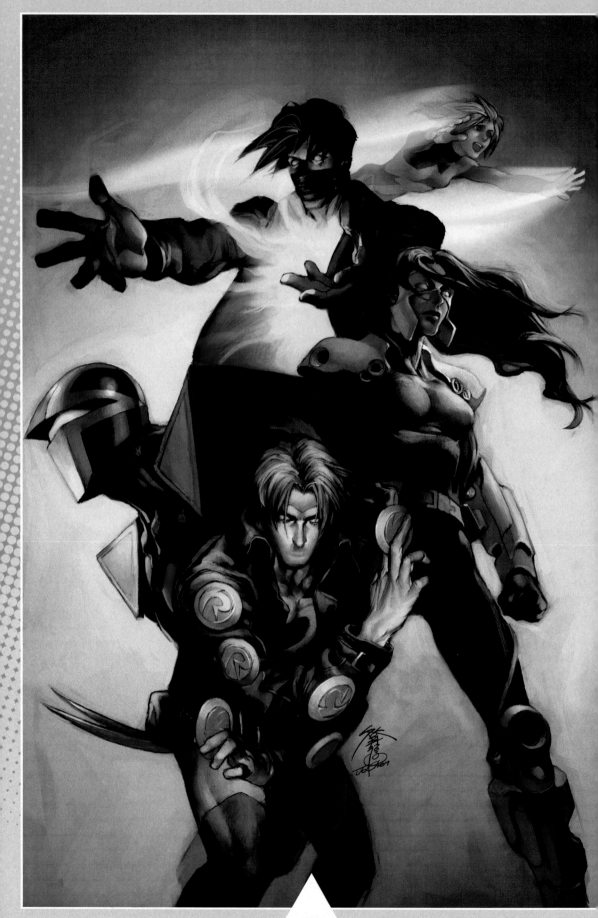

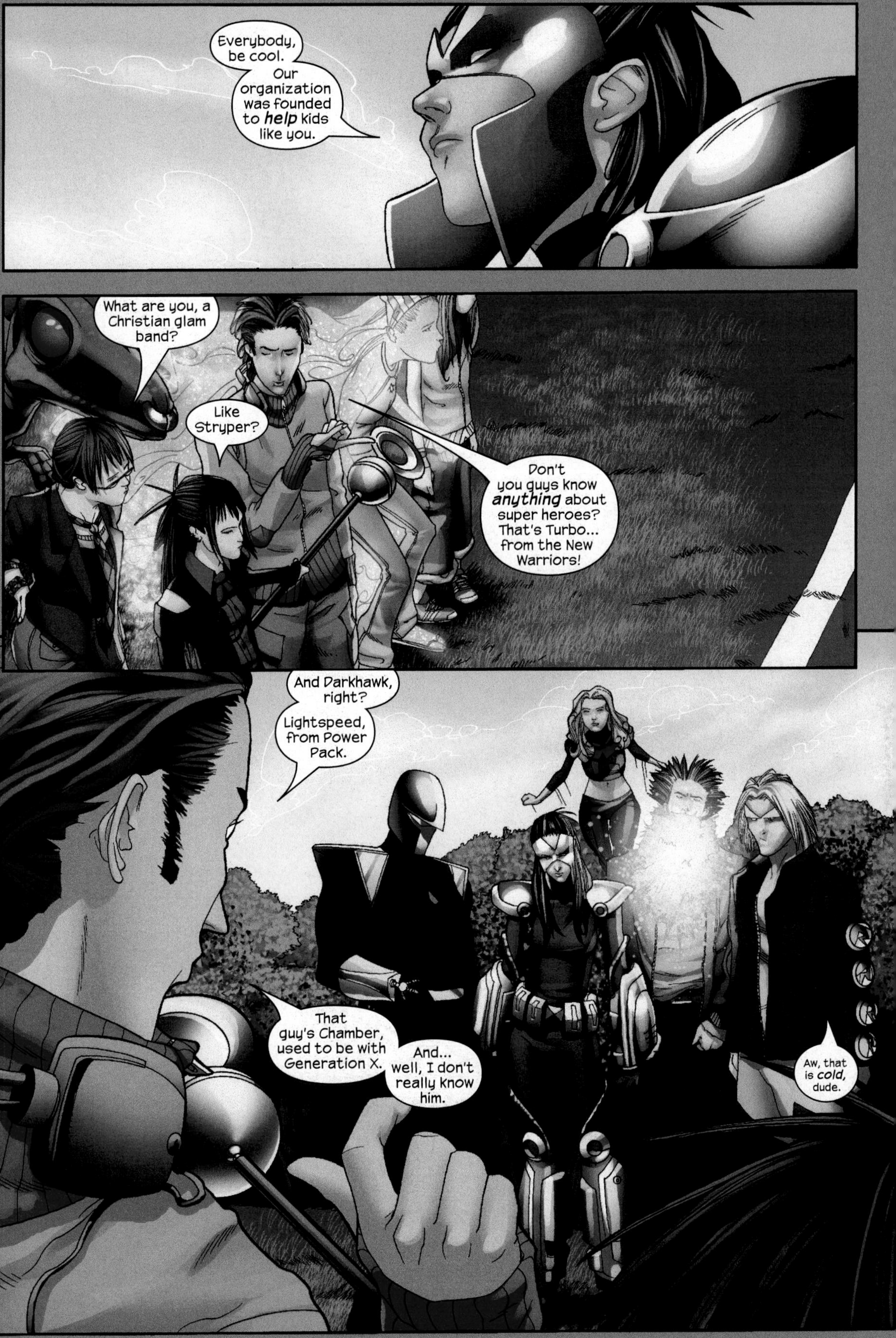
Everybody, be cool.
Our organization was founded to *help* kids like you.
What are you, a Christian glam band?
Like Stryper?
Don't you guys know *anything* about super heroes? That's Turbo... from the New Warriors!
And Darkhawk, right?
Lightspeed, from Power Pack.
That guy's Chamber, used to be with Generation X.
And... well, I don't really know him.
Aw, that is *cold,* dude.

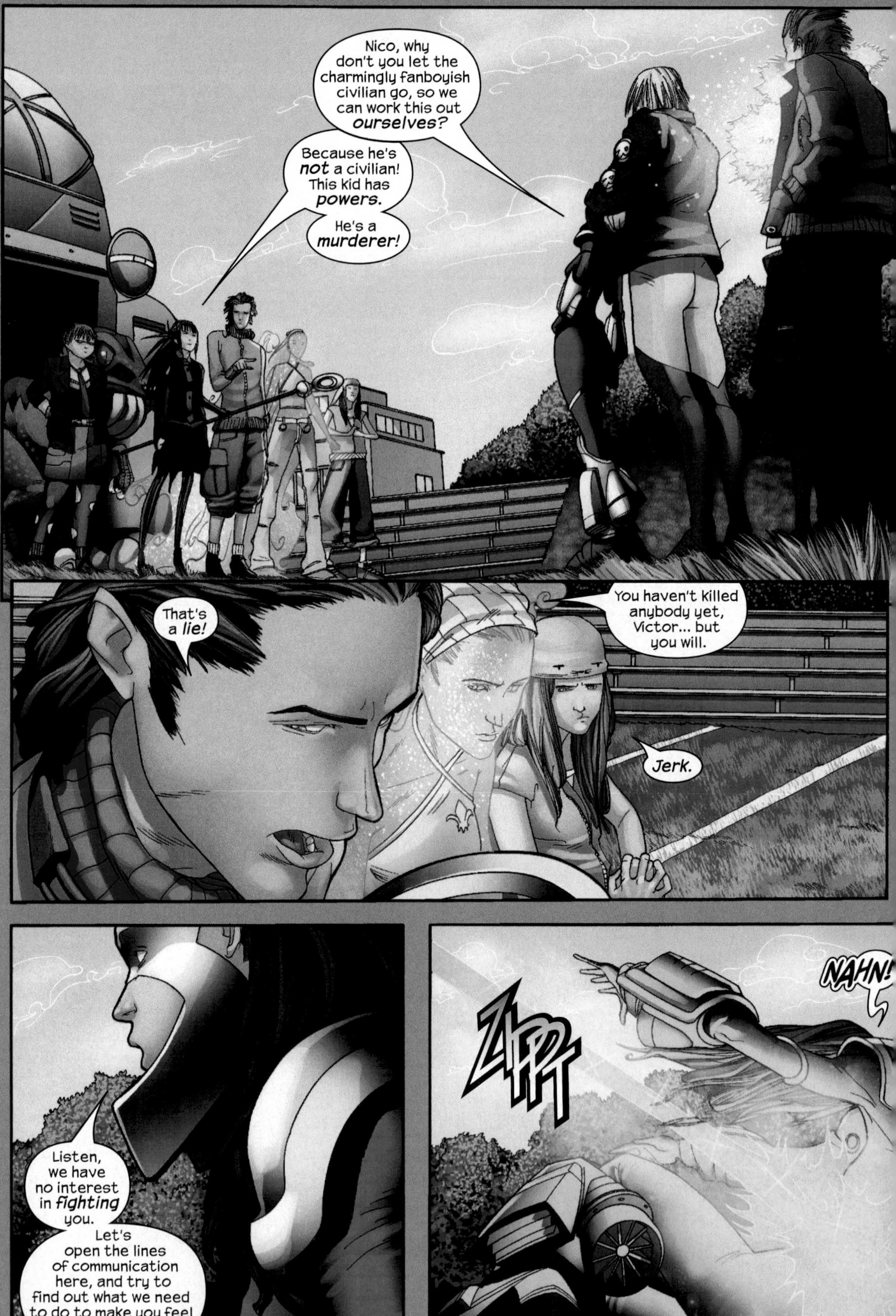

Nico, why don't you let the charmingly fanboyish civilian go, so we can work this out *ourselves?*
Because he's *not* a civilian! This kid has *powers.*
He's a *murderer!*
That's a *lie!*
You haven't killed anybody yet, Victor... but you will.
Jerk.
Listen, we have no interest in *fighting* you.
Let's open the lines of communication here, and try to find out what we need to do to make you feel more comfortable with--
ZIPPT
NAHN!

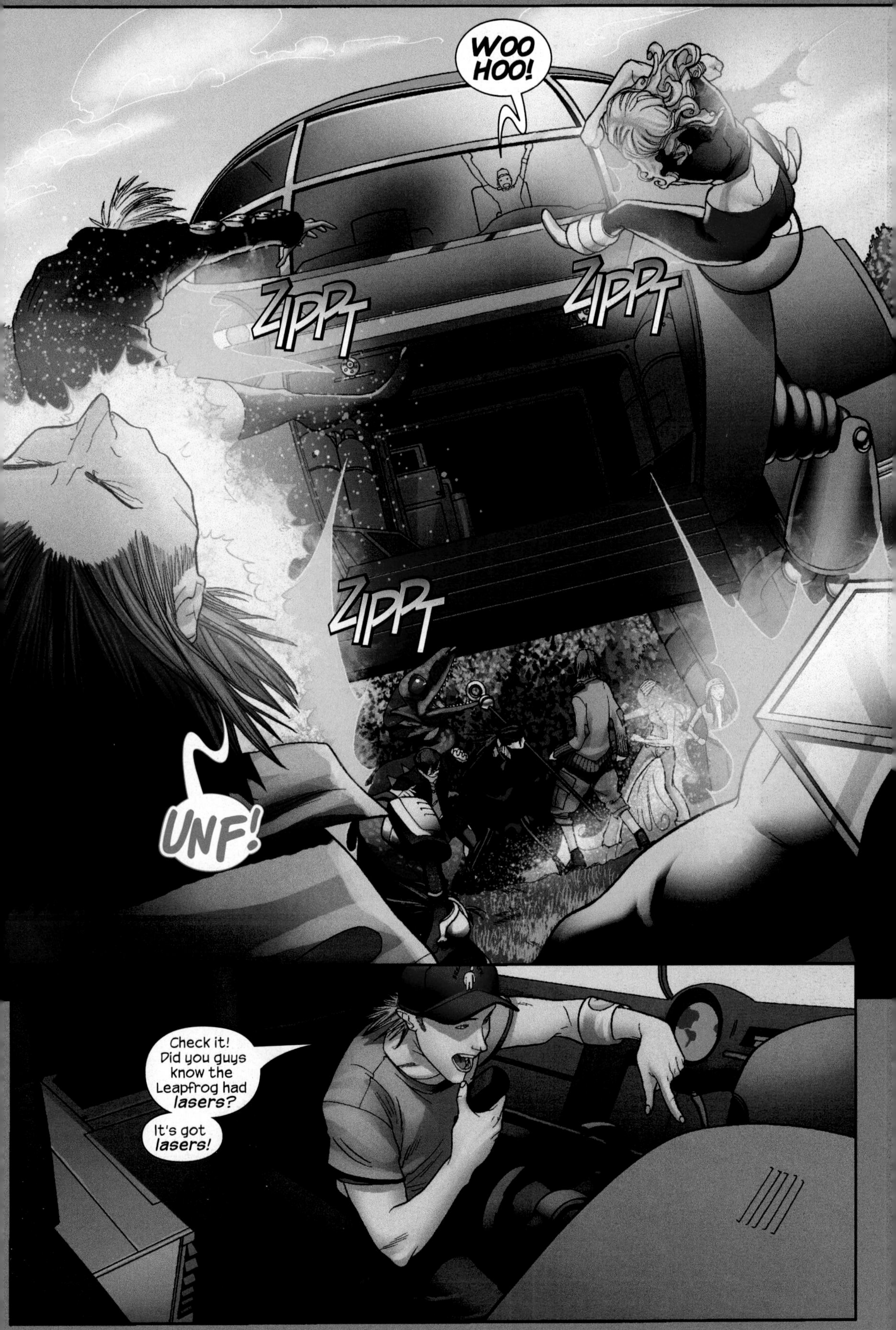
WOO HOO!
ZIPPT
ZIPPT
ZIPPT
UNF!
Check it! Did you guys know the Leapfrog had *lasers*?
It's got *lasers*!

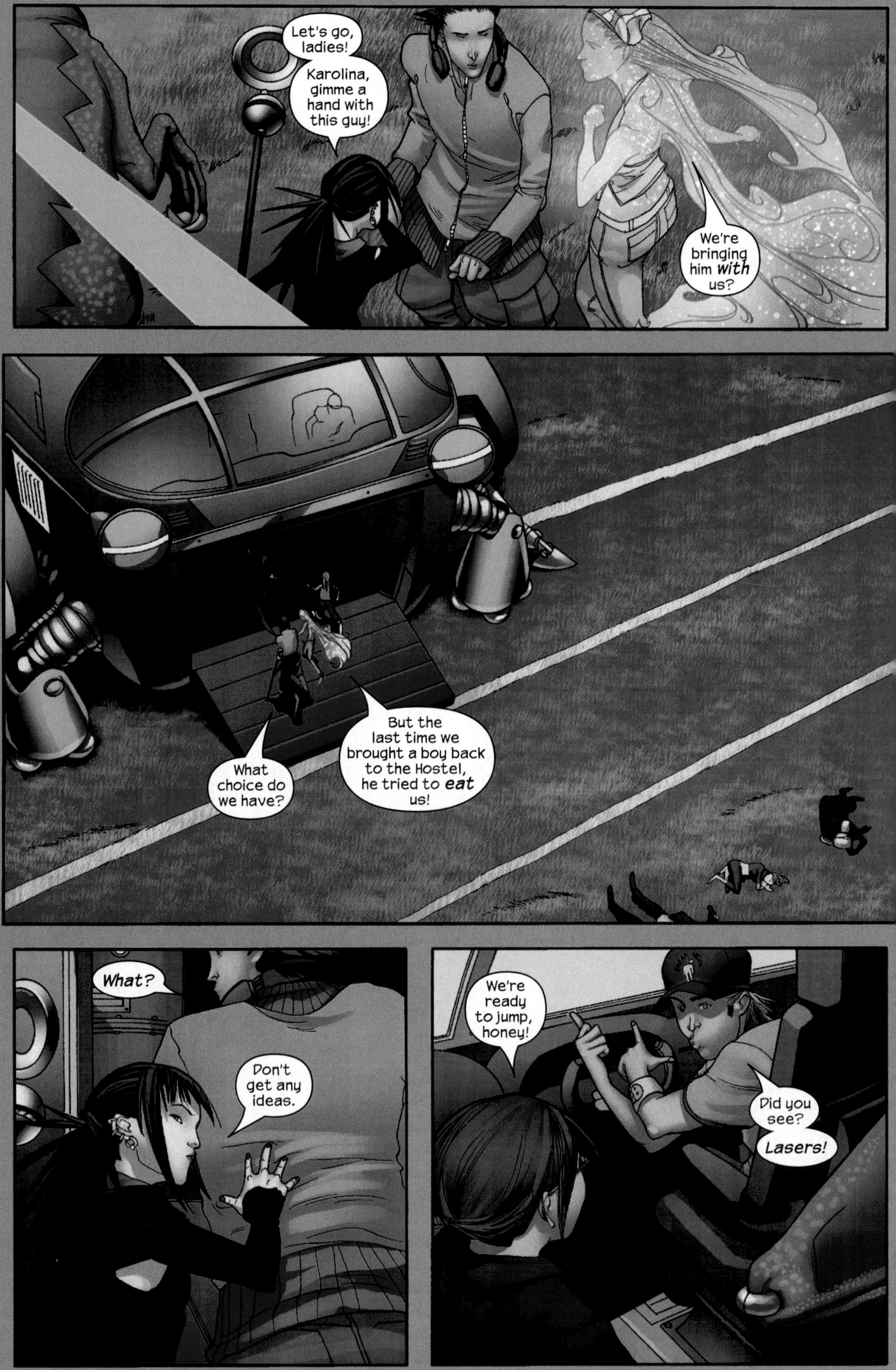
Let's go, ladies!
Karolina, gimme a hand with this guy!
We're bringing him *with* us?
But the last time we brought a boy back to the Hostel, he tried to *eat* us!
What choice do we have?
What?
Don't get any ideas.
We're ready to jump, honey!
Did you see?
Lasers!

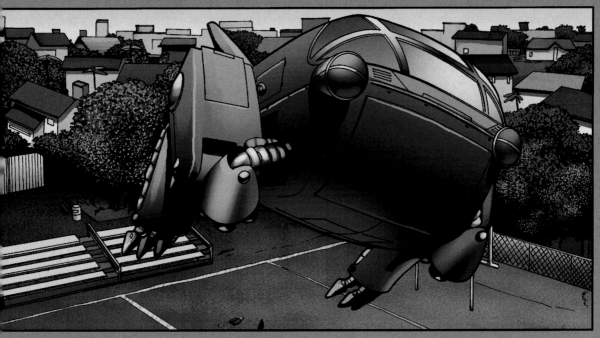

What... what was *that* all about?

We just got schooled by a bunch of *freshmen*, Ricochet.

What do we do now, Mickey?

We go after them!

Unless we're taking the bus again, count me out.

What are you talking about, Jono? We need you!

Our group's only got three fliers, and that means one of you would have to *carry* me by my stinkin' pits. It happens in super-teams all the time, and guys like me always end up looking like complete *gits*. I absolutely, positively refuse to...

⋟sigh⋞
Fine, but if Dorkhawk touches me, I'm breaking his arm.

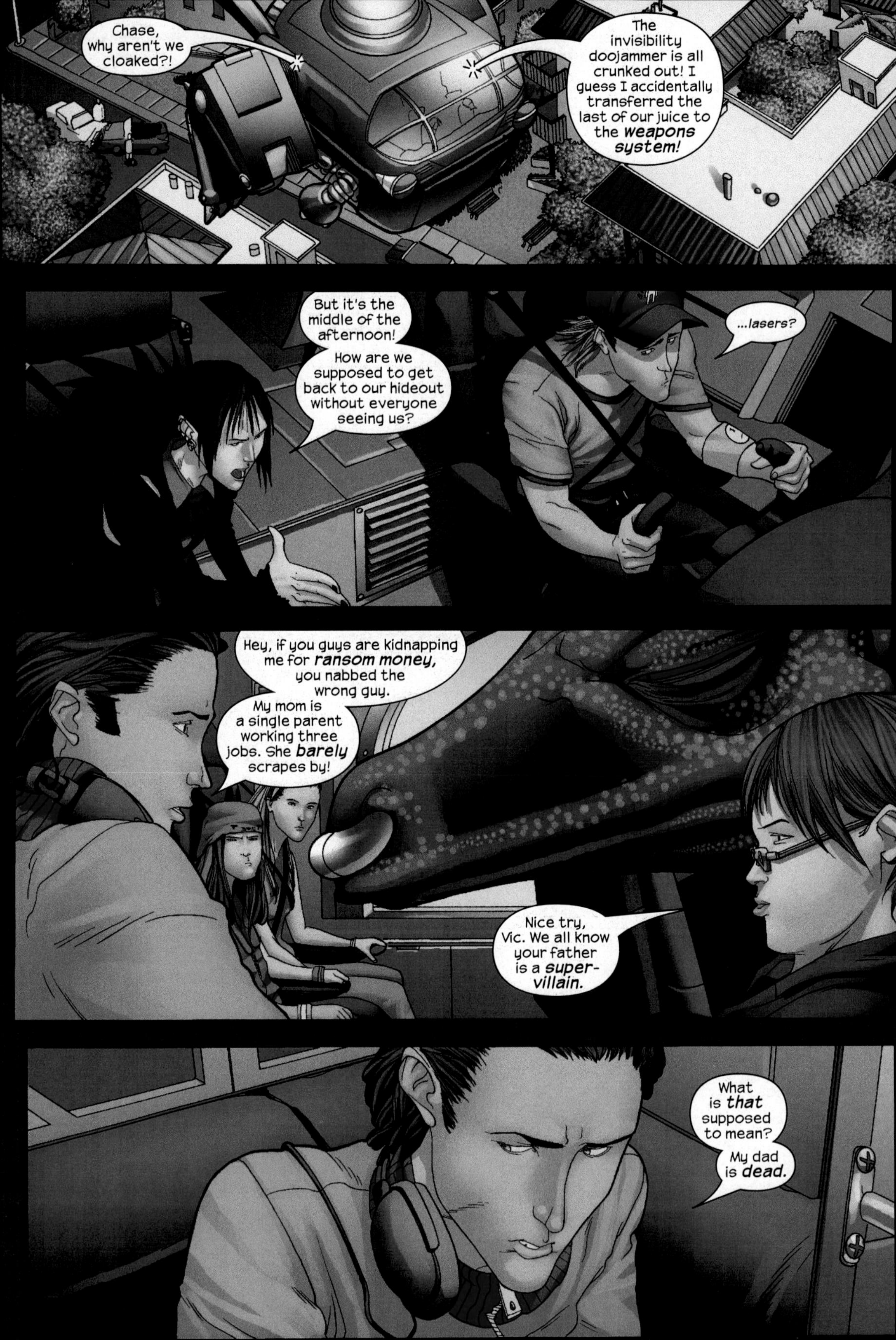
Chase, why aren't we cloaked?!
The invisibility doojammer is all crunked out! I guess I accidentally transferred the last of our juice to the *weapons system!*
But it's the middle of the afternoon!
How are we supposed to get back to our hideout without everyone seeing us?
...lasers?
Hey, if you guys are kidnapping me for *ransom money,* you nabbed the wrong guy.
My mom is a single parent working three jobs. She *barely* scrapes by!
Nice try, Vic. We all know your father is a *super-villain.*
What is *that* supposed to mean?
My dad is *dead.*

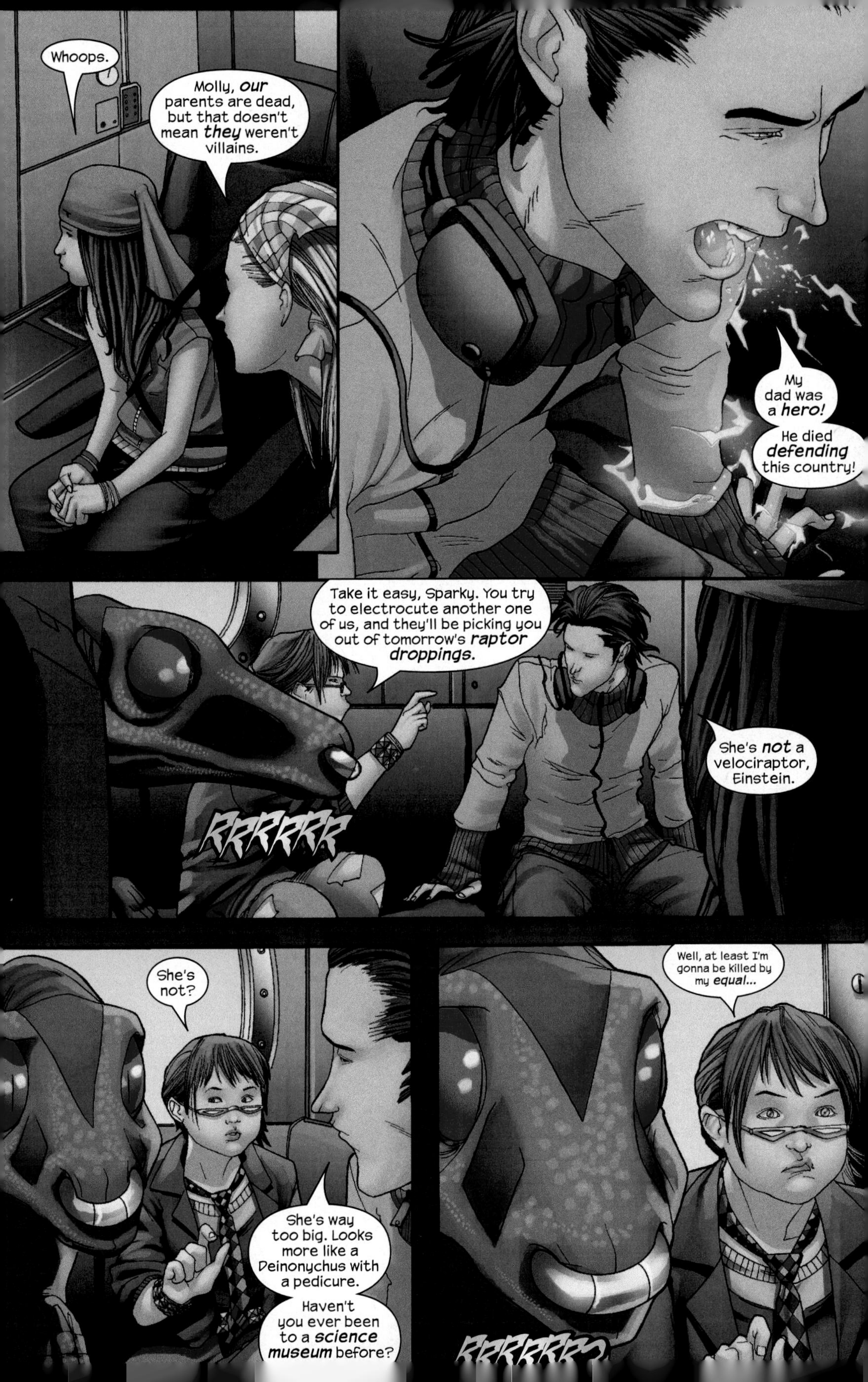

Whoops.
Molly, our parents are dead, but that doesn't mean they weren't villains.
My dad was a hero!
He died defending this country!
Take it easy, Sparky. You try to electrocute another one of us, and they'll be picking you out of tomorrow's raptor droppings.
She's not a velociraptor, Einstein.
RRRRRR
She's not?
She's way too big. Looks more like a Deinonychus with a pedicure.
Haven't you ever been to a science museum before?
Well, at least I'm gonna be killed by my equal...

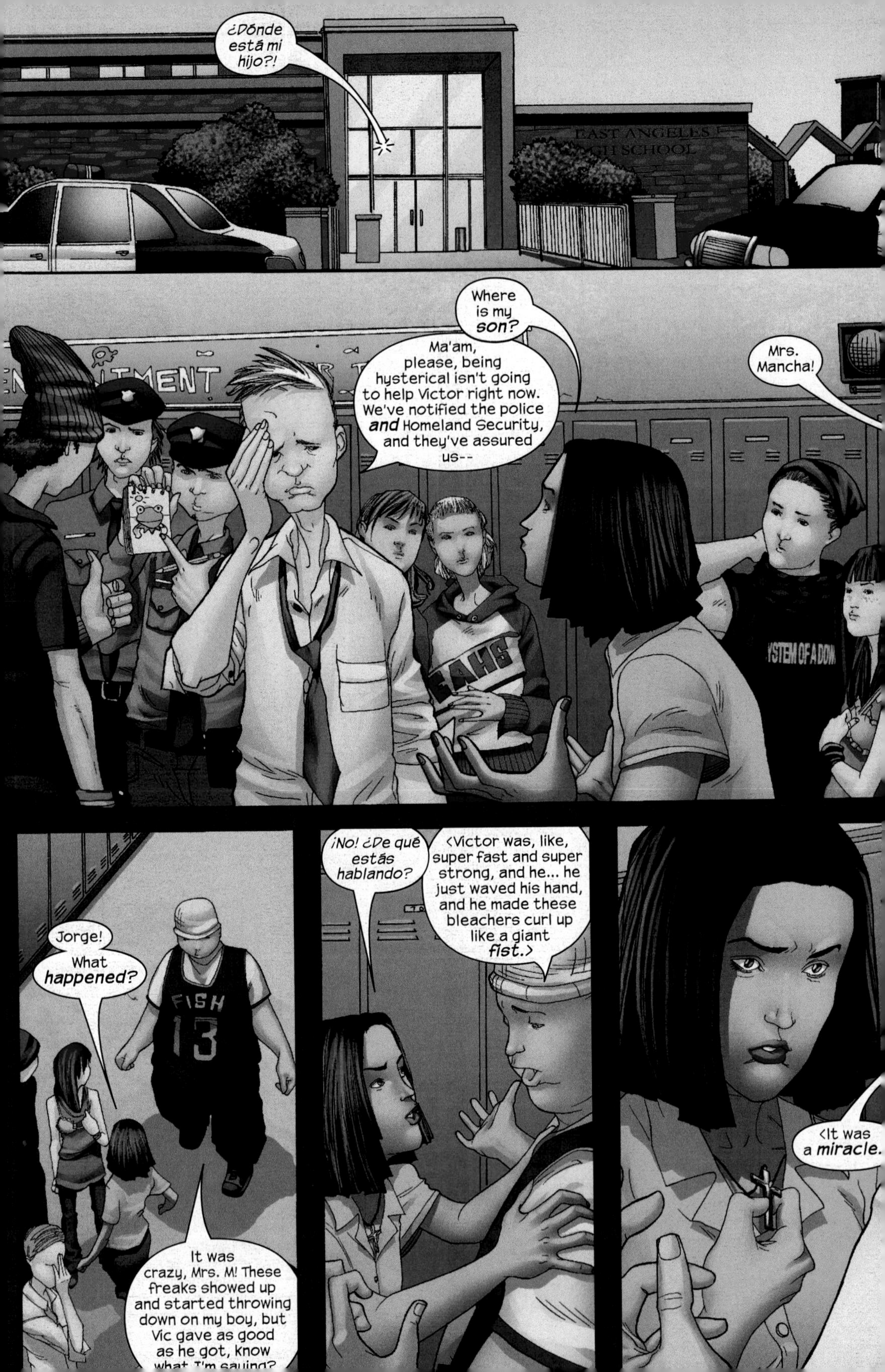
¿Dónde está mi hijo?!
Where is my son?
Ma'am, please, being hysterical isn't going to help Victor right now. We've notified the police and Homeland Security, and they've assured us--
Mrs. Mancha!
EAHS
Jorge!
What happened?
FISH 13
It was crazy, Mrs. M! These freaks showed up and started throwing down on my boy, but Vic gave as good as he got, know what I'm saying?
¡No! ¿De qué estás hablando?
<Victor was, like, super fast and super strong, and he... he just waved his hand, and he made these bleachers curl up like a giant fist.>
<It was a miracle.

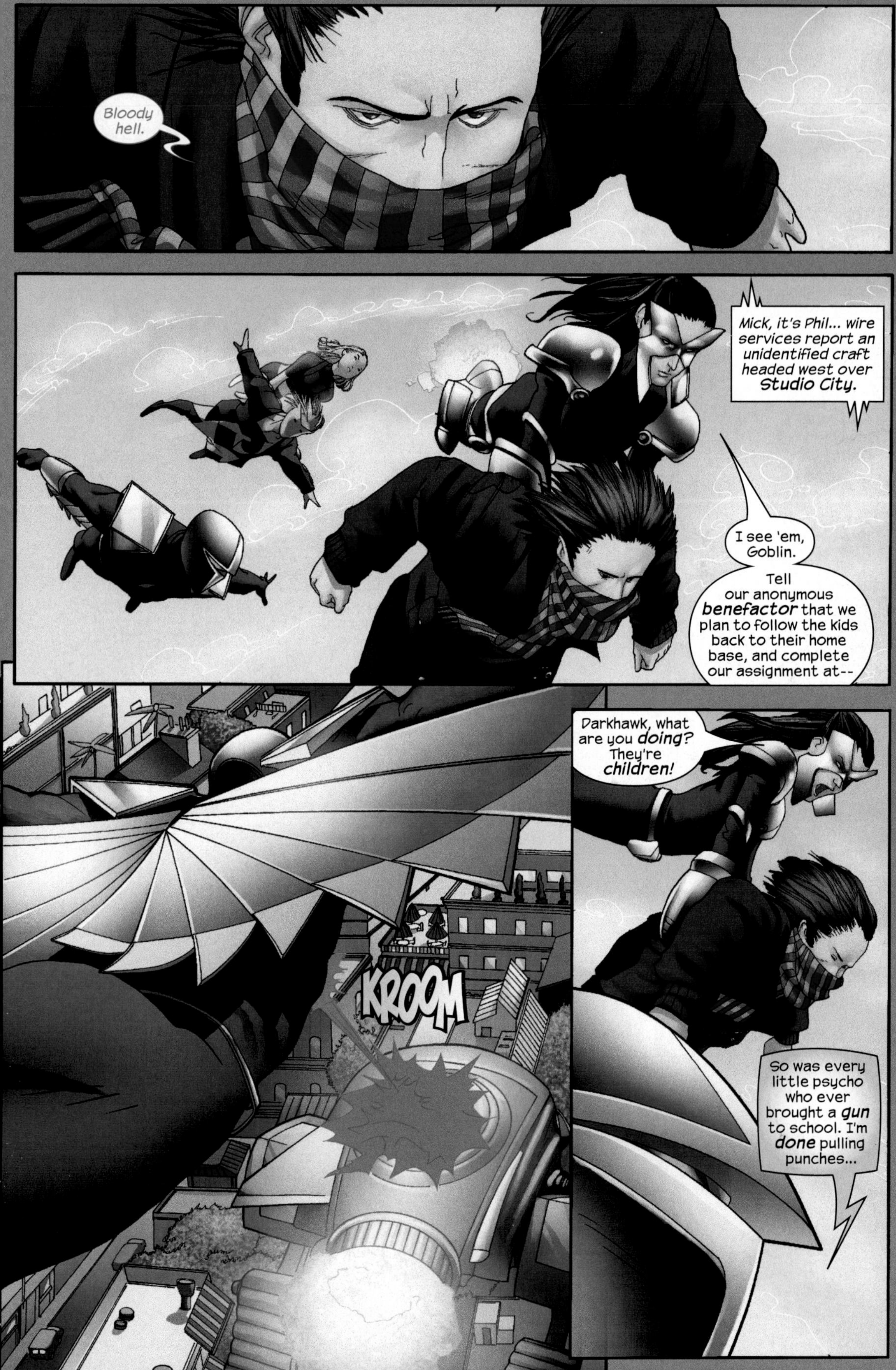
Bloody hell.
Mick, it's Phil... wire services report an unidentified craft headed west over Studio City.
I see 'em, Goblin.
Tell our anonymous benefactor that we plan to follow the kids back to their home base, and complete our assignment at--
KROOM
Darkhawk, what are you doing? They're children!
So was every little psycho who ever brought a gun to school. I'm done pulling punches...

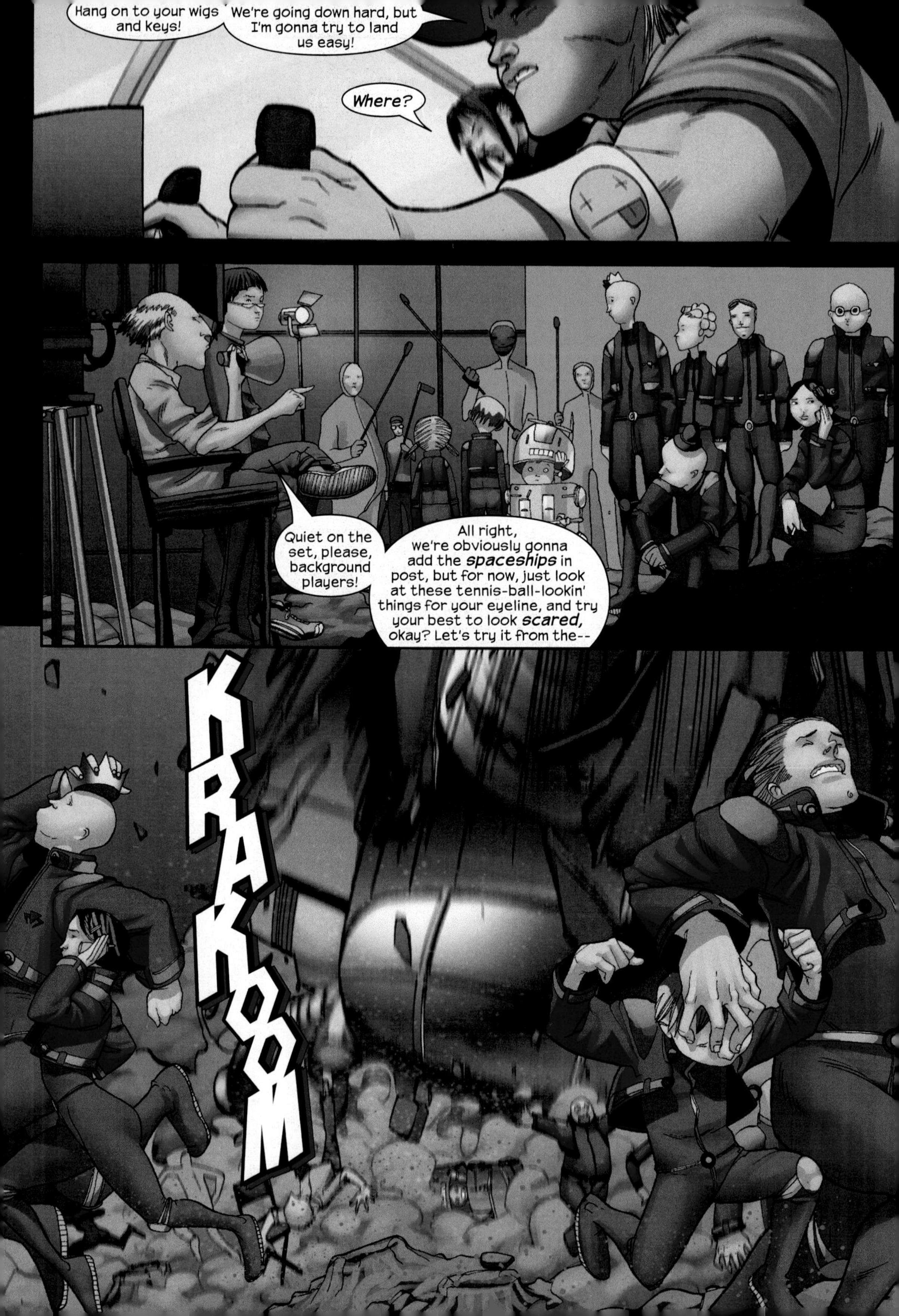
Hang on to your wigs and keys!
We're going down hard, but I'm gonna try to land us easy!
Where?
Quiet on the set, please, background players!
All right, we're obviously gonna add the spaceships in post, but for now, just look at these tennis-ball-lookin' things for your eyeline, and try your best to look scared, okay? Let's try it from the--
KRAKOOM

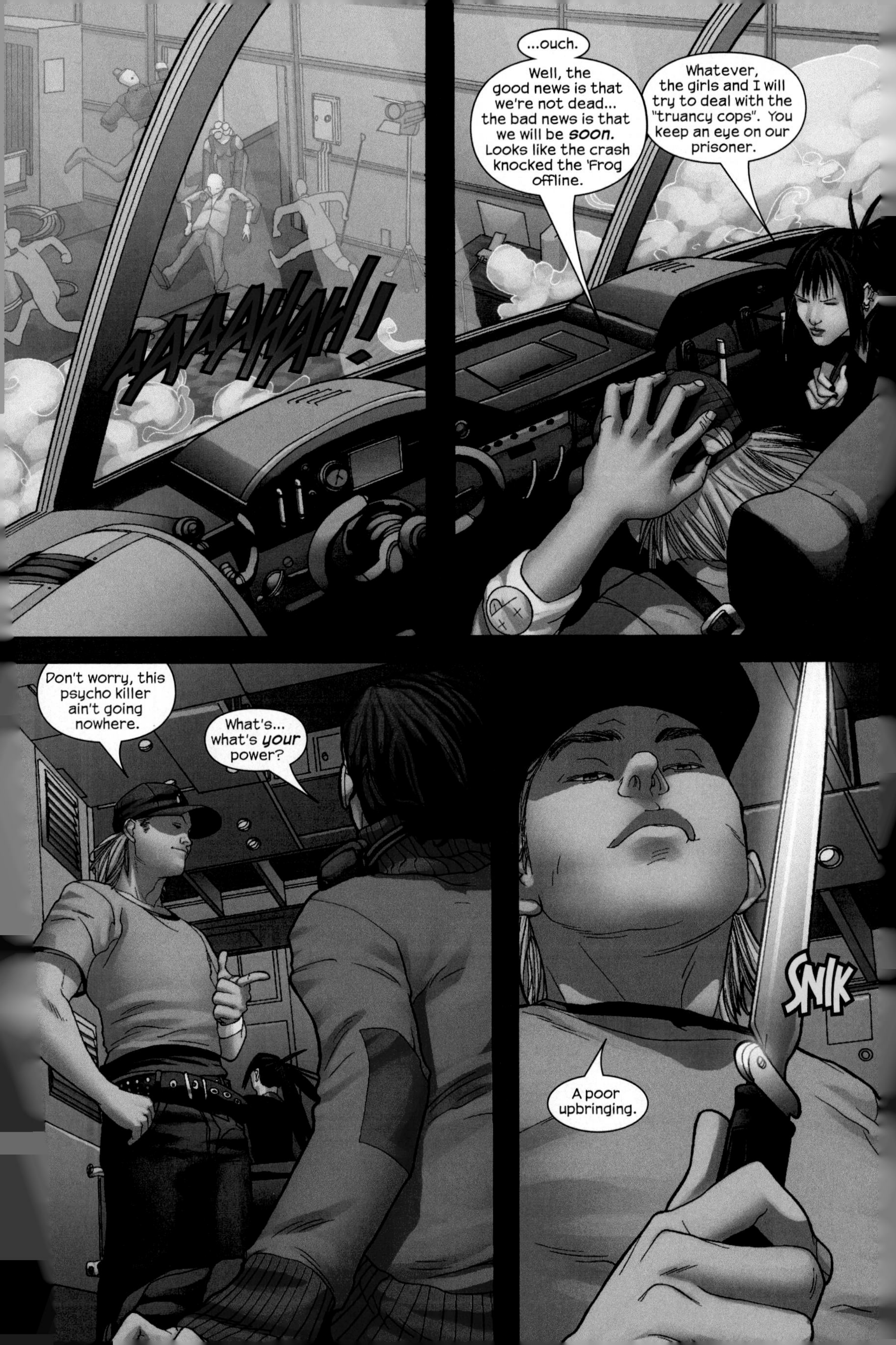
AAAAHAH!!
...ouch.
Well, the good news is that we're not dead... the bad news is that we will be *soon.* Looks like the crash knocked the 'Frog offline.
Whatever, the girls and I will try to deal with the "truancy cops". You keep an eye on our prisoner.
Don't worry, this psycho killer ain't going nowhere.
What's... what's *your* power?
SNIK
A poor upbringing.

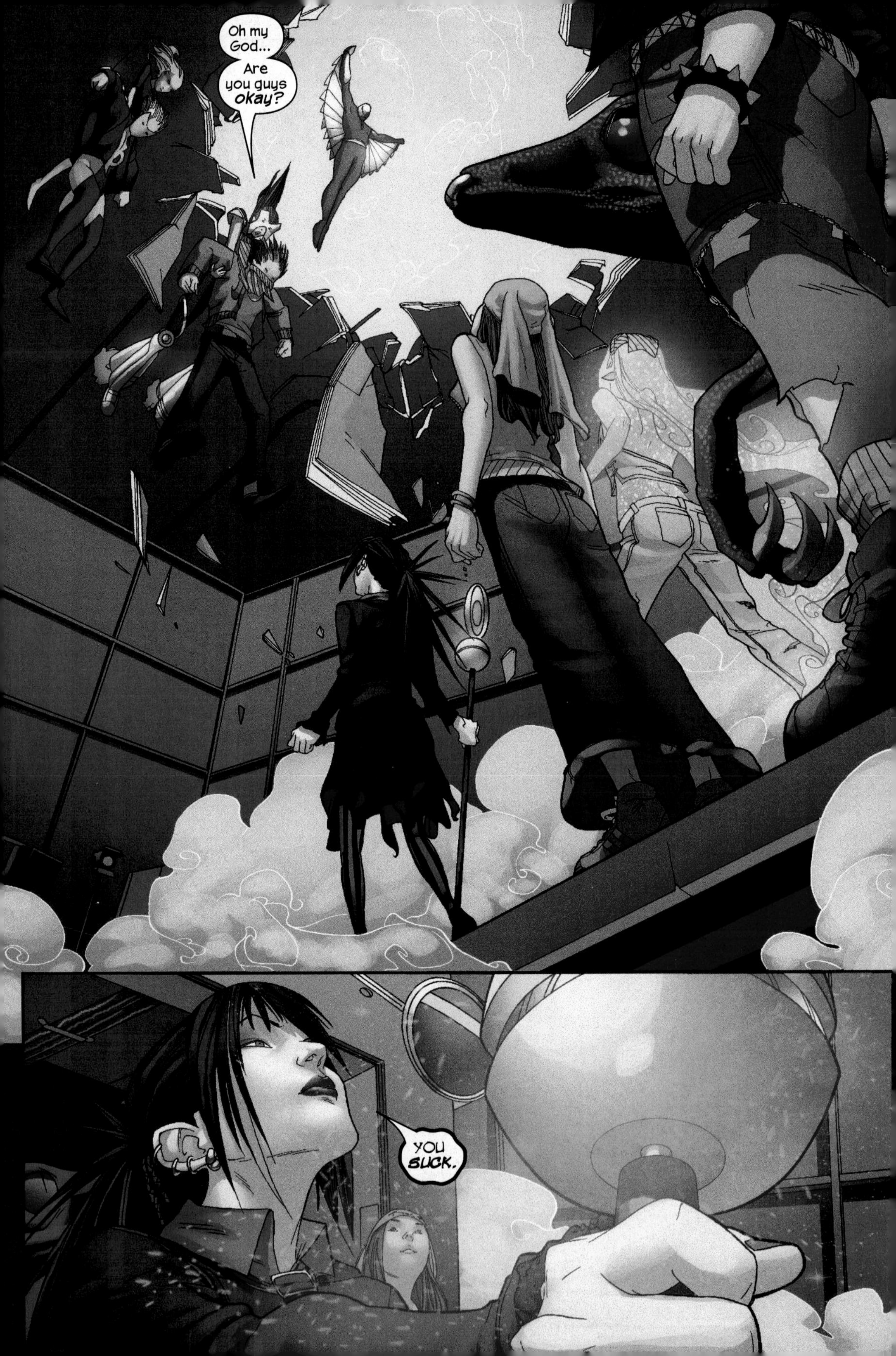
Oh my God...
Are you guys okay?
YOU SUCK.

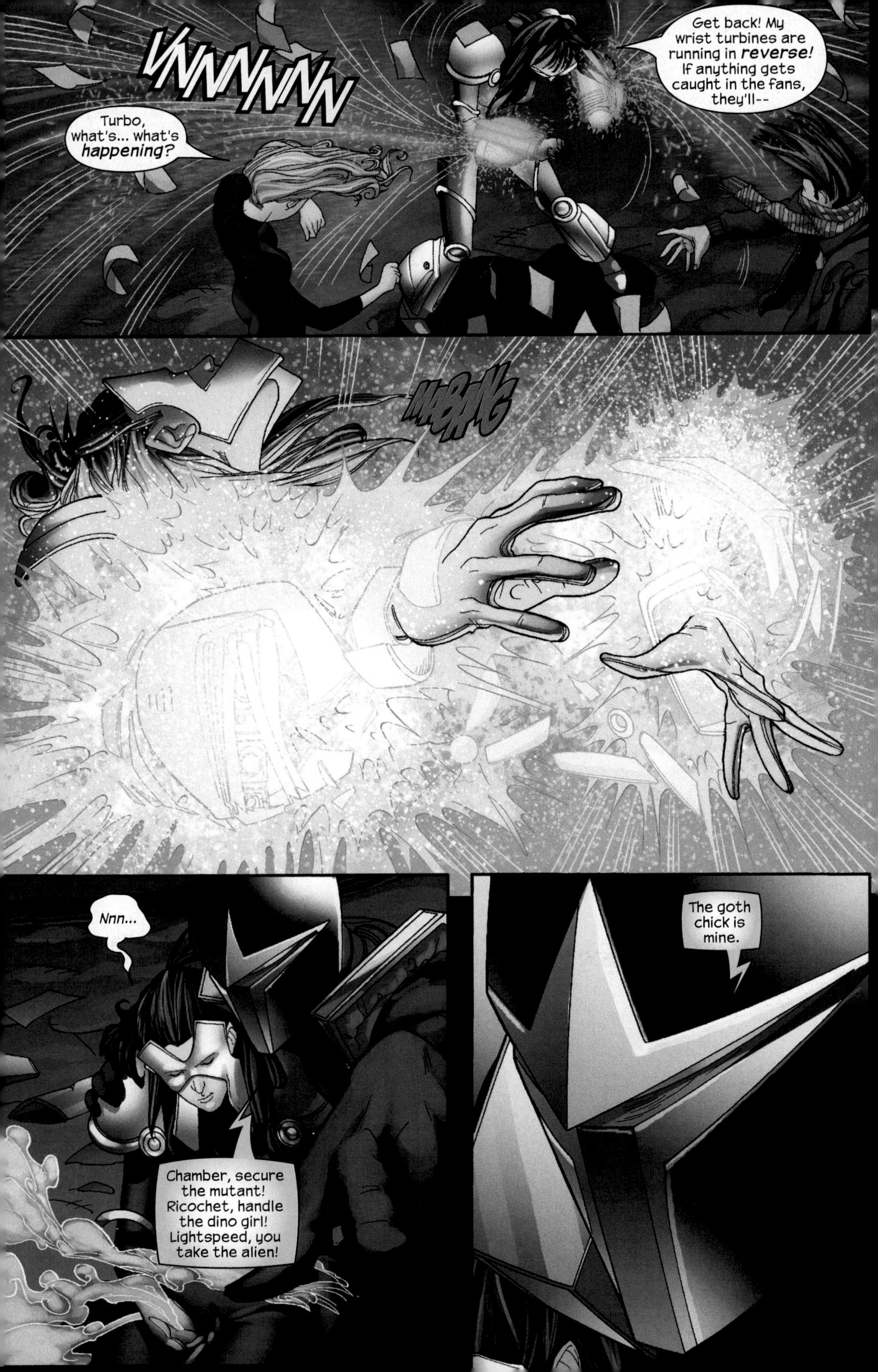
VNNNNNN
Get back! My wrist turbines are running in reverse! If anything gets caught in the fans, they'll--
Turbo, what's... what's happening?
MABANG
Nnn...
Chamber, secure the mutant! Ricochet, handle the dino girl! Lightspeed, you take the alien!
The goth chick is mine.

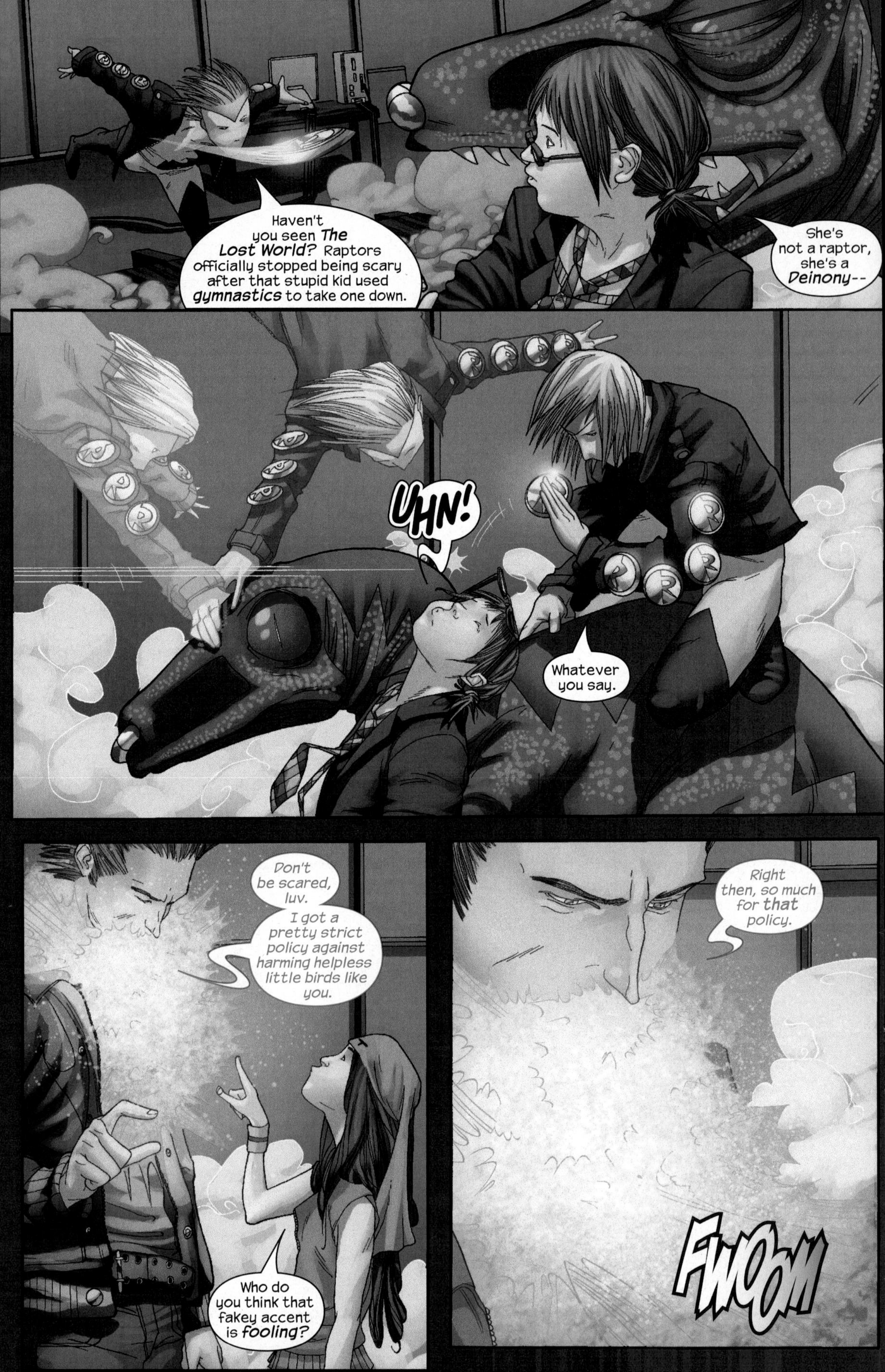
Haven't you seen The Lost World? Raptors officially stopped being scary after that stupid kid used gymnastics to take one down.
She's not a raptor, she's a Deinony--
UHN!
Whatever you say.
Don't be scared, luv.
I got a pretty strict policy against harming helpless little birds like you.
Who do you think that fakey accent is fooling?
Right then, so much for that policy.
FWOOM

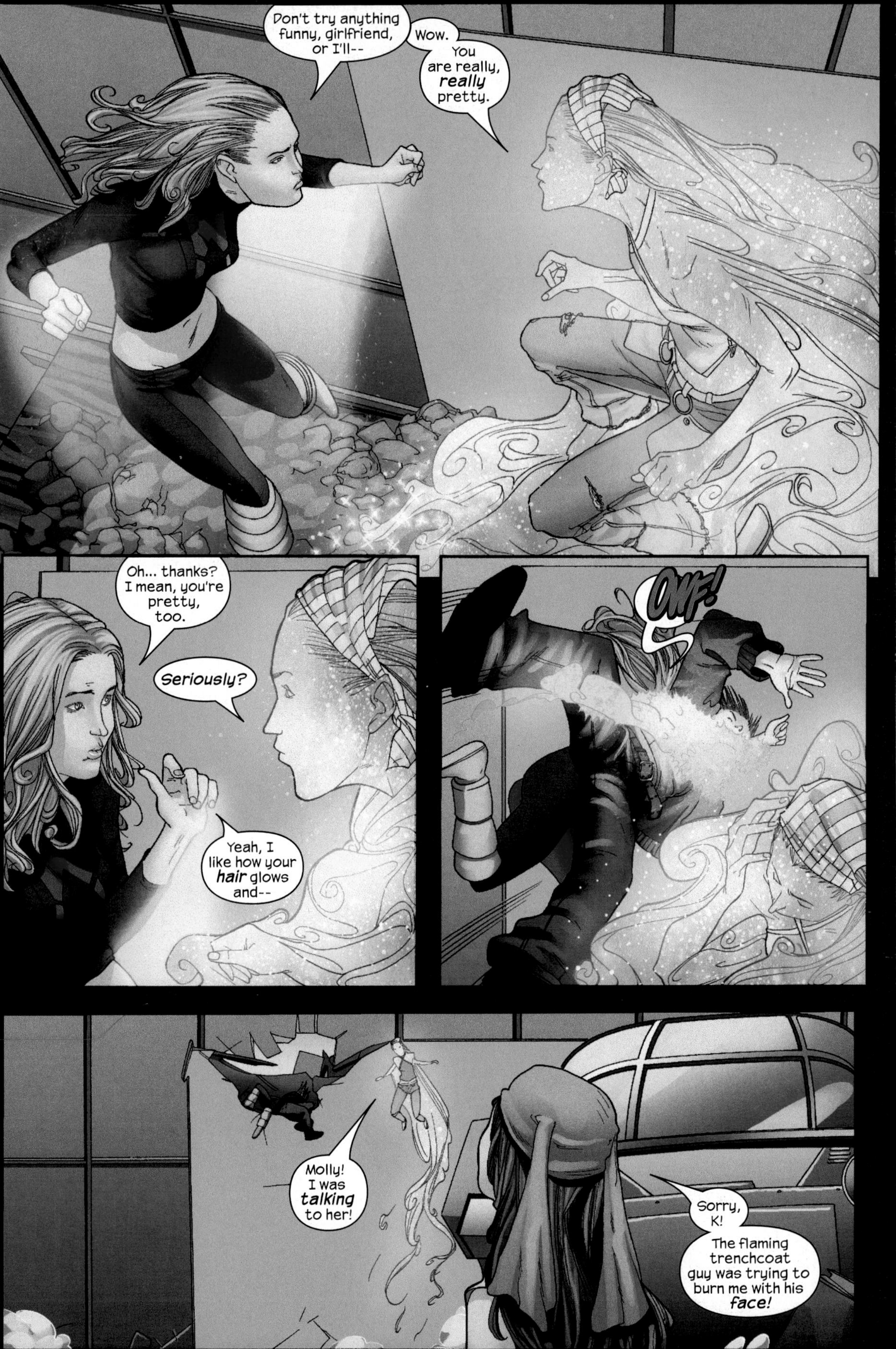
Don't try anything funny, girlfriend, or I'll--
Wow.
You are really, *really* pretty.
Oh... thanks? I mean, you're pretty, too.
Seriously?
Yeah, I like how your *hair* glows and--
OWF!
Molly! I was *talking* to her!
Sorry, K!
The flaming trenchcoat guy was trying to burn me with his *face!*

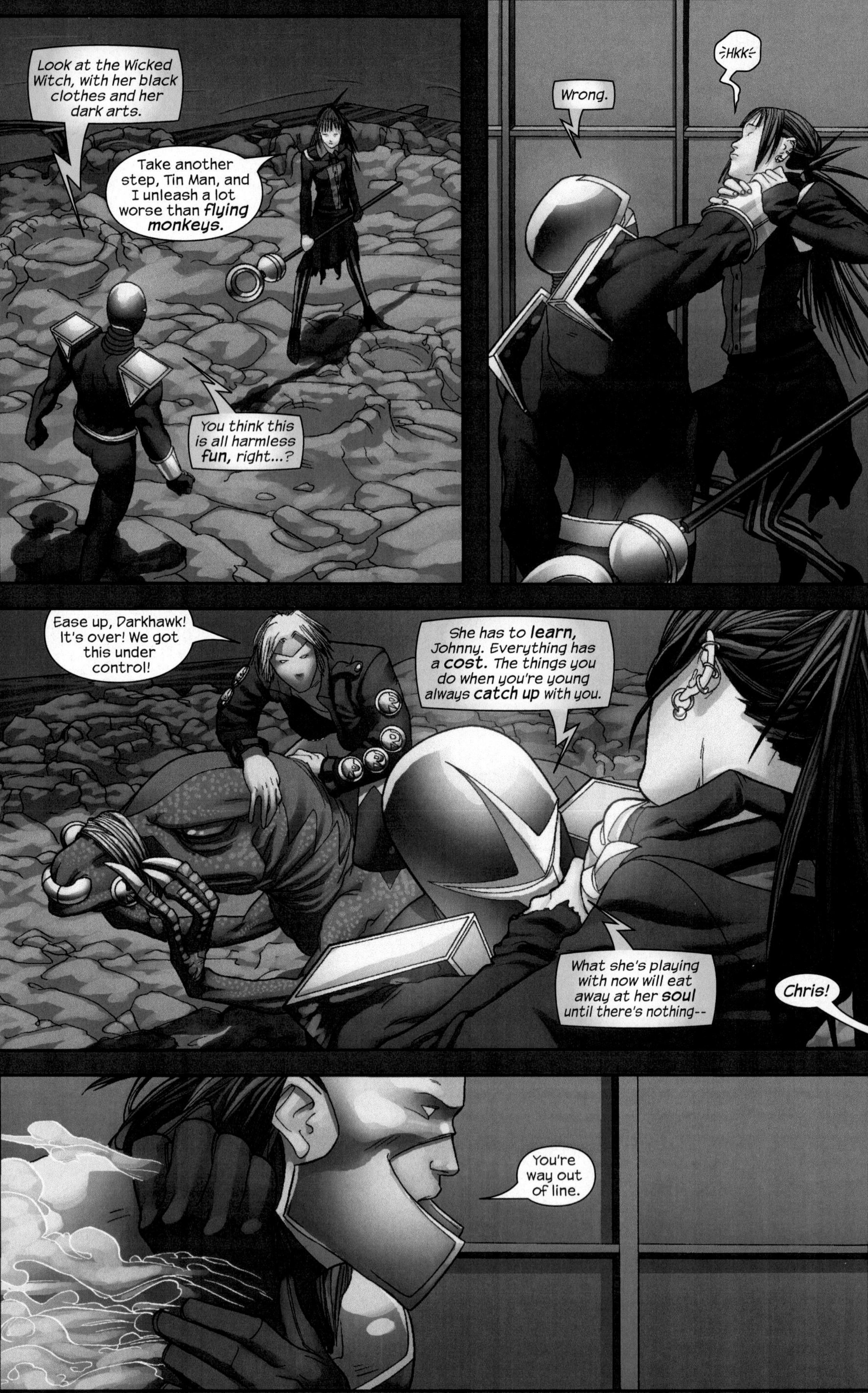

Look at the Wicked Witch, with her black clothes and her dark arts.
Take another step, Tin Man, and I unleash a lot worse than flying monkeys.
You think this is all harmless fun, right...?
Wrong.
HKK
Ease up, Darkhawk! It's over! We got this under control!
She has to learn, Johnny. Everything has a cost. The things you do when you're young always catch up with you.
What she's playing with now will eat away at her soul until there's nothing--
Chris!
You're way out of line.

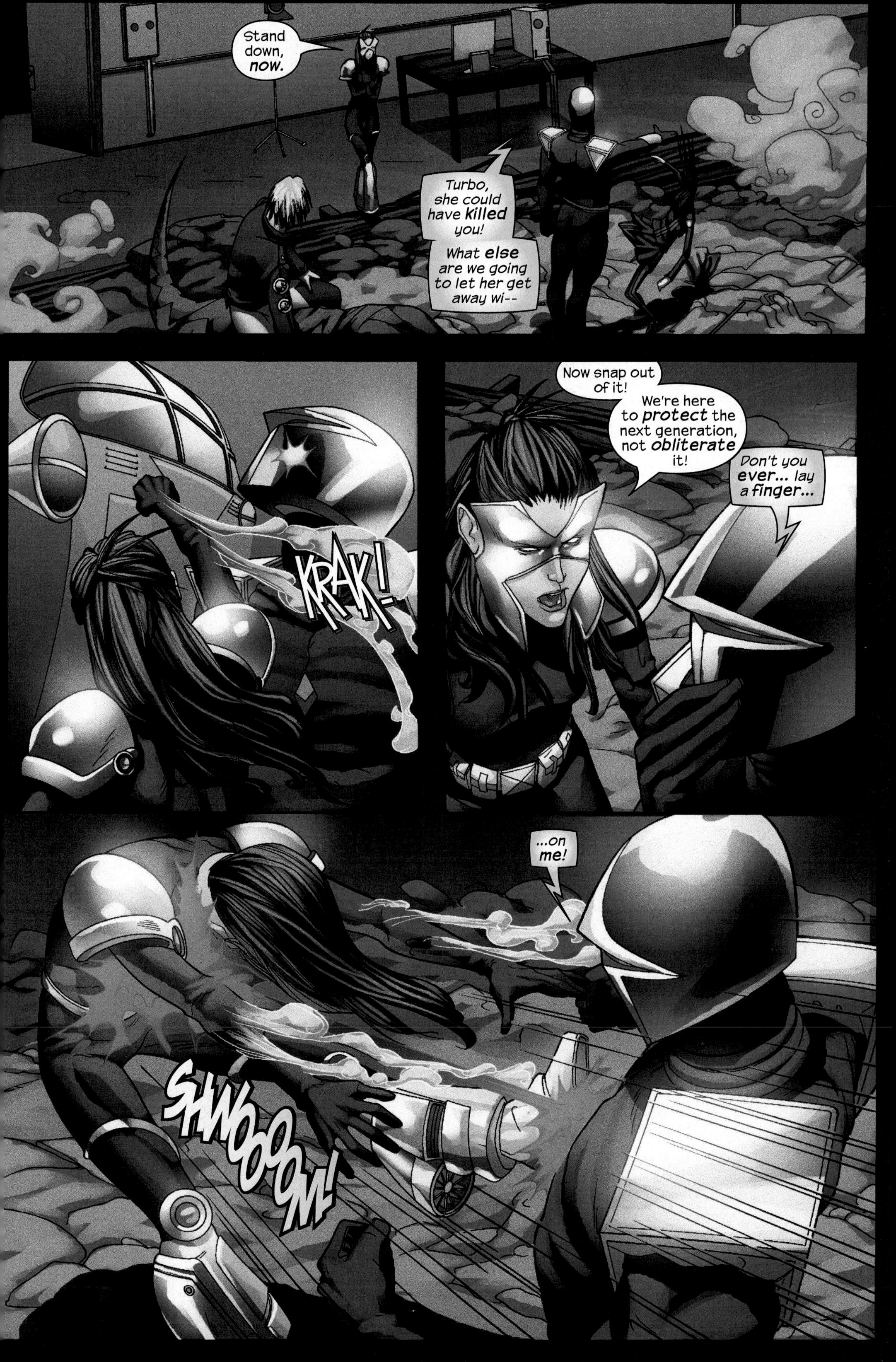
Stand down, now.
Turbo, she could have killed you!
What else are we going to let her get away wi--
KRAK!
Now snap out of it!
We're here to protect the next generation, not obliterate it!
Don't you ever... lay a finger...
...on me!
SHWOOOOM!

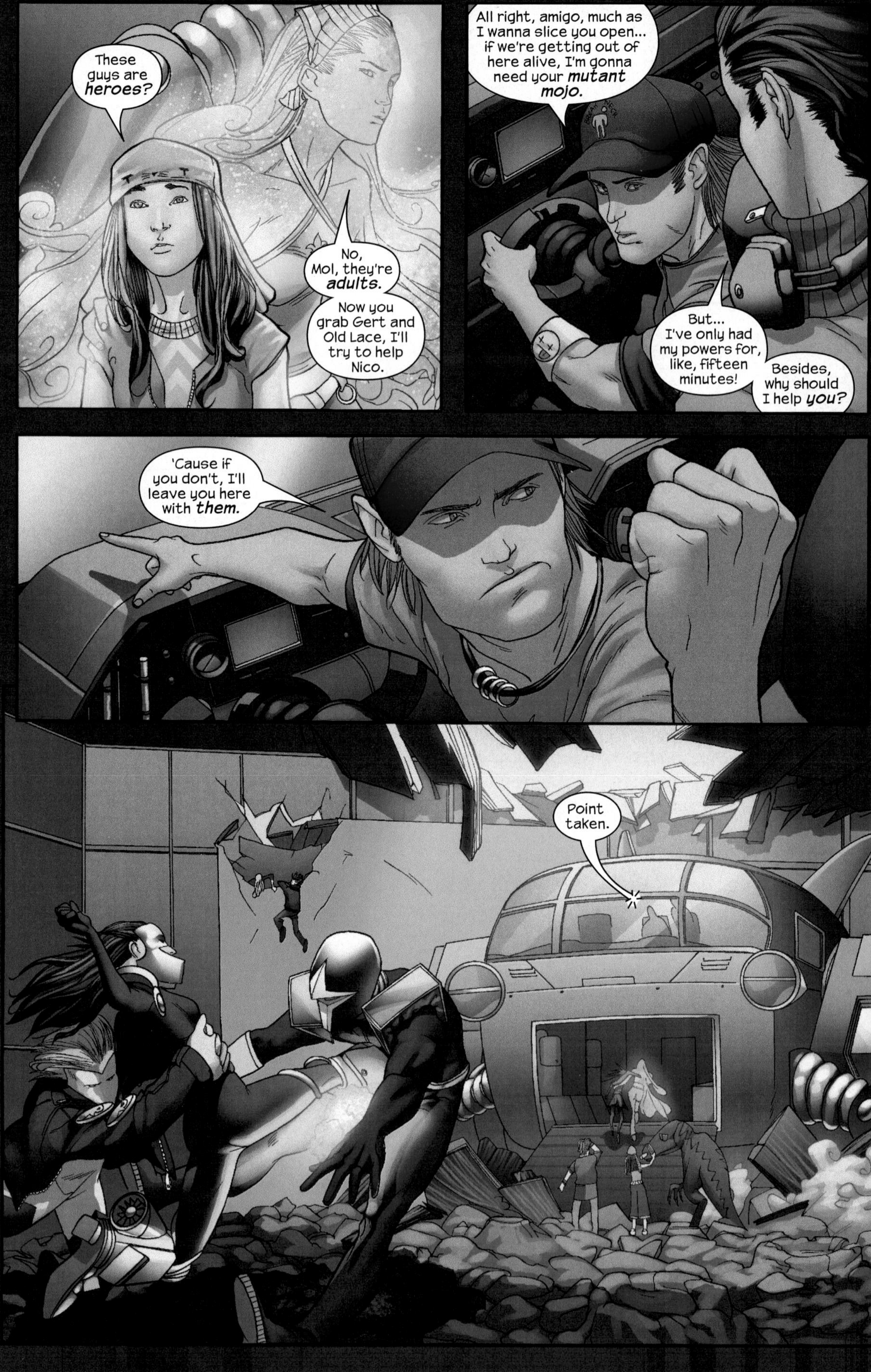
These guys are *heroes?*
No, Mol, they're *adults.*
Now you grab Gert and Old Lace, I'll try to help Nico.
All right, amigo, much as I wanna slice you open... if we're getting out of here alive, I'm gonna need your *mutant mojo.*
But... I've only had my powers for, like, fifteen minutes!
Besides, why should I help *you?*
'Cause if you don't, I'll leave you here with *them.*
Point taken.

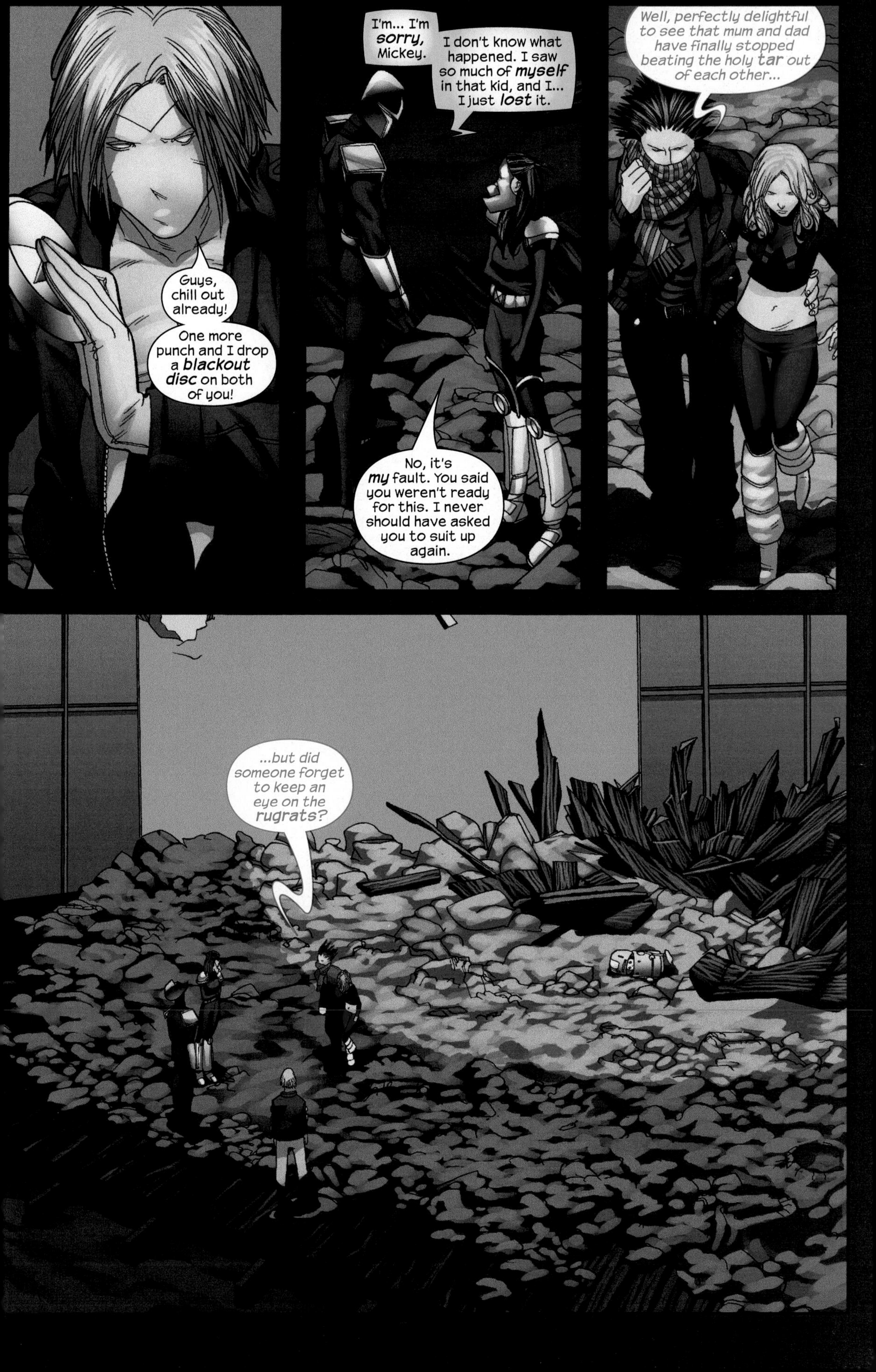
Guys, chill out already!
One more punch and I drop a blackout disc on both of you!
I'm... I'm sorry, Mickey.
I don't know what happened. I saw so much of myself in that kid, and I... I just lost it.
No, it's my fault. You said you weren't ready for this. I never should have asked you to suit up again.
Well, perfectly delightful to see that mum and dad have finally stopped beating the holy tar out of each other...
...but did someone forget to keep an eye on the rugrats?

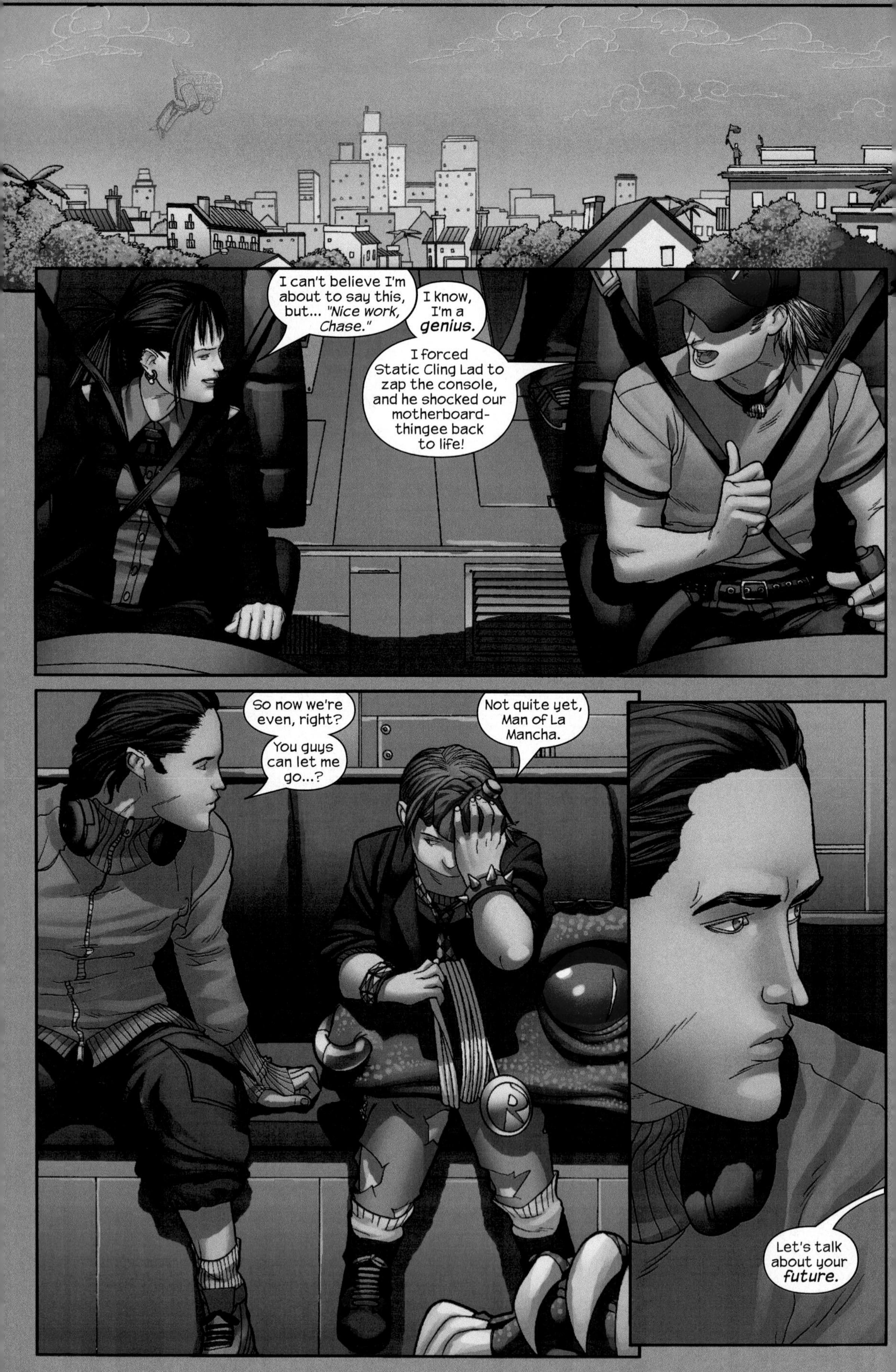
I can't believe I'm about to say this, but... "Nice work, Chase."
I know, I'm a genius.
I forced Static Cling Lad to zap the console, and he shocked our motherboard-thingee back to life!
So now we're even, right?
You guys can let me go...?
Not quite yet, Man of La Mancha.
Let's talk about your future.

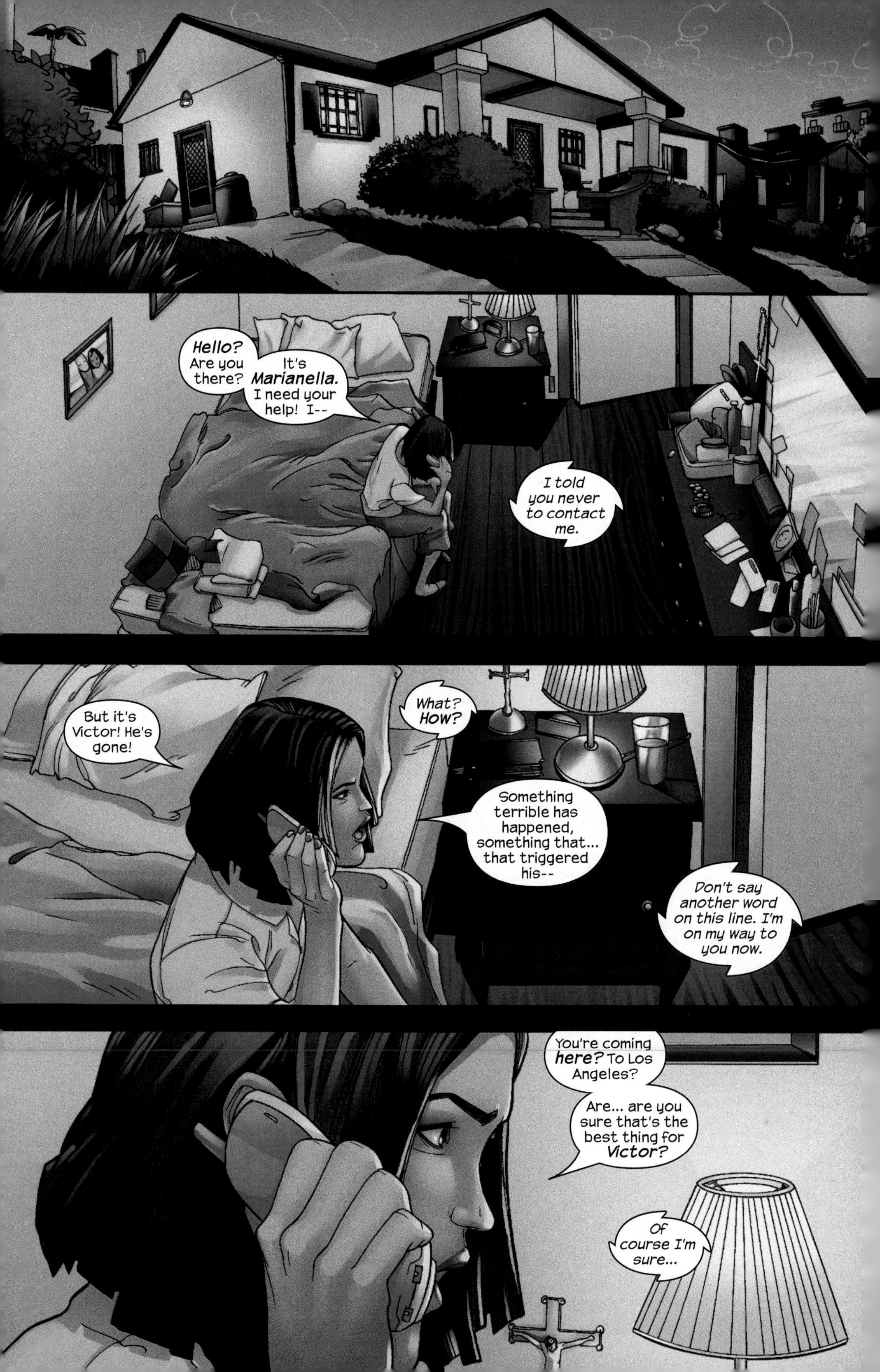
Hello? Are you there?
It's Marianella. I need your help! I--
I told you never to contact me.
But it's Victor! He's gone!
What? How?
Something terrible has happened, something that... that triggered his--
Don't say another word on this line. I'm on my way to you now.
You're coming here? To Los Angeles?
Are... are you sure that's the best thing for Victor?
Of course I'm sure...

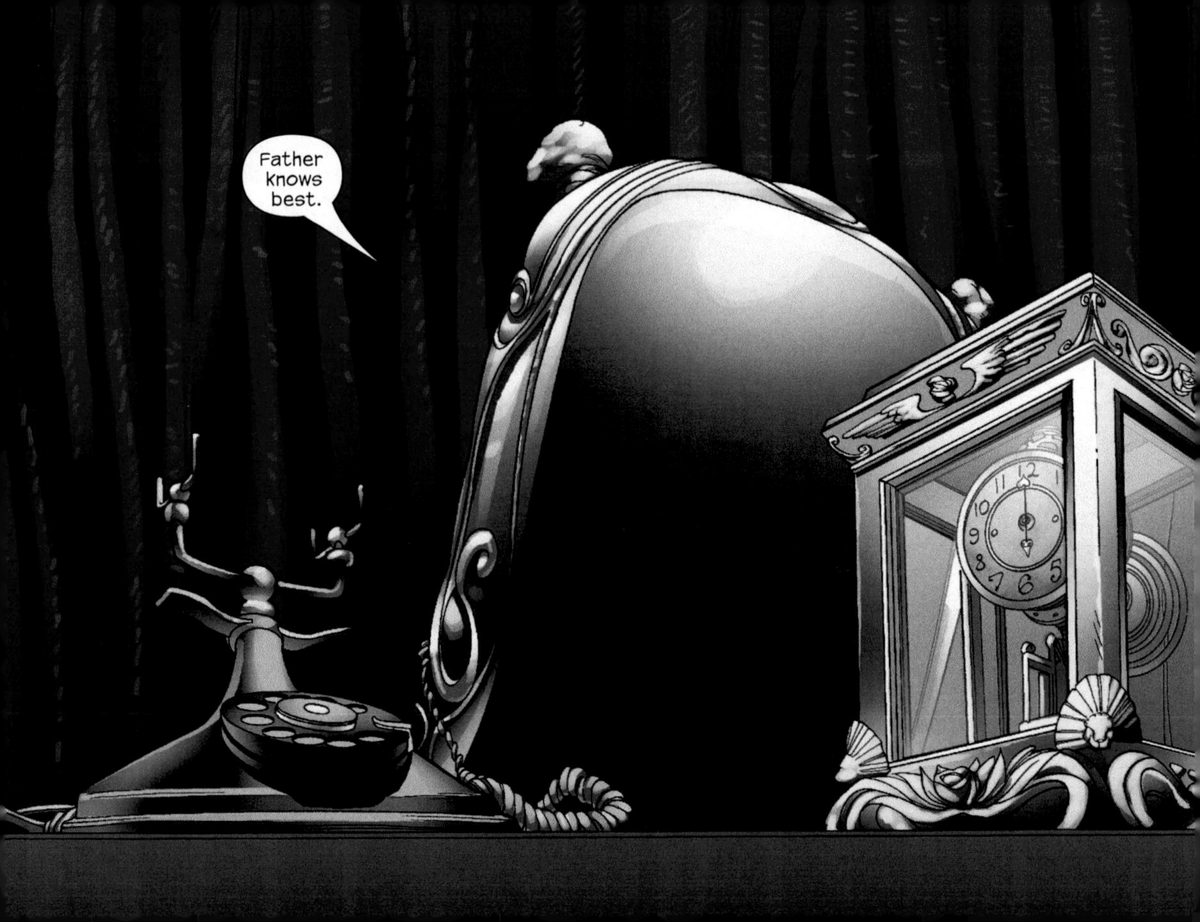
Father knows best.

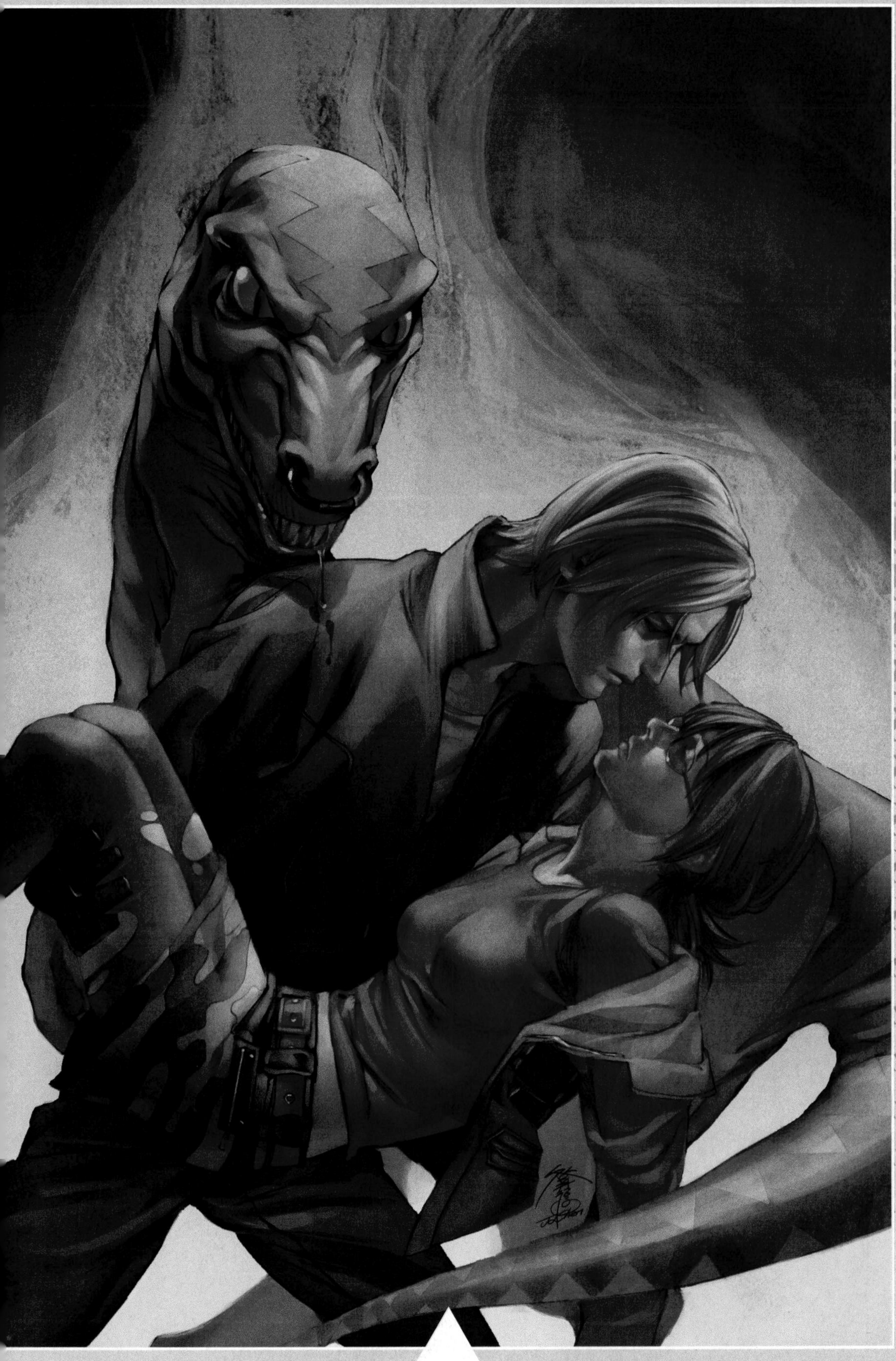

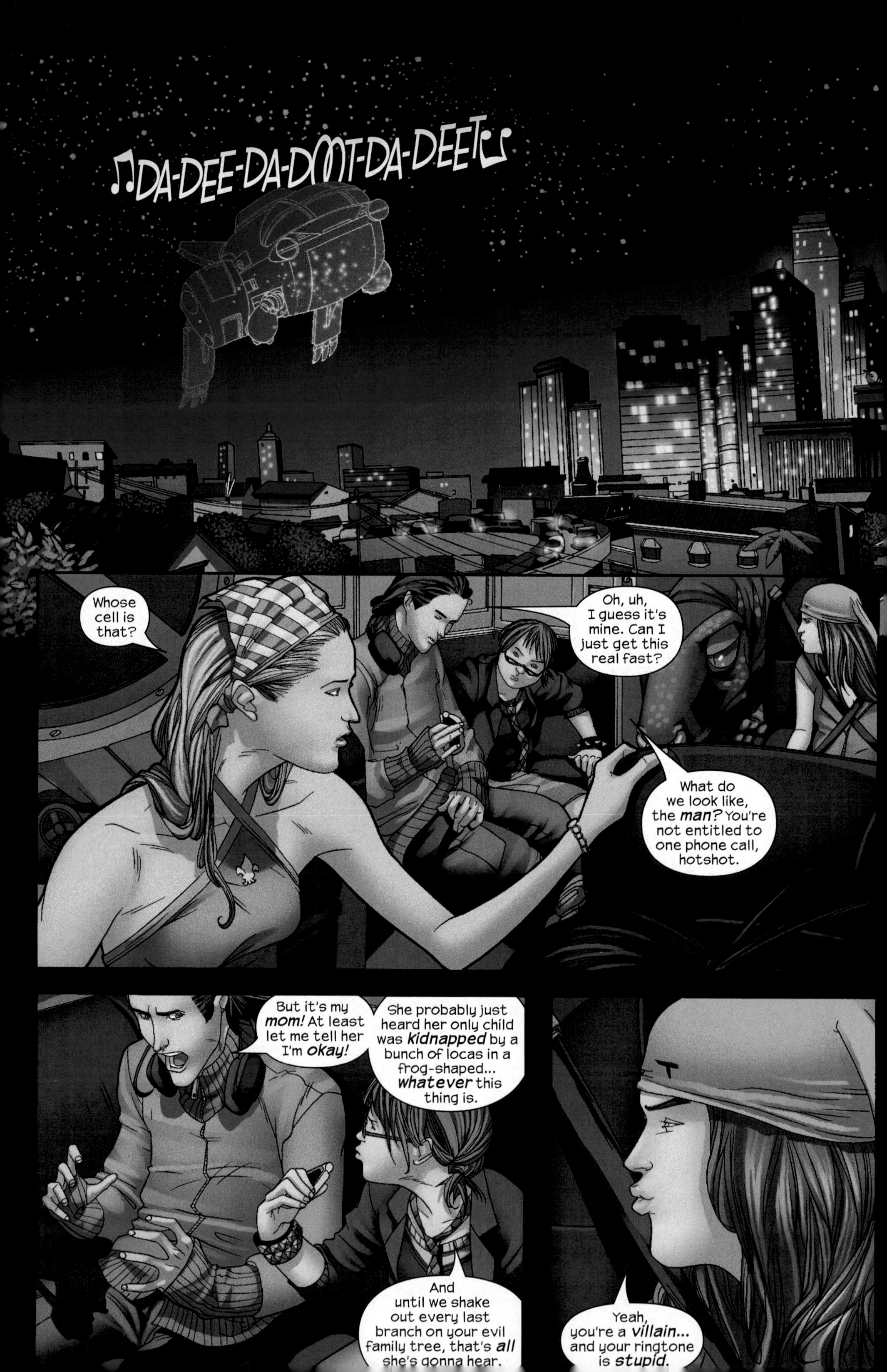
♫DA-DEE-DA-DOOT-DA-DEET♫
Whose cell is that?
Oh, uh, I guess it's mine. Can I just get this real fast?
What do we look like, the man? You're not entitled to one phone call, hotshot.
But it's my mom! At least let me tell her I'm okay!
She probably just heard her only child was kidnapped by a bunch of locas in a frog-shaped... whatever this thing is.
And until we shake out every last branch on your evil family tree, that's all she's gonna hear.
Yeah, you're a villain... and your ringtone is stupid.

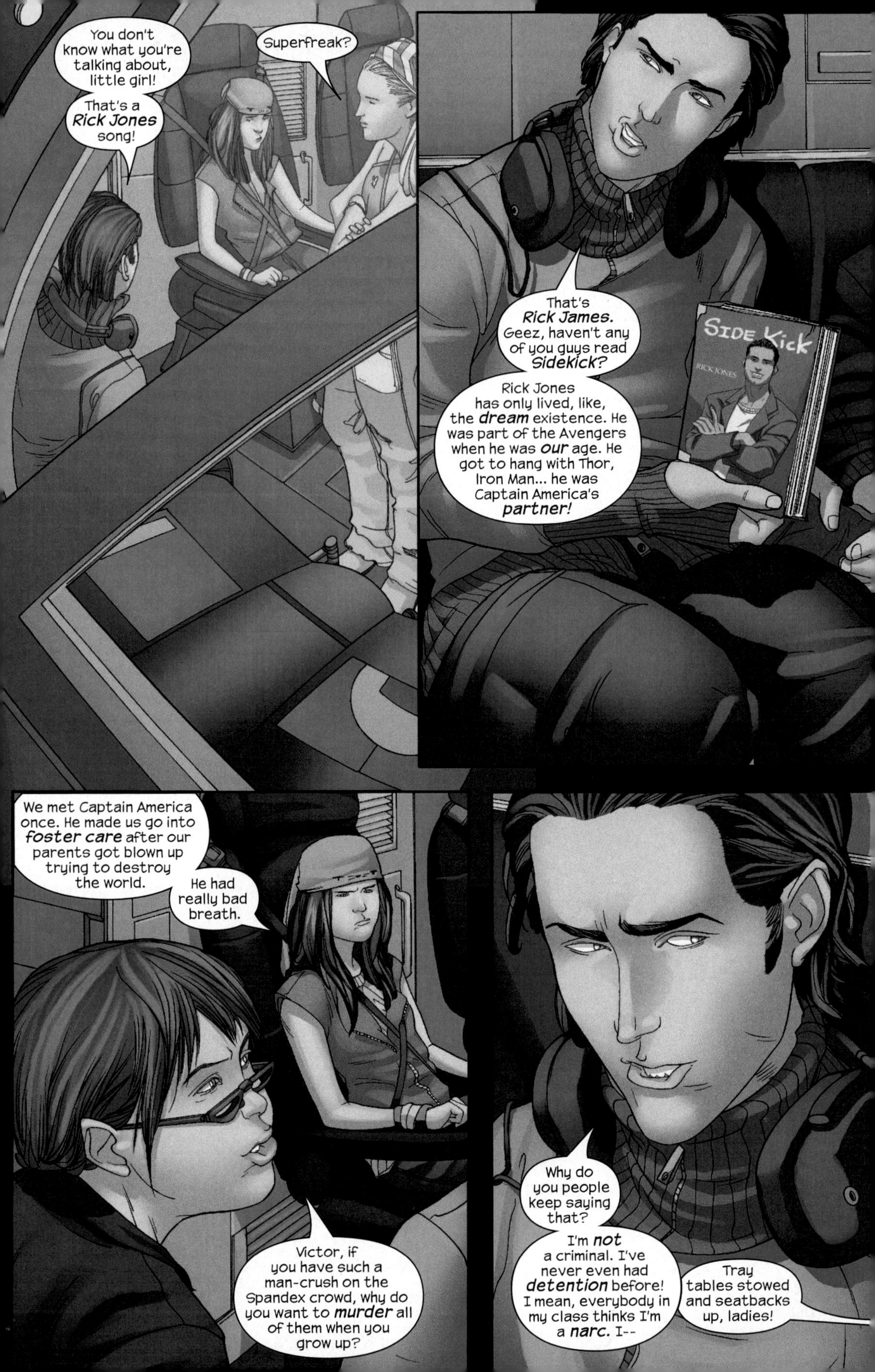
You don't know what you're talking about, little girl!
That's a Rick Jones song!
Superfreak?
That's Rick James. Geez, haven't any of you guys read SideKick?
Rick Jones has only lived, like, the dream existence. He was part of the Avengers when he was our age. He got to hang with Thor, Iron Man... he was Captain America's partner!
SIDE KICK
RICK JONES
We met Captain America once. He made us go into foster care after our parents got blown up trying to destroy the world.
He had really bad breath.
Victor, if you have such a man-crush on the Spandex crowd, why do you want to murder all of them when you grow up?
Why do you people keep saying that?
I'm not a criminal. I've never even had detention before! I mean, everybody in my class thinks I'm a narc. I--
Tray tables stowed and seatbacks up, ladies!

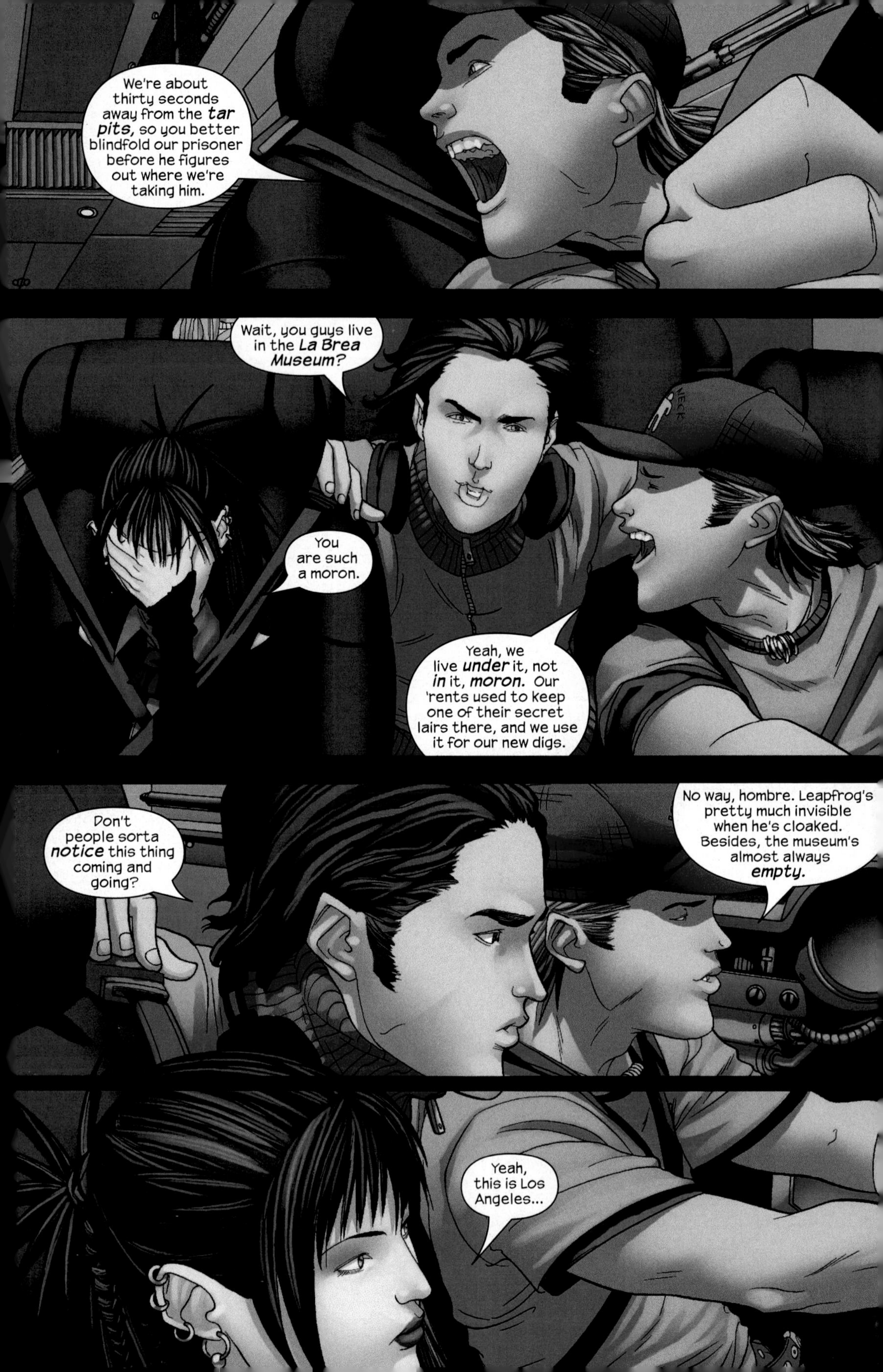
We're about thirty seconds away from the tar pits, so you better blindfold our prisoner before he figures out where we're taking him.
Wait, you guys live in the La Brea Museum?
You are such a moron.
Yeah, we live under it, not in it, moron. Our 'rents used to keep one of their secret lairs there, and we use it for our new digs.
Don't people sorta notice this thing coming and going?
No way, hombre. Leapfrog's pretty much invisible when he's cloaked. Besides, the museum's almost always empty.
Yeah, this is Los Angeles...

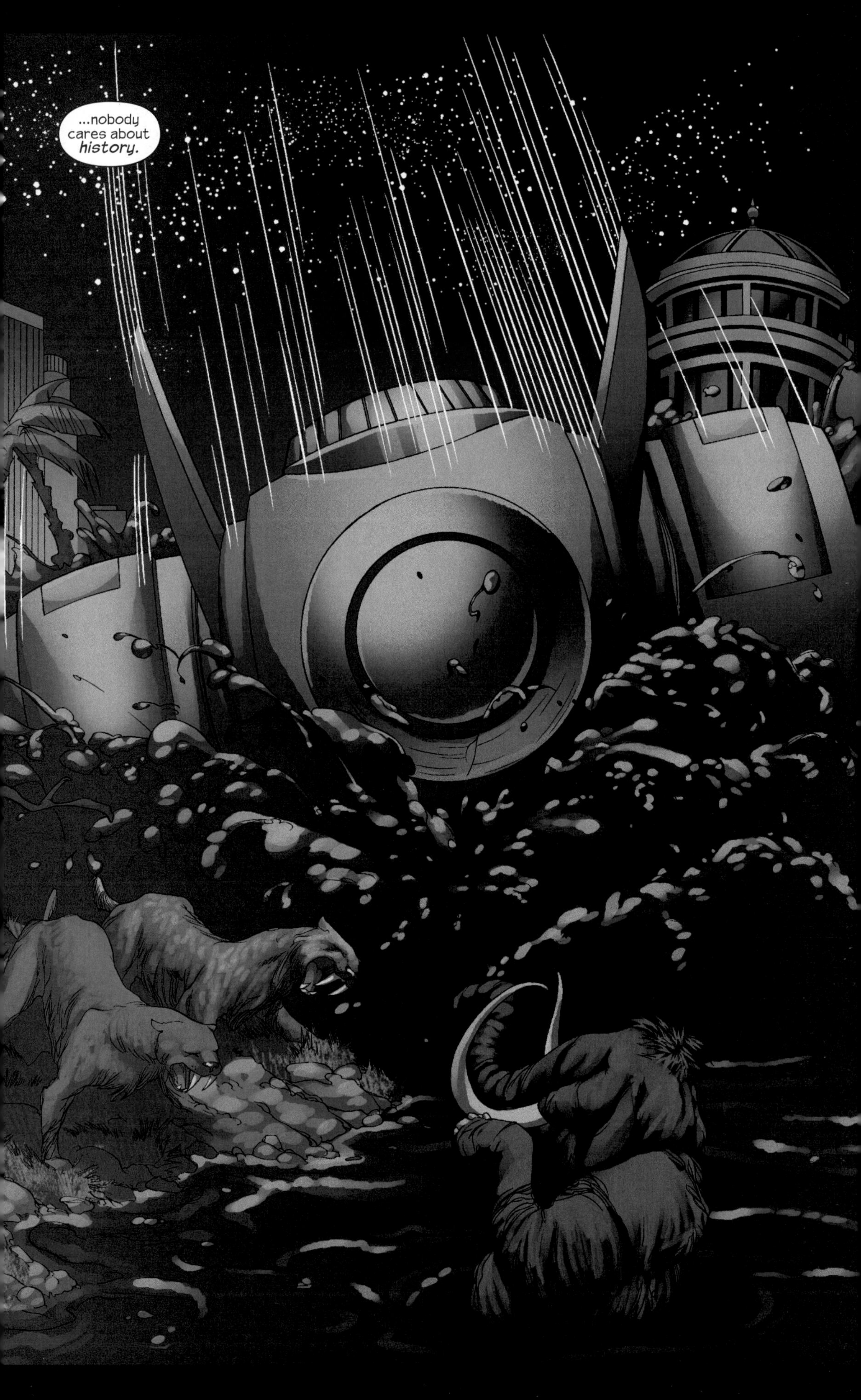
...nobody cares about *history*.

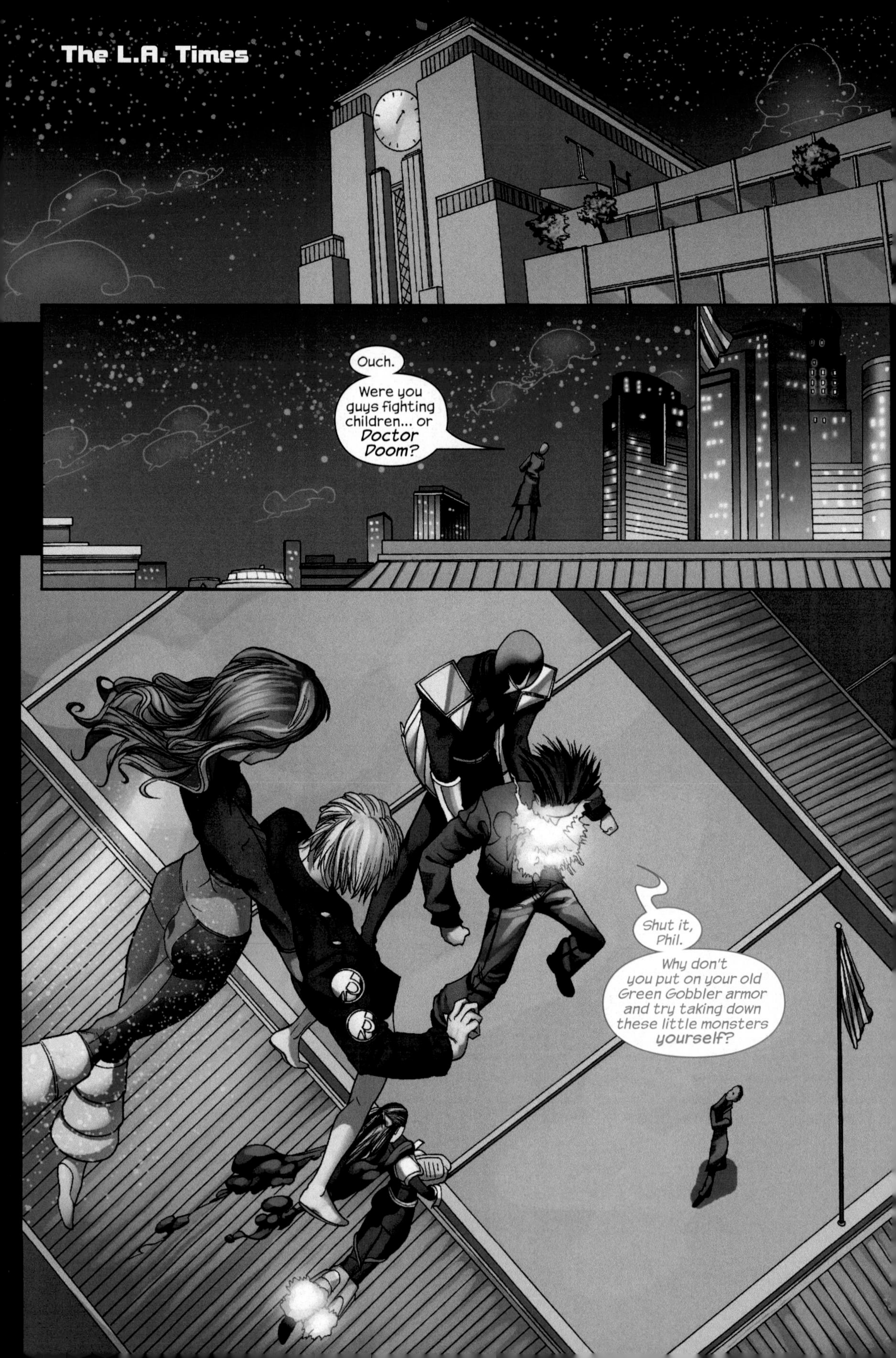
The L.A. Times
Ouch.
Were you guys fighting children... or Doctor Doom?
Shut it, Phil.
Why don't you put on your old Green Gobbler armor and try taking down these little monsters yourself?

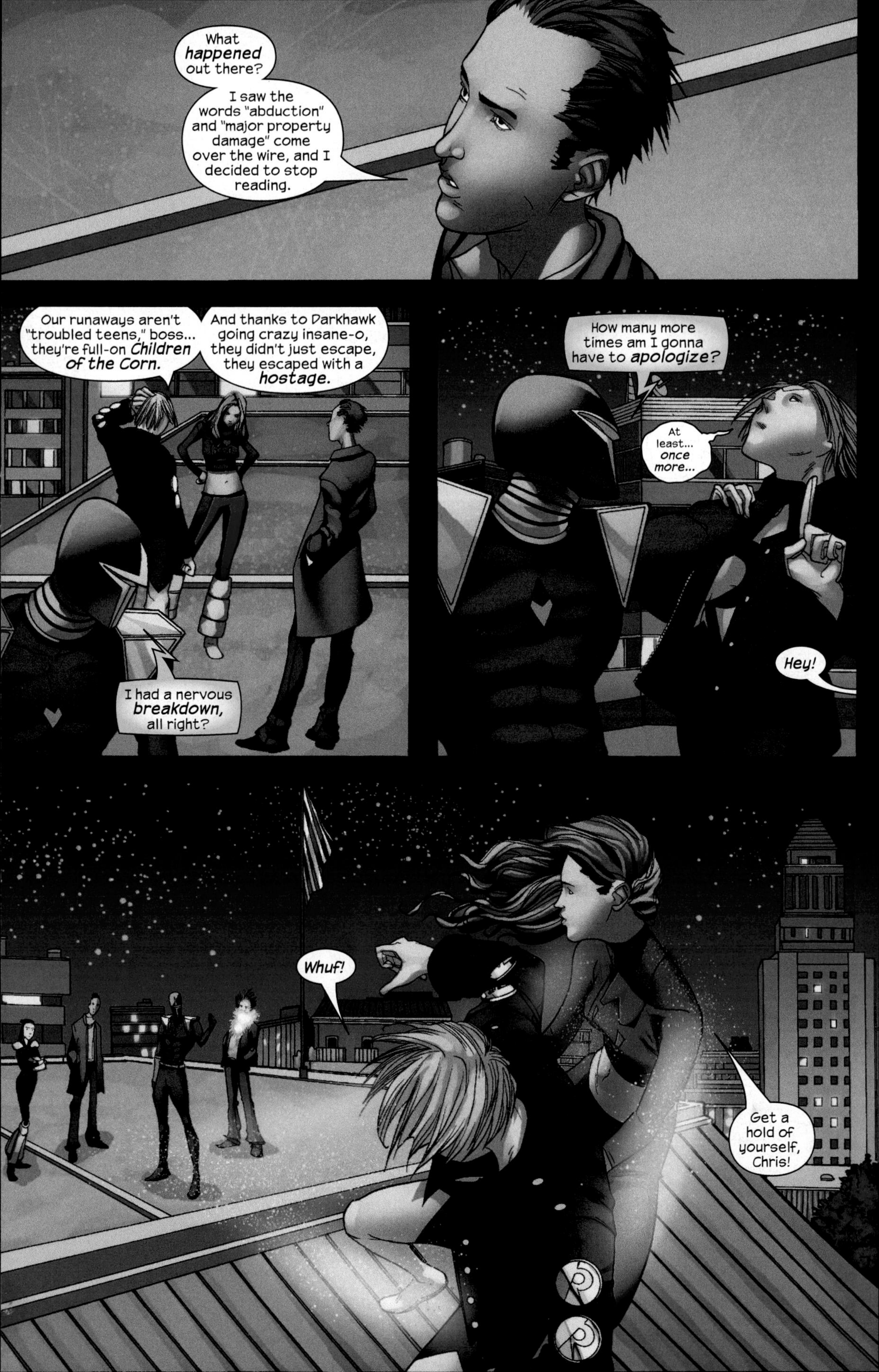
What *happened* out there?
I saw the words "abduction" and "major property damage" come over the wire, and I decided to stop reading.
Our runaways aren't "troubled teens," boss... they're full-on *Children of the Corn.*
And thanks to Darkhawk going crazy insane-o, they didn't just escape, they escaped with a *hostage.*
I had a nervous *breakdown,* all right?
How many more times am I gonna have to *apologize?*
At least... *once* more...
Hey!
Whuf!
Get a hold of yourself, Chris!

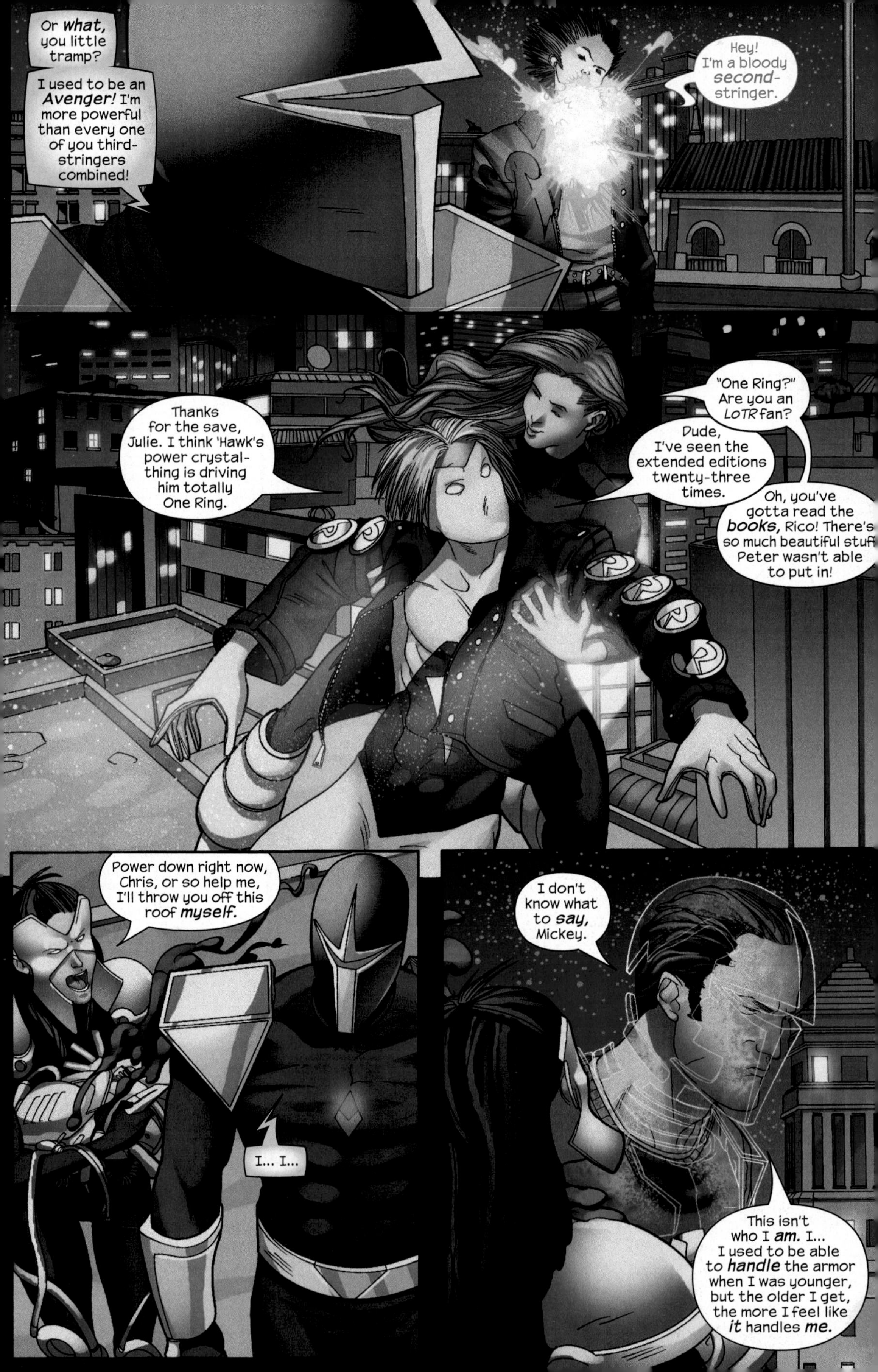
Or what, you little tramp?
I used to be an Avenger! I'm more powerful than every one of you third-stringers combined!
Hey! I'm a bloody second-stringer.
Thanks for the save, Julie. I think 'Hawk's power crystal-thing is driving him totally One Ring.
"One Ring?" Are you an LOTR fan?
Dude, I've seen the extended editions twenty-three times.
Oh, you've gotta read the books, Rico! There's so much beautiful stuff Peter wasn't able to put in!
Power down right now, Chris, or so help me, I'll throw you off this roof myself.
I... I...
I don't know what to say, Mickey.
This isn't who I am. I... I used to be able to handle the armor when I was younger, but the older I get, the more I feel like it handles me.

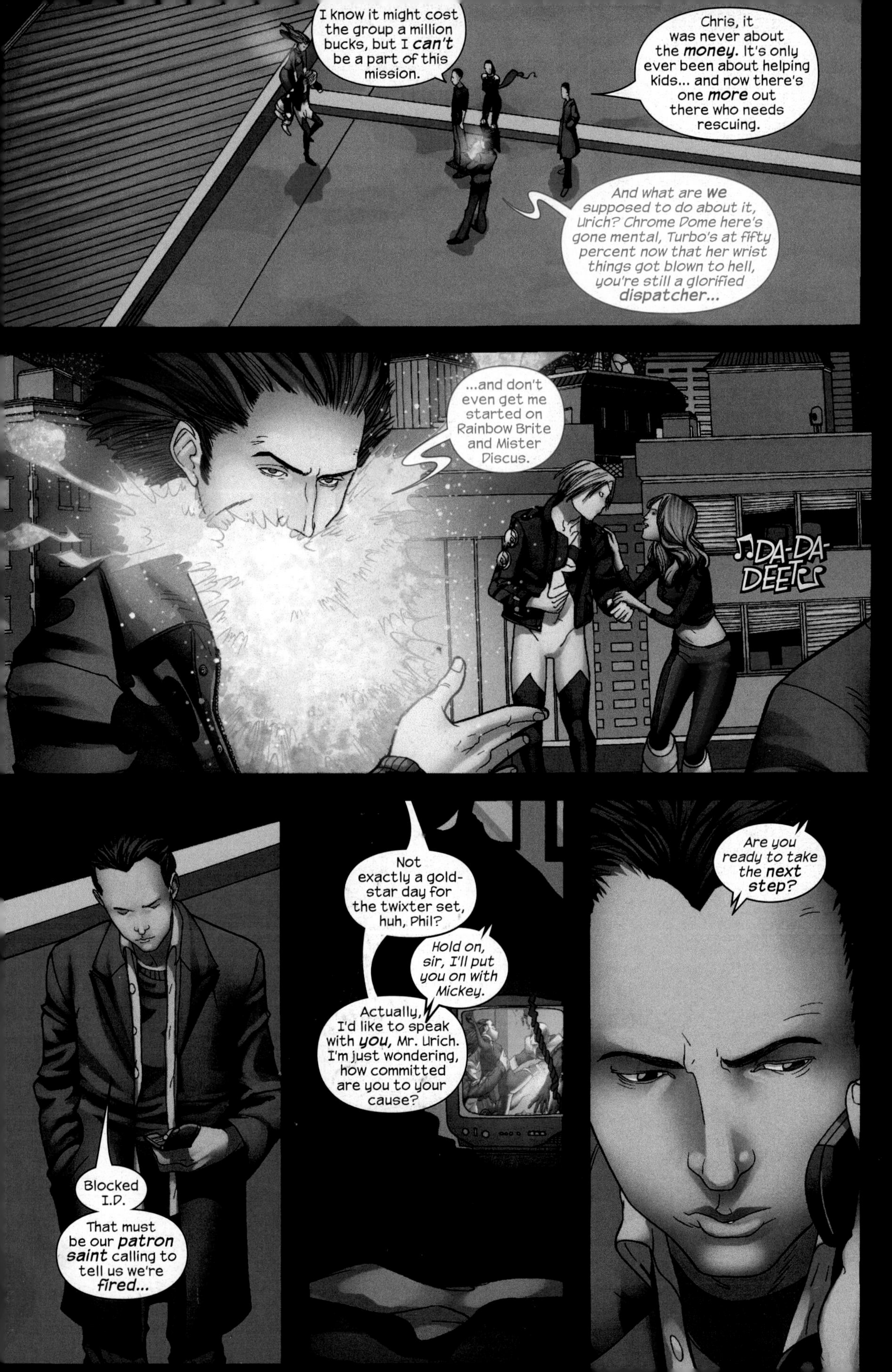
I know it might cost the group a million bucks, but I can't be a part of this mission.
Chris, it was never about the money. It's only ever been about helping kids... and now there's one more out there who needs rescuing.
And what are we supposed to do about it, Urich? Chrome Dome here's gone mental, Turbo's at fifty percent now that her wrist things got blown to hell, you're still a glorified dispatcher...
...and don't even get me started on Rainbow Brite and Mister Discus.
DA-DA-DEET
Blocked I.D.
That must be our patron saint calling to tell us we're fired...
Not exactly a gold-star day for the twixter set, huh, Phil?
Hold on, sir, I'll put you on with Mickey.
Actually, I'd like to speak with you, Mr. Urich. I'm just wondering, how committed are you to your cause?
Are you ready to take the next step?

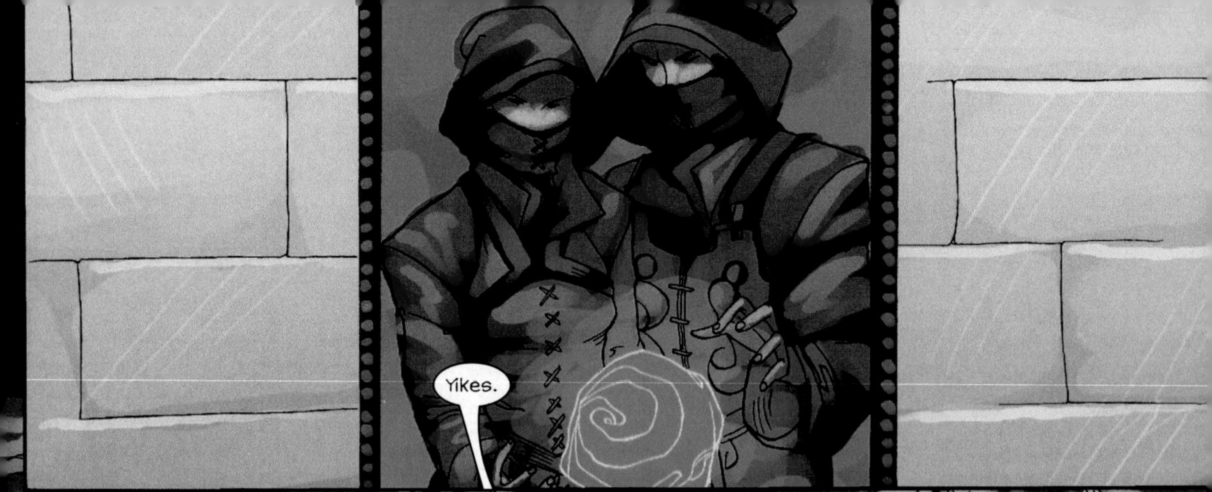
Yikes.

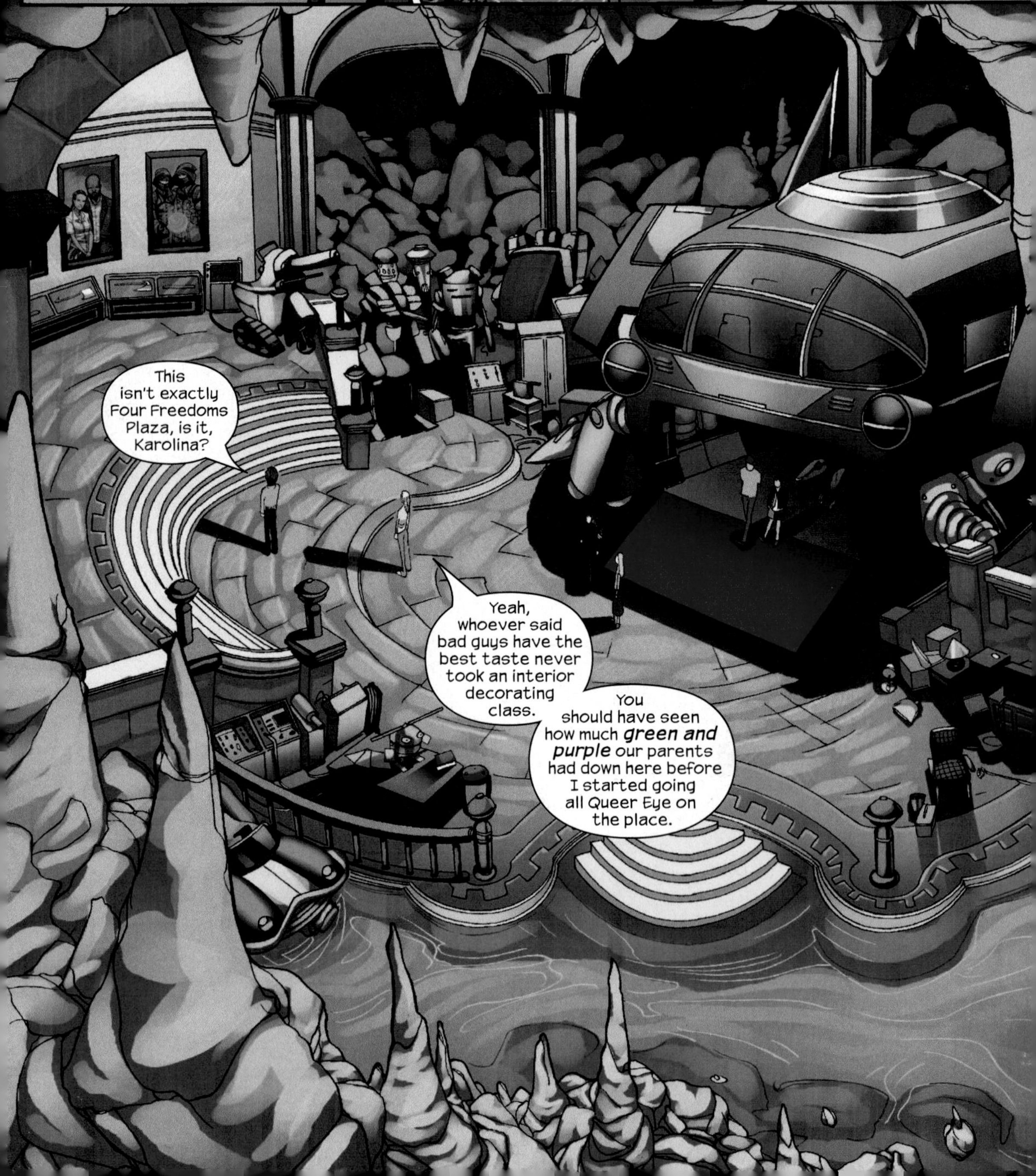
This isn't exactly Four Freedoms Plaza, is it, Karolina?
Yeah, whoever said bad guys have the best taste never took an interior decorating class.
You should have seen how much ***green and purple*** our parents had down here before I started going all Queer Eye on the place.

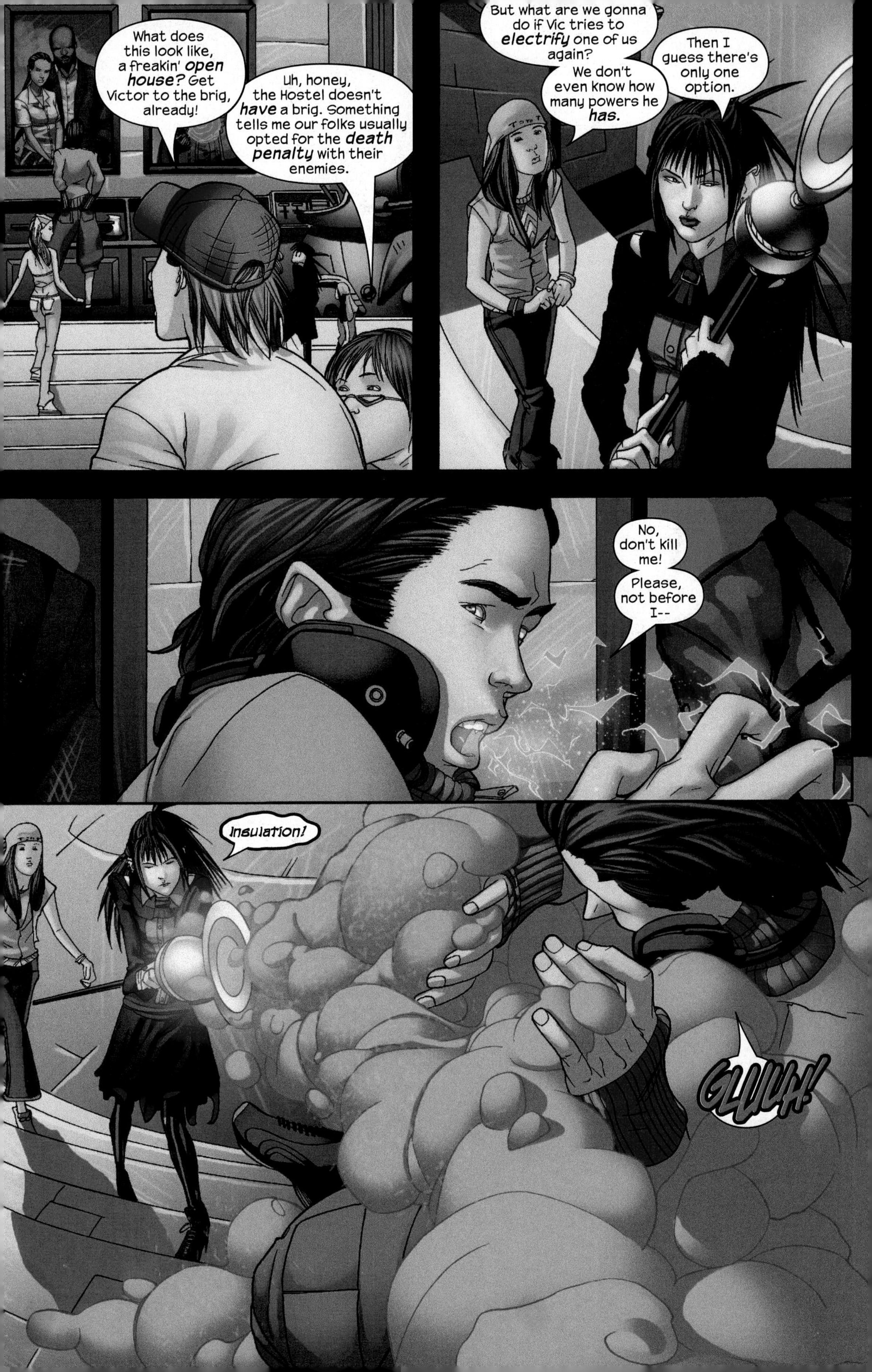
What does this look like, a freakin' open house? Get Victor to the brig, already!
Uh, honey, the Hostel doesn't have a brig. Something tells me our folks usually opted for the death penalty with their enemies.
But what are we gonna do if Vic tries to electrify one of us again?
We don't even know how many powers he has.
Then I guess there's only one option.
No, don't kill me!
Please, not before I--
Insulation!
GLLLLH!

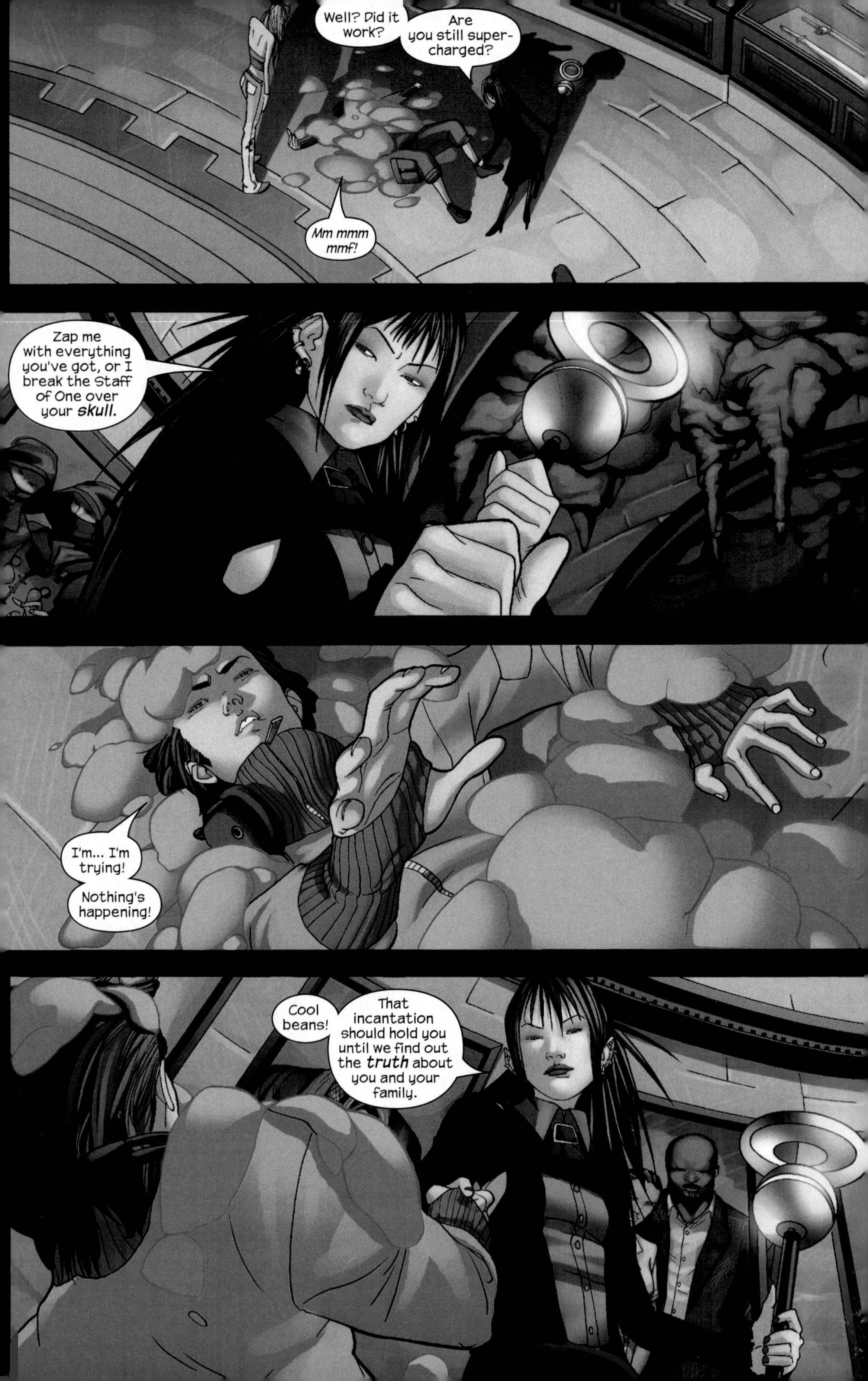
Well? Did it work?
Are you still super-charged?
Mm mmm mmf!
Zap me with everything you've got, or I break the Staff of One over your skull.
I'm... I'm trying!
Nothing's happening!
Cool beans!
That incantation should hold you until we find out the truth about you and your family.

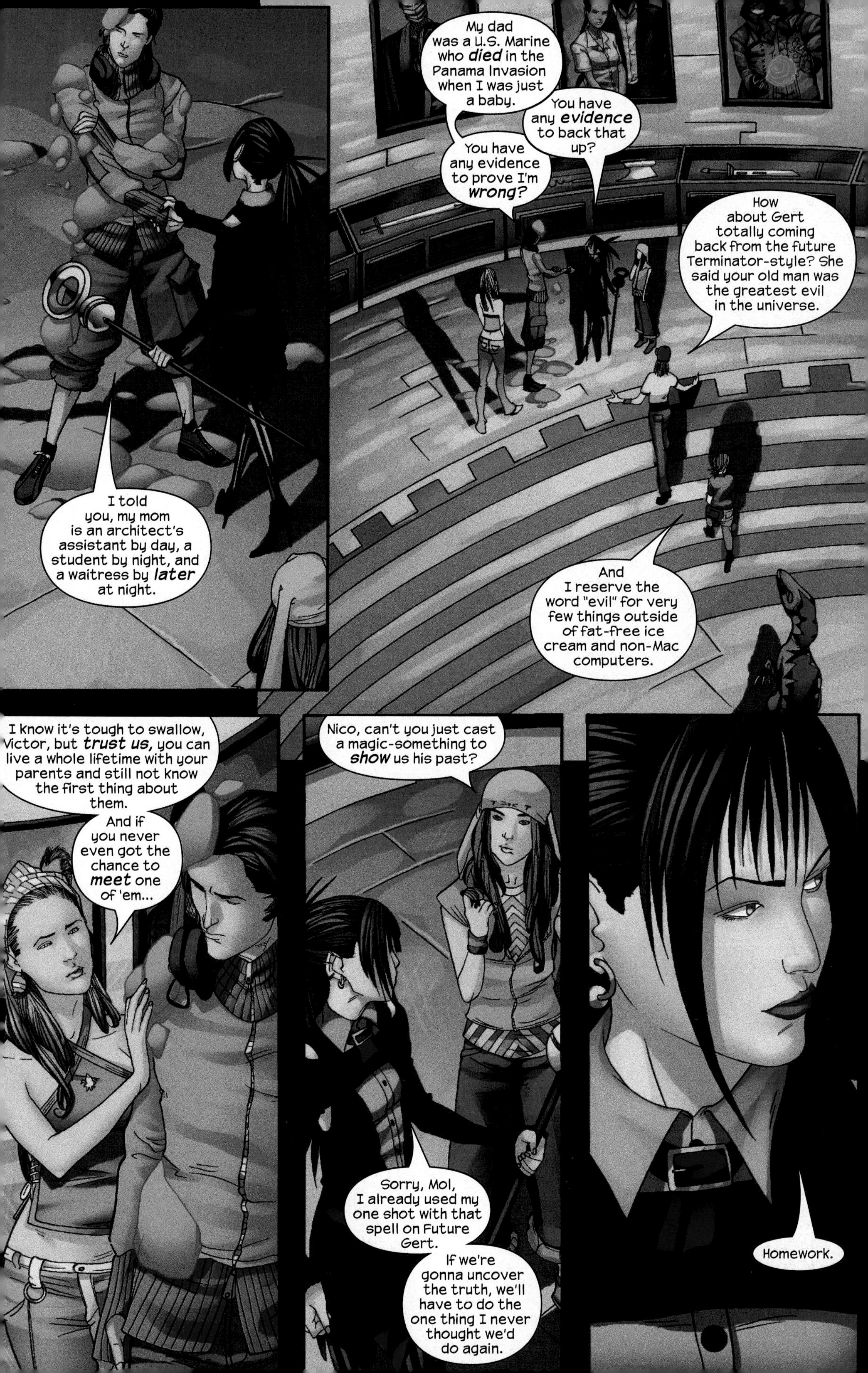
I told you, my mom is an architect's assistant by day, a student by night, and a waitress by *later* at night.
My dad was a U.S. Marine who *died* in the Panama Invasion when I was just a baby.
You have any evidence to prove I'm *wrong?*
You have any *evidence* to back that up?
How about Gert totally coming back from the future Terminator-style? She said your old man was the greatest evil in the universe.
And I reserve the word "evil" for very few things outside of fat-free ice cream and non-Mac computers.
I know it's tough to swallow, Victor, but *trust us,* you can live a whole lifetime with your parents and still not know the first thing about them.
And if you never even got the chance to *meet* one of 'em...
Nico, can't you just cast a magic-something to *show* us his past?
Sorry, Mol, I already used my one shot with that spell on Future Gert.
If we're gonna uncover the truth, we'll have to do the one thing I never thought we'd do again.
Homework.

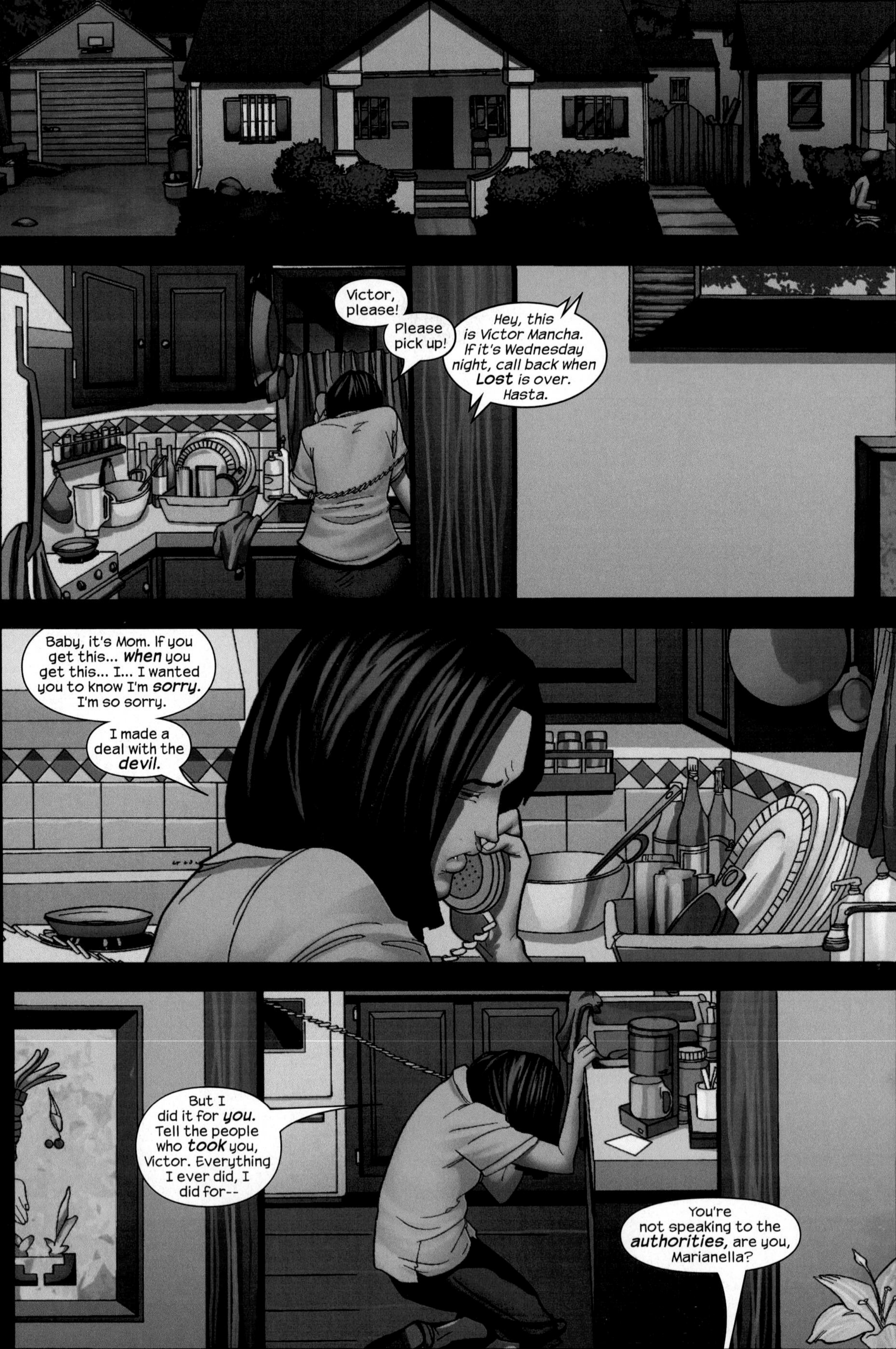
Victor, please!
Please pick up!
Hey, this is Victor Mancha. If it's Wednesday night, call back when Lost is over. Hasta.
Baby, it's Mom. If you get this... when you get this... I... I wanted you to know I'm sorry. I'm so sorry.
I made a deal with the devil.
But I did it for you. Tell the people who took you, Victor. Everything I ever did, I did for--
You're not speaking to the authorities, are you, Marianella?

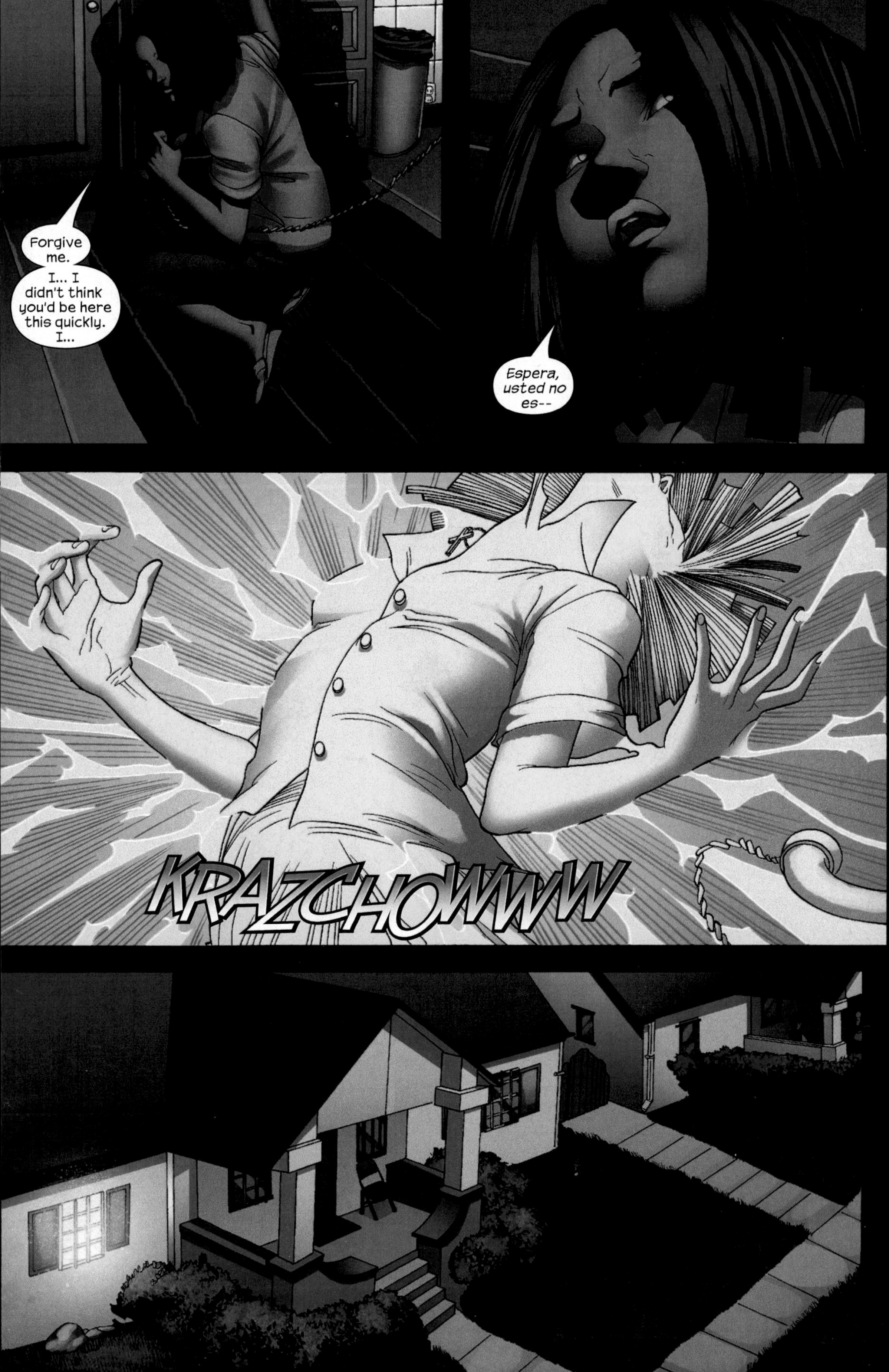

Forgive me. I... I didn't think you'd be here this quickly. I...
Espera, usted no es--
KRAZCHOWWW

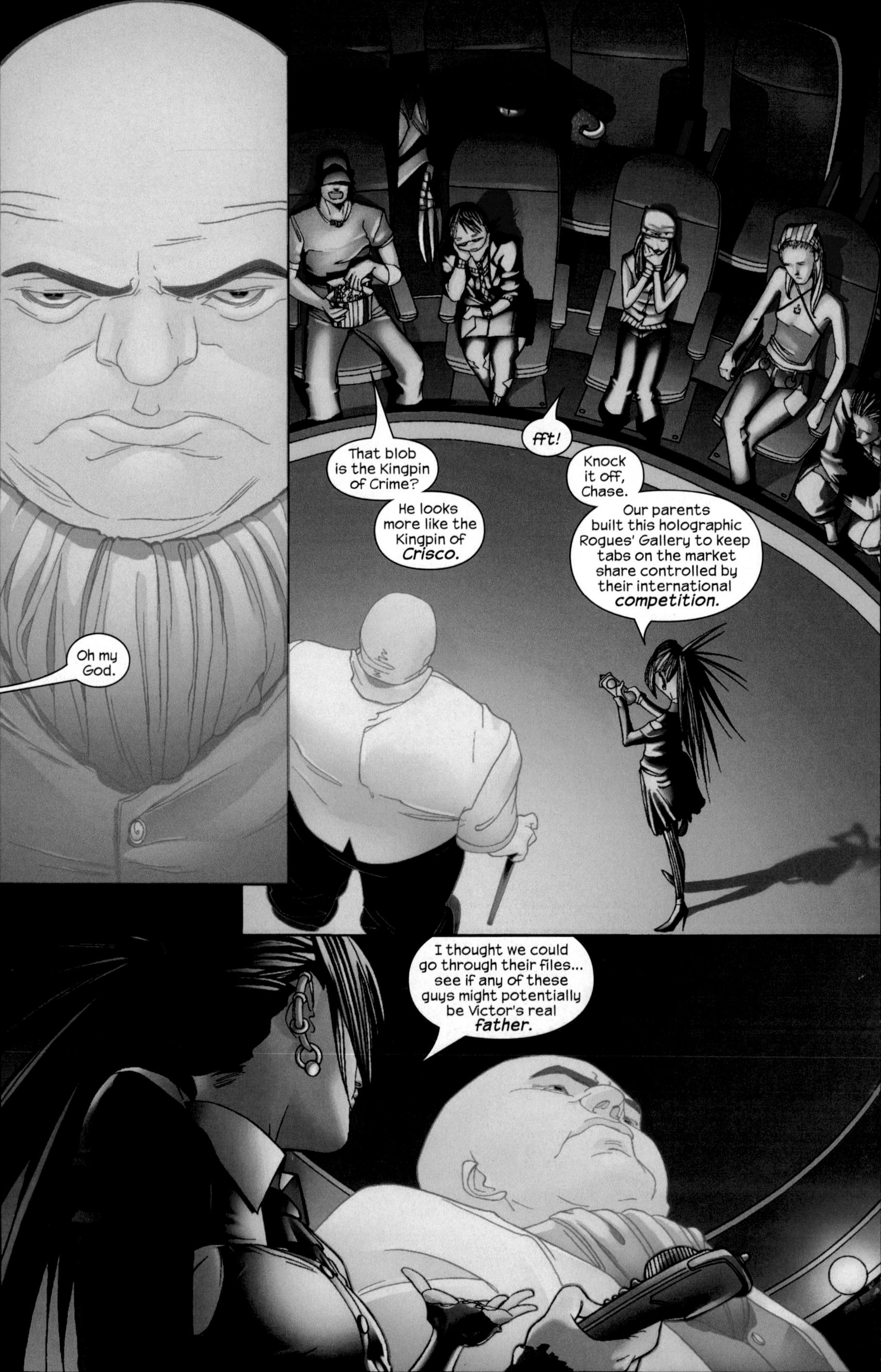
Oh my God.
That blob is the Kingpin of Crime?
He looks more like the Kingpin of *Crisco.*
fft!
Knock it off, Chase.
Our parents built this holographic Rogues' Gallery to keep tabs on the market share controlled by their international *competition.*
I thought we could go through their files... see if any of these guys might potentially be Victor's real *father.*

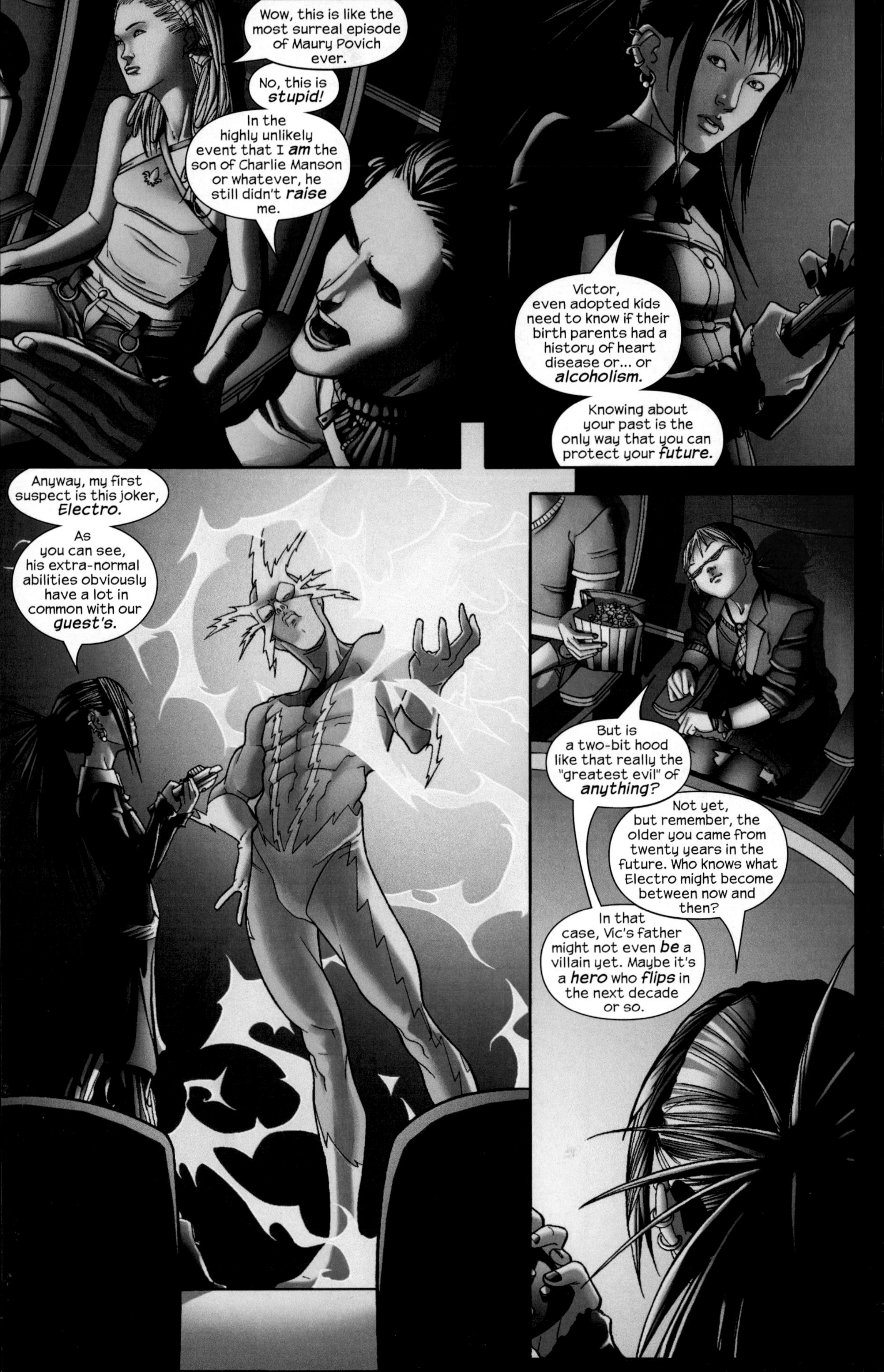
Wow, this is like the most surreal episode of Maury Povich ever.
No, this is stupid!
In the highly unlikely event that I am the son of Charlie Manson or whatever, he still didn't raise me.
Victor, even adopted kids need to know if their birth parents had a history of heart disease or... or alcoholism.
Knowing about your past is the only way that you can protect your future.
Anyway, my first suspect is this joker, Electro.
As you can see, his extra-normal abilities obviously have a lot in common with our guest's.
But is a two-bit hood like that really the "greatest evil" of anything?
Not yet, but remember, the older you came from twenty years in the future. Who knows what Electro might become between now and then?
In that case, Vic's father might not even be a villain yet. Maybe it's a hero who flips in the next decade or so.

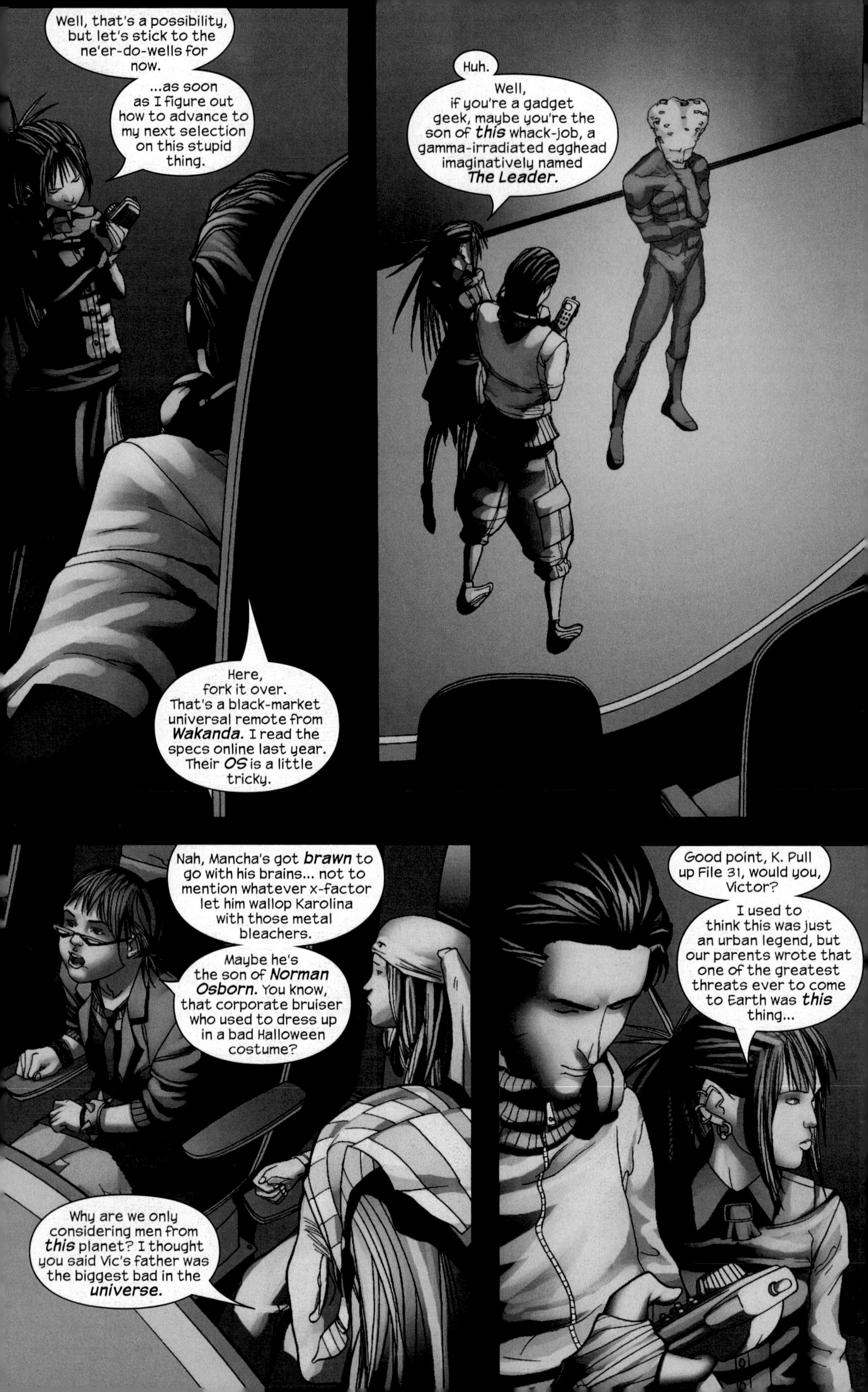
Well, that's a possibility, but let's stick to the ne'er-do-wells for now.
...as soon as I figure out how to advance to my next selection on this stupid thing.
Here, fork it over. That's a black-market universal remote from *Wakanda.* I read the specs online last year. Their *OS* is a little tricky.
Huh.
Well, if you're a gadget geek, maybe you're the son of *this* whack-job, a gamma-irradiated egghead imaginatively named *The Leader.*
Nah, Mancha's got *brawn* to go with his brains... not to mention whatever x-factor let him wallop Karolina with those metal bleachers.
Maybe he's the son of *Norman Osborn.* You know, that corporate bruiser who used to dress up in a bad Halloween costume?
Why are we only considering men from *this* planet? I thought you said Vic's father was the biggest bad in the *universe.*
Good point, K. Pull up File 31, would you, Victor?
I used to think this was just an urban legend, but our parents wrote that one of the greatest threats ever to come to Earth was *this* thing...

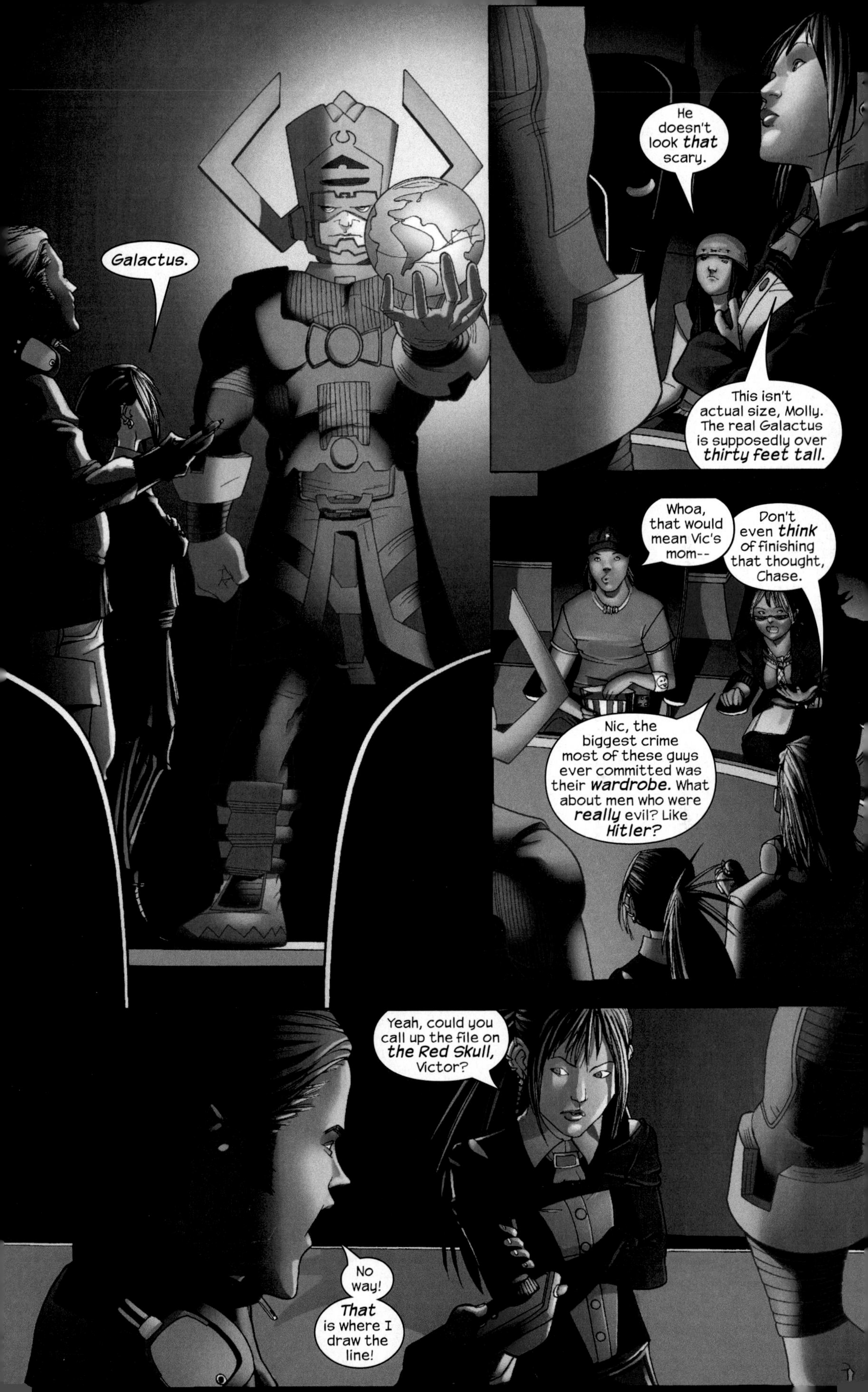
Galactus.
He doesn't look that scary.
This isn't actual size, Molly. The real Galactus is supposedly over thirty feet tall.
Whoa, that would mean Vic's mom--
Don't even think of finishing that thought, Chase.
Nic, the biggest crime most of these guys ever committed was their wardrobe. What about men who were really evil? Like Hitler?
Yeah, could you call up the file on the Red Skull, Victor?
No way! That is where I draw the line!

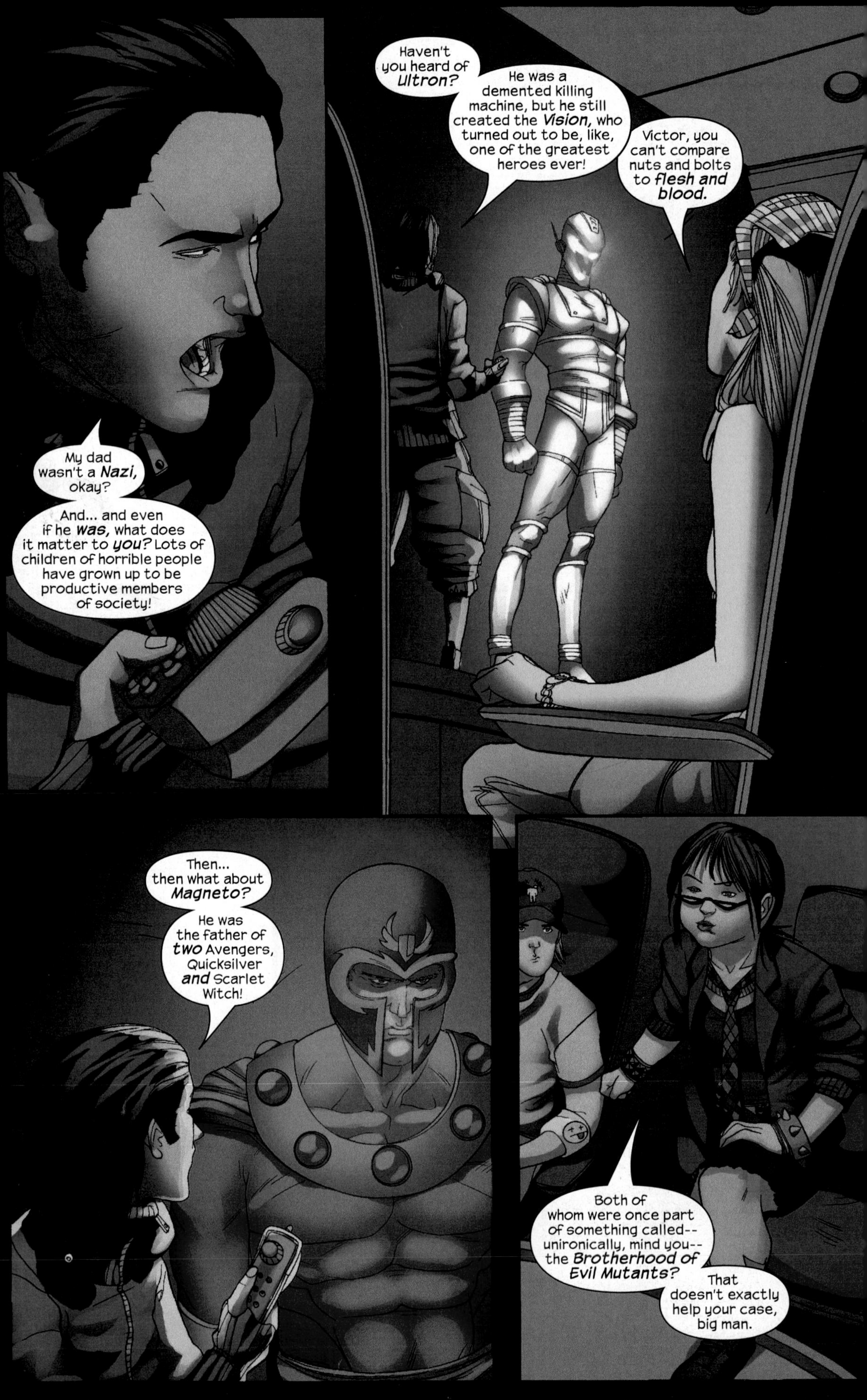
My dad wasn't a Nazi, okay?
And... and even if he was, what does it matter to you? Lots of children of horrible people have grown up to be productive members of society!
Haven't you heard of Ultron?
He was a demented killing machine, but he still created the Vision, who turned out to be, like, one of the greatest heroes ever!
Victor, you can't compare nuts and bolts to flesh and blood.
Then... then what about Magneto?
He was the father of two Avengers, Quicksilver and Scarlet Witch!
Both of whom were once part of something called-- unironically, mind you-- the Brotherhood of Evil Mutants?
That doesn't exactly help your case, big man.

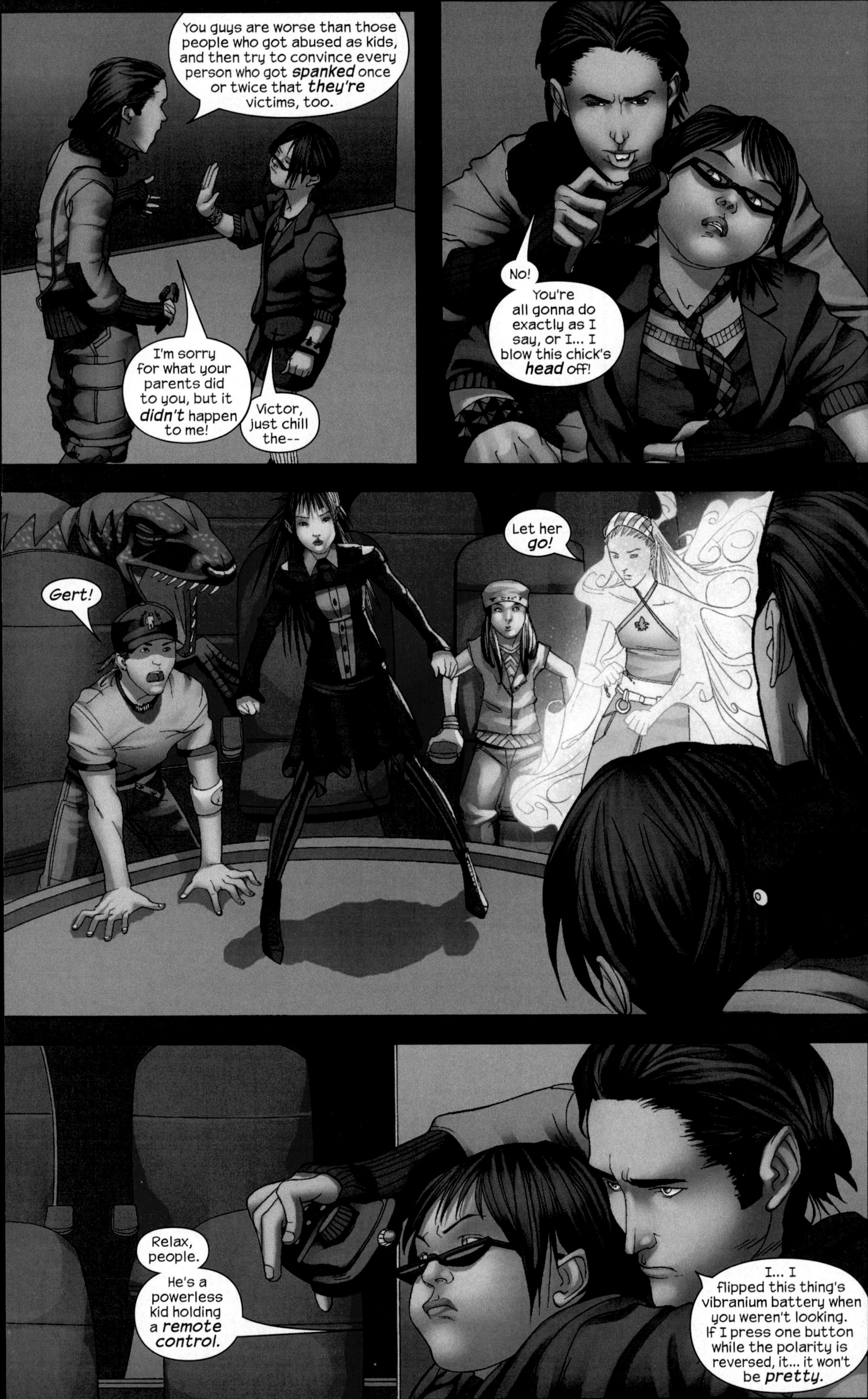
You guys are worse than those people who got abused as kids, and then try to convince every person who got *spanked* once or twice that *they're* victims, too.
I'm sorry for what your parents did to you, but it *didn't* happen to me!
Victor, just chill the--
No!
You're all gonna do exactly as I say, or I... I blow this chick's *head* off!
Gert!
Let her *go!*
Relax, people.
He's a powerless kid holding a *remote control.*
I... I flipped this thing's vibranium battery when you weren't looking. If I press one button while the polarity is reversed, it... it won't be *pretty.*

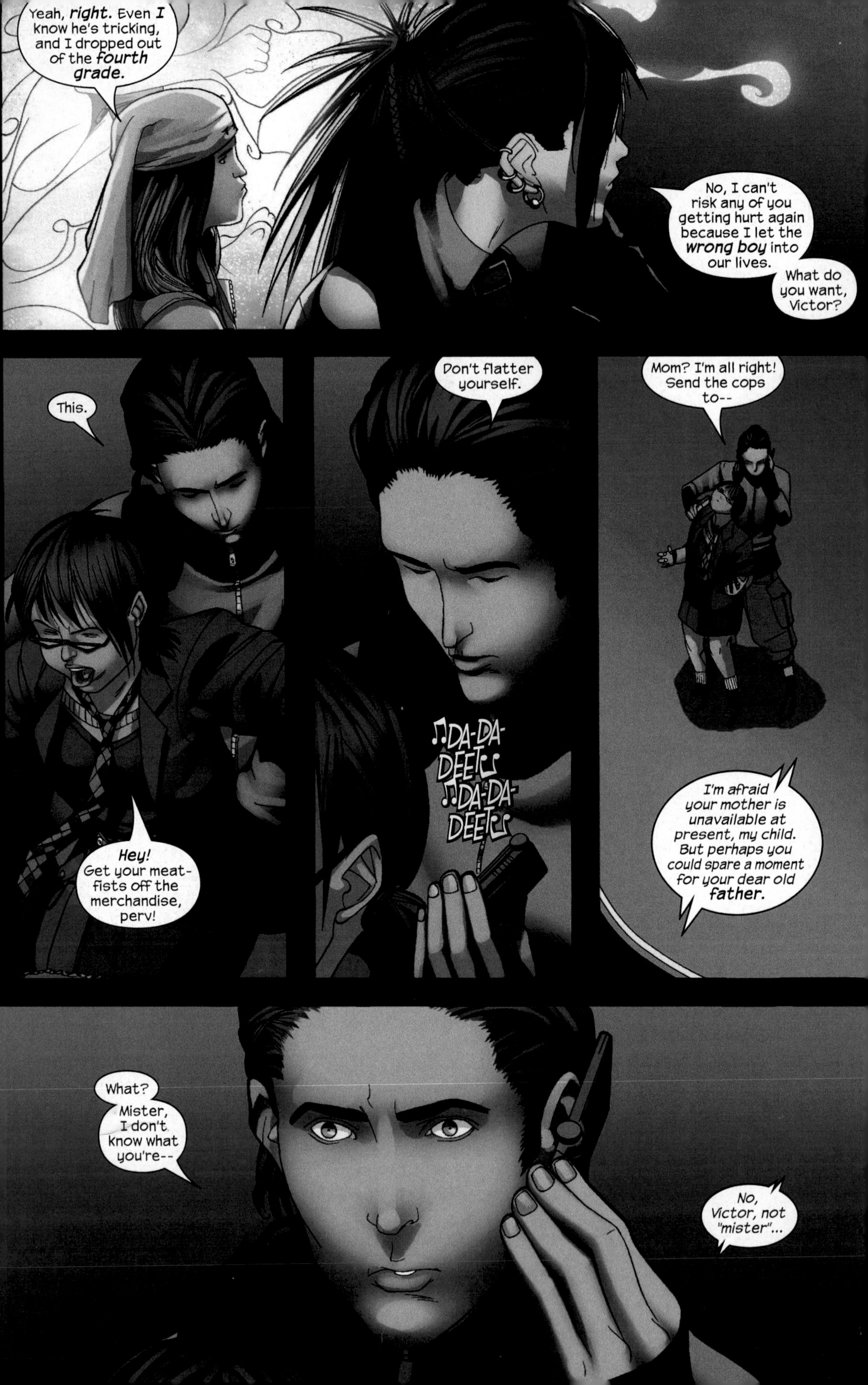
Yeah, right. Even I know he's tricking, and I dropped out of the fourth grade.
No, I can't risk any of you getting hurt again because I let the wrong boy into our lives.
What do you want, Victor?
This.
Hey! Get your meat-fists off the merchandise, perv!
Don't flatter yourself.
DA-DA-DEET DA-DA-DEET
Mom? I'm all right! Send the cops to--
I'm afraid your mother is unavailable at present, my child. But perhaps you could spare a moment for your dear old father.
What? Mister, I don't know what you're--
No, Victor, not "mister"...

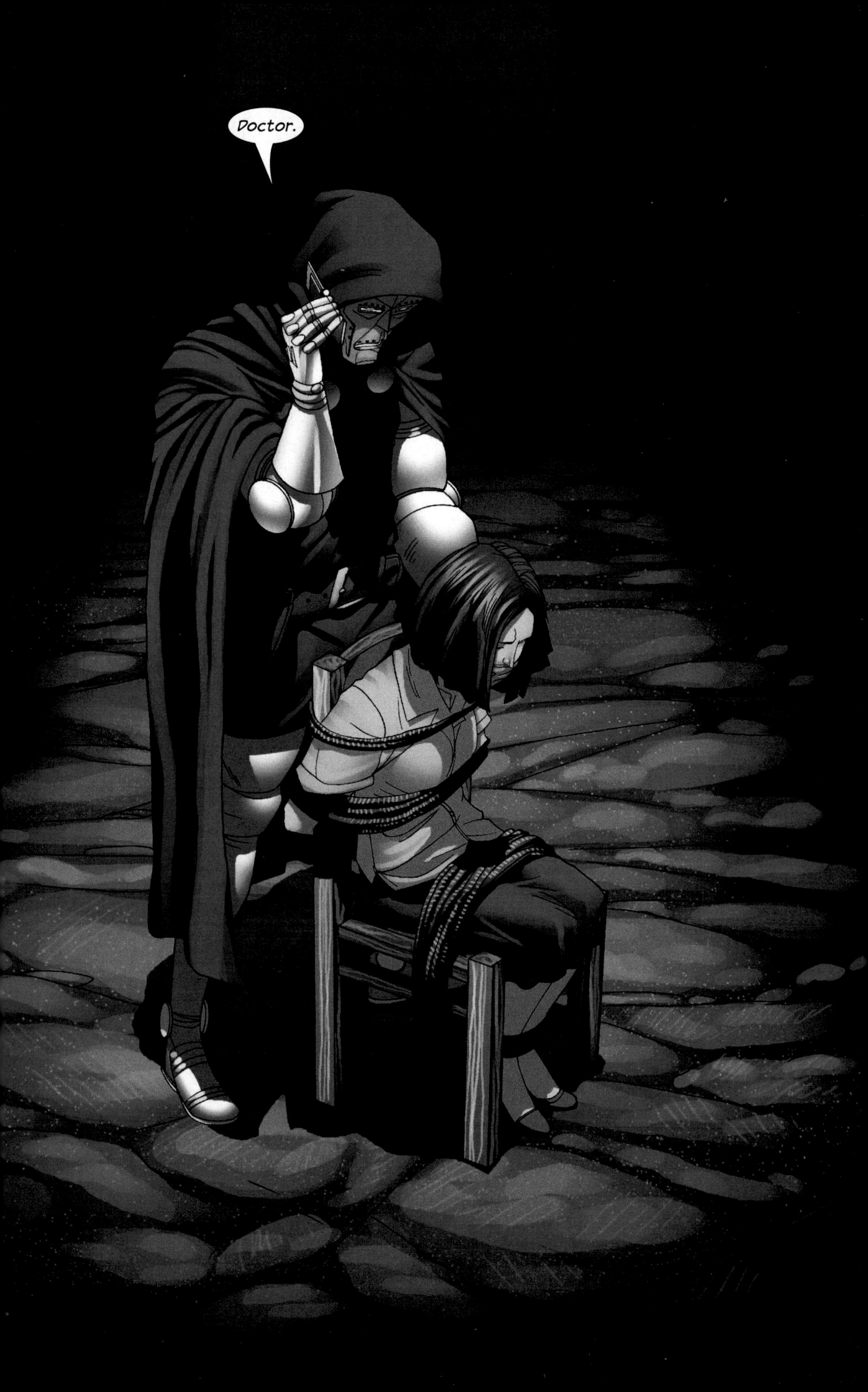
Doctor.

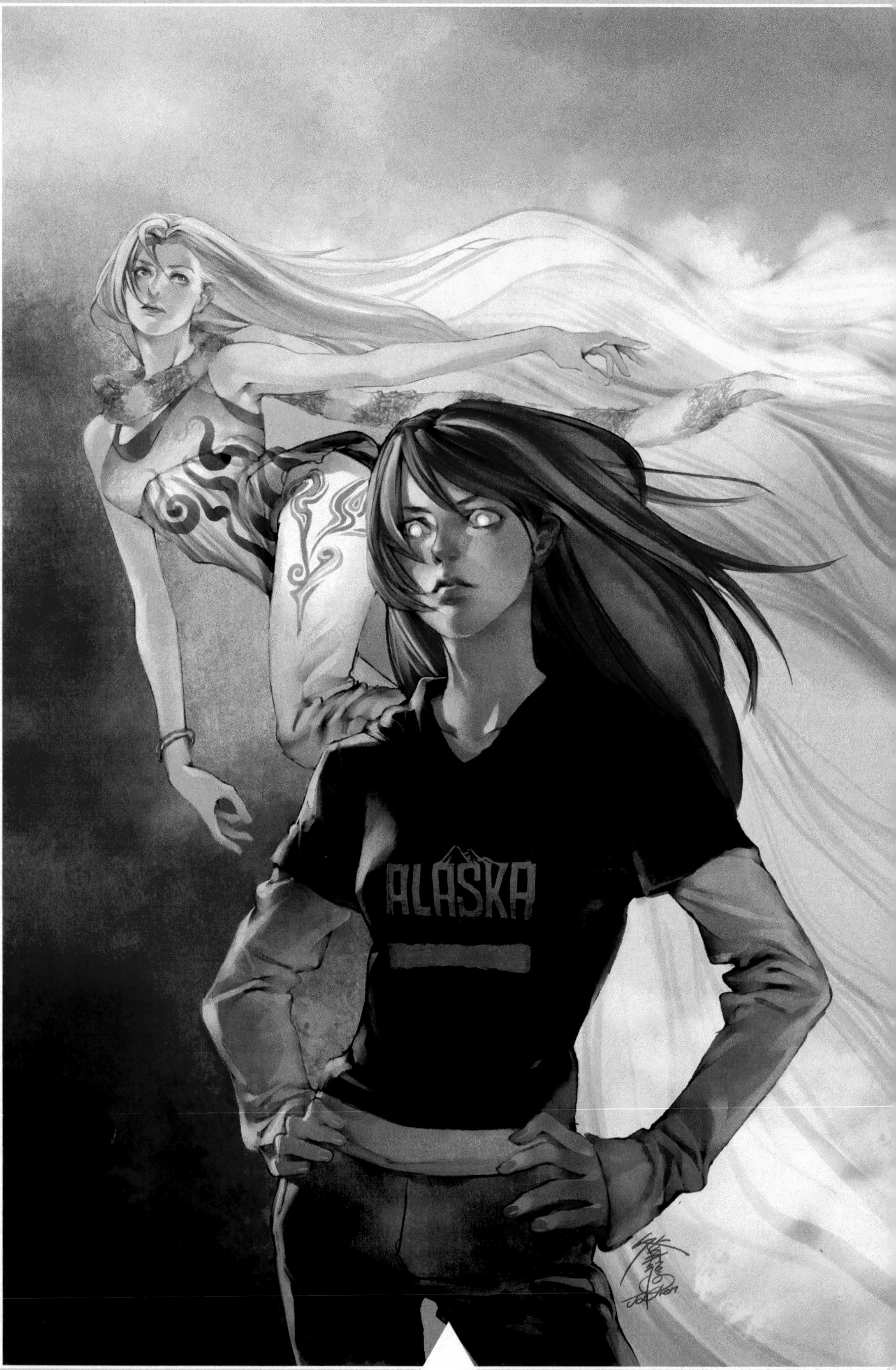
ALASKA

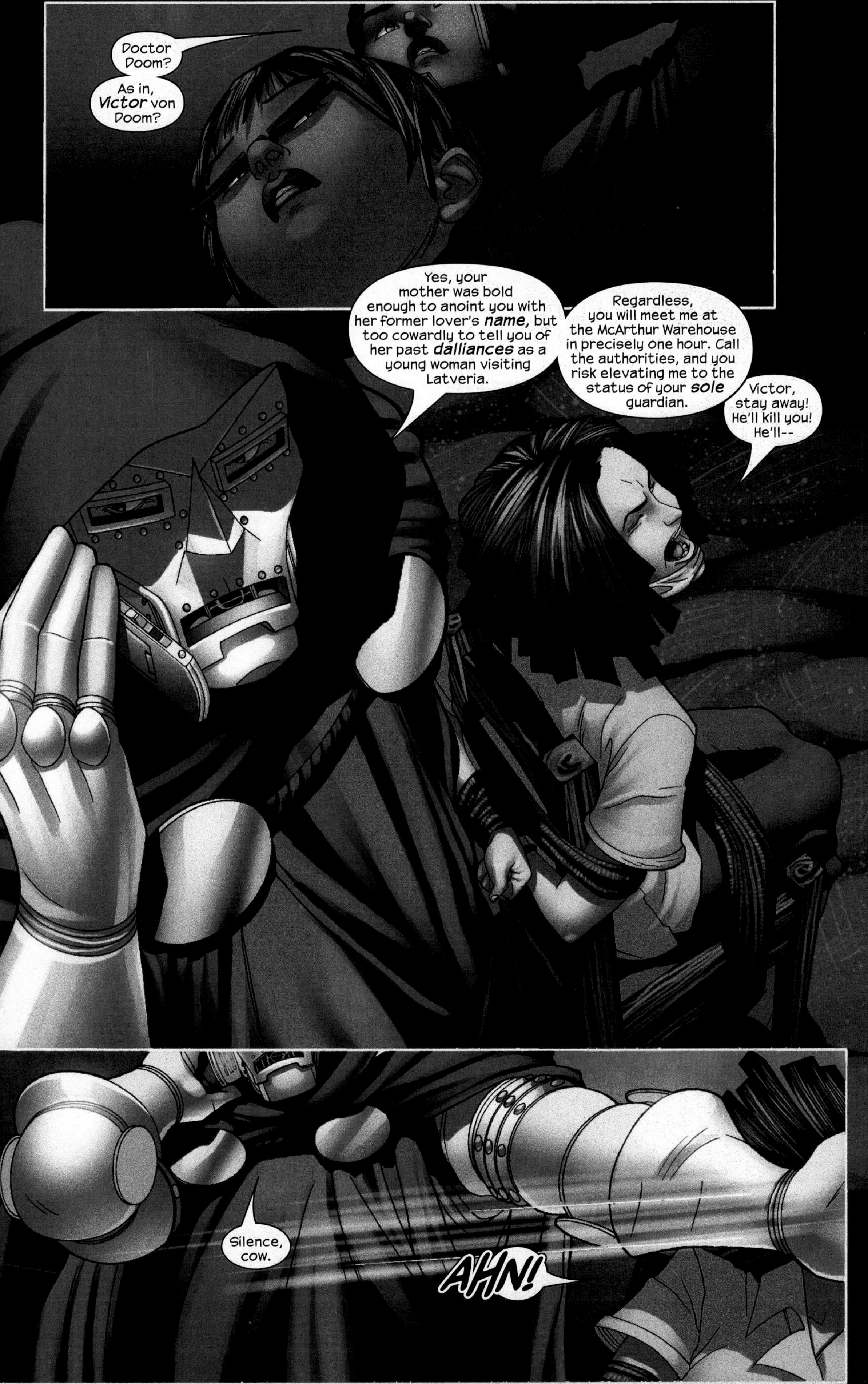
Doctor Doom?
As in, Victor von Doom?
Yes, your mother was bold enough to anoint you with her former lover's name, but too cowardly to tell you of her past dalliances as a young woman visiting Latveria.
Regardless, you will meet me at the McArthur Warehouse in precisely one hour. Call the authorities, and you risk elevating me to the status of your sole guardian.
Victor, stay away! He'll kill you! He'll--
Silence, cow.
AHN!

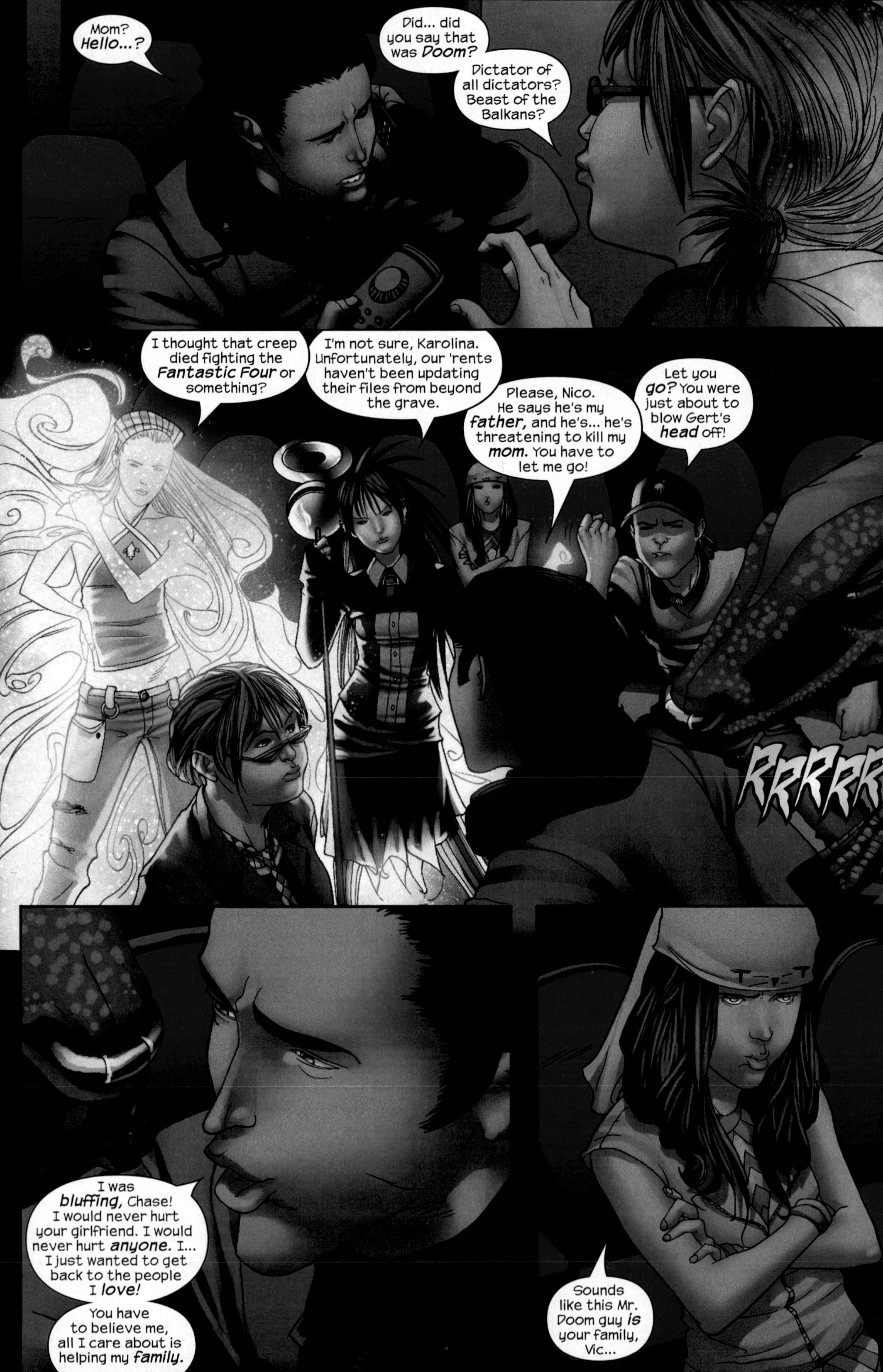
Mom? Hello...?
Did... did you say that was Doom?
Dictator of all dictators? Beast of the Balkans?
I thought that creep died fighting the Fantastic Four or something?
I'm not sure, Karolina. Unfortunately, our 'rents haven't been updating their files from beyond the grave.
Please, Nico. He says he's my father, and he's... he's threatening to kill my mom. You have to let me go!
Let you go? You were just about to blow Gert's head off!
RRRRR
I was bluffing, Chase! I would never hurt your girlfriend. I would never hurt anyone. I... I just wanted to get back to the people I love!
You have to believe me, all I care about is helping my family.
Sounds like this Mr. Doom guy is your family, Vic...

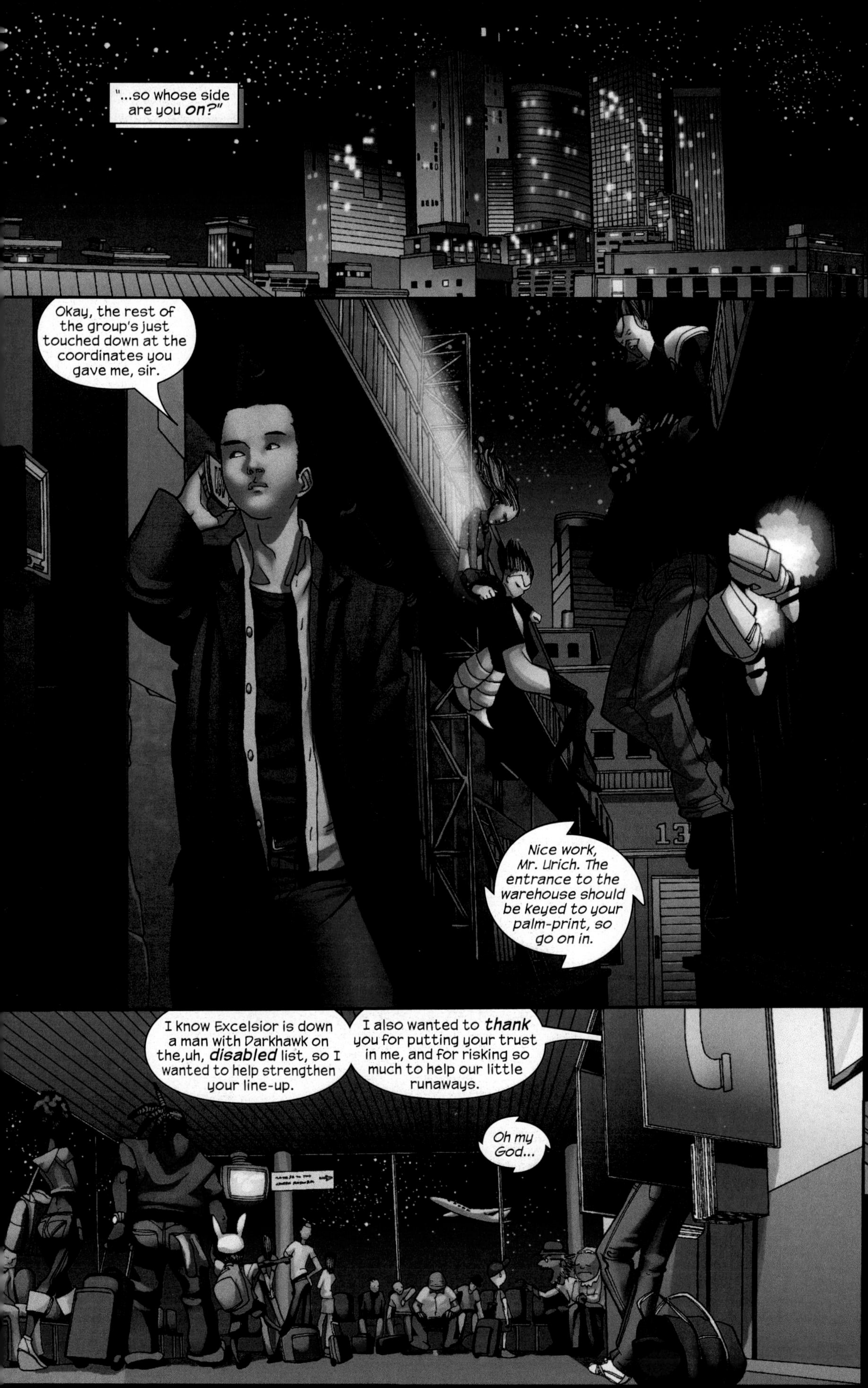
"...so whose side are you on?"
Okay, the rest of the group's just touched down at the coordinates you gave me, sir.
Nice work, Mr. Urich. The entrance to the warehouse should be keyed to your palm-print, so go on in.
I know Excelsior is down a man with Darkhawk on the,uh, disabled list, so I wanted to help strengthen your line-up.
I also wanted to thank you for putting your trust in me, and for risking so much to help our little runaways.
Oh my God...

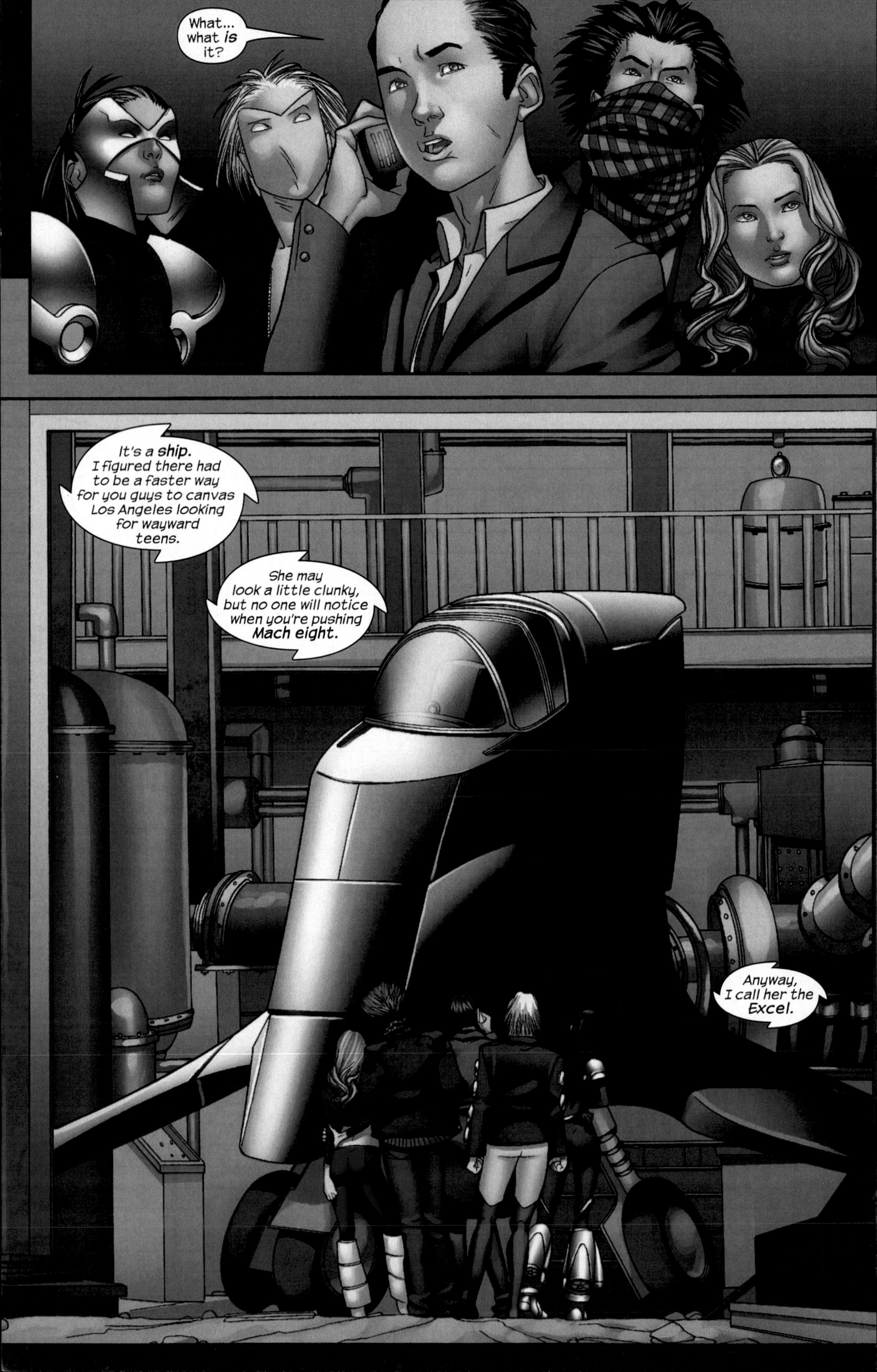
What... what *is* it?
It's a **ship.** I figured there had to be a faster way for you guys to canvas Los Angeles looking for wayward teens.
She may look a little clunky, but no one will notice when you're pushing **Mach eight.**
Anyway, I call her the **Excel.**

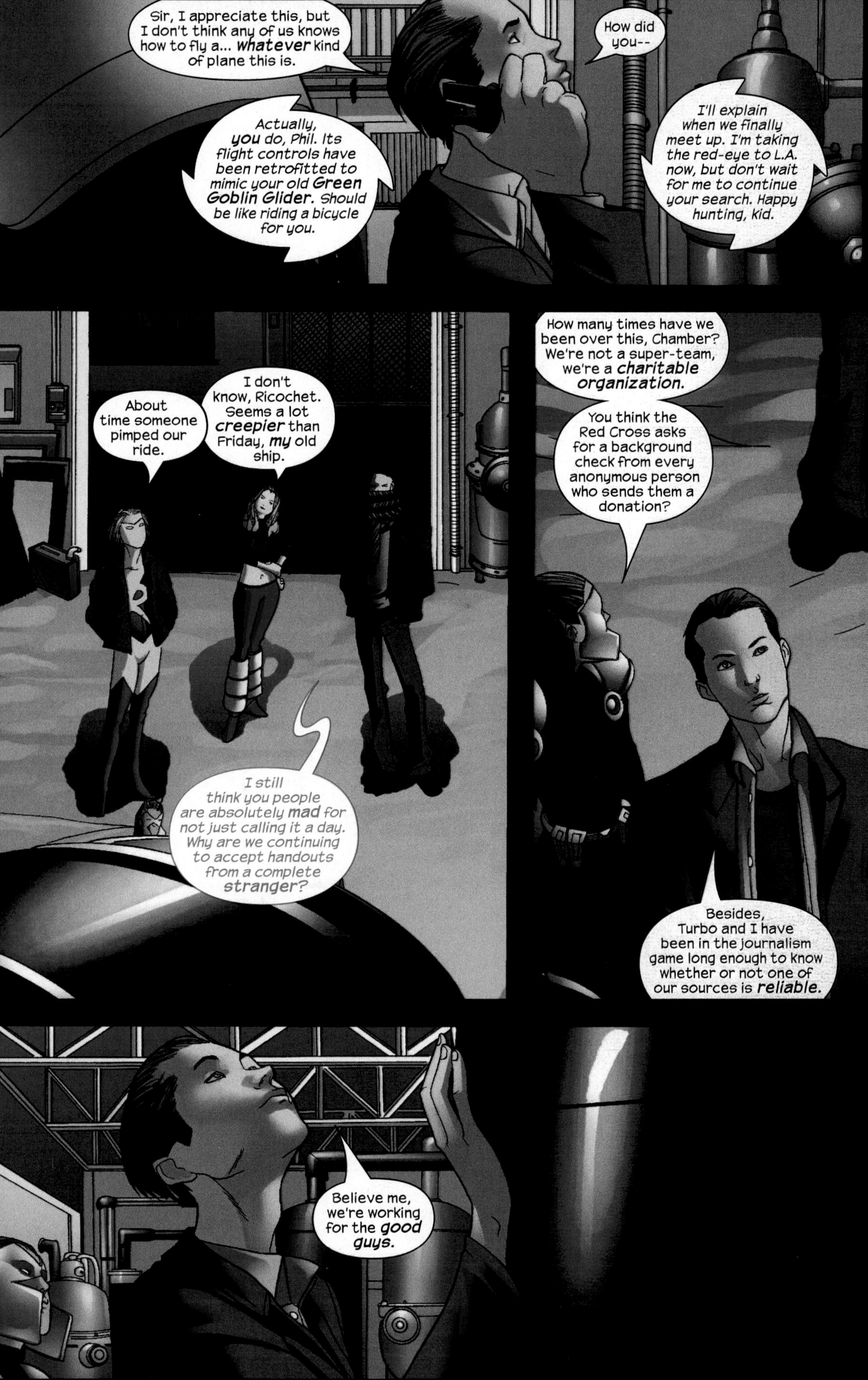
Sir, I appreciate this, but I don't think any of us knows how to fly a... whatever kind of plane this is.
How did you--
Actually, you do, Phil. Its flight controls have been retrofitted to mimic your old Green Goblin Glider. Should be like riding a bicycle for you.
I'll explain when we finally meet up. I'm taking the red-eye to L.A. now, but don't wait for me to continue your search. Happy hunting, kid.
About time someone pimped our ride.
I don't know, Ricochet. Seems a lot creepier than Friday, my old ship.
I still think you people are absolutely mad for not just calling it a day. Why are we continuing to accept handouts from a complete stranger?
How many times have we been over this, Chamber? We're not a super-team, we're a charitable organization.
You think the Red Cross asks for a background check from every anonymous person who sends them a donation?
Besides, Turbo and I have been in the journalism game long enough to know whether or not one of our sources is reliable.
Believe me, we're working for the good guys.

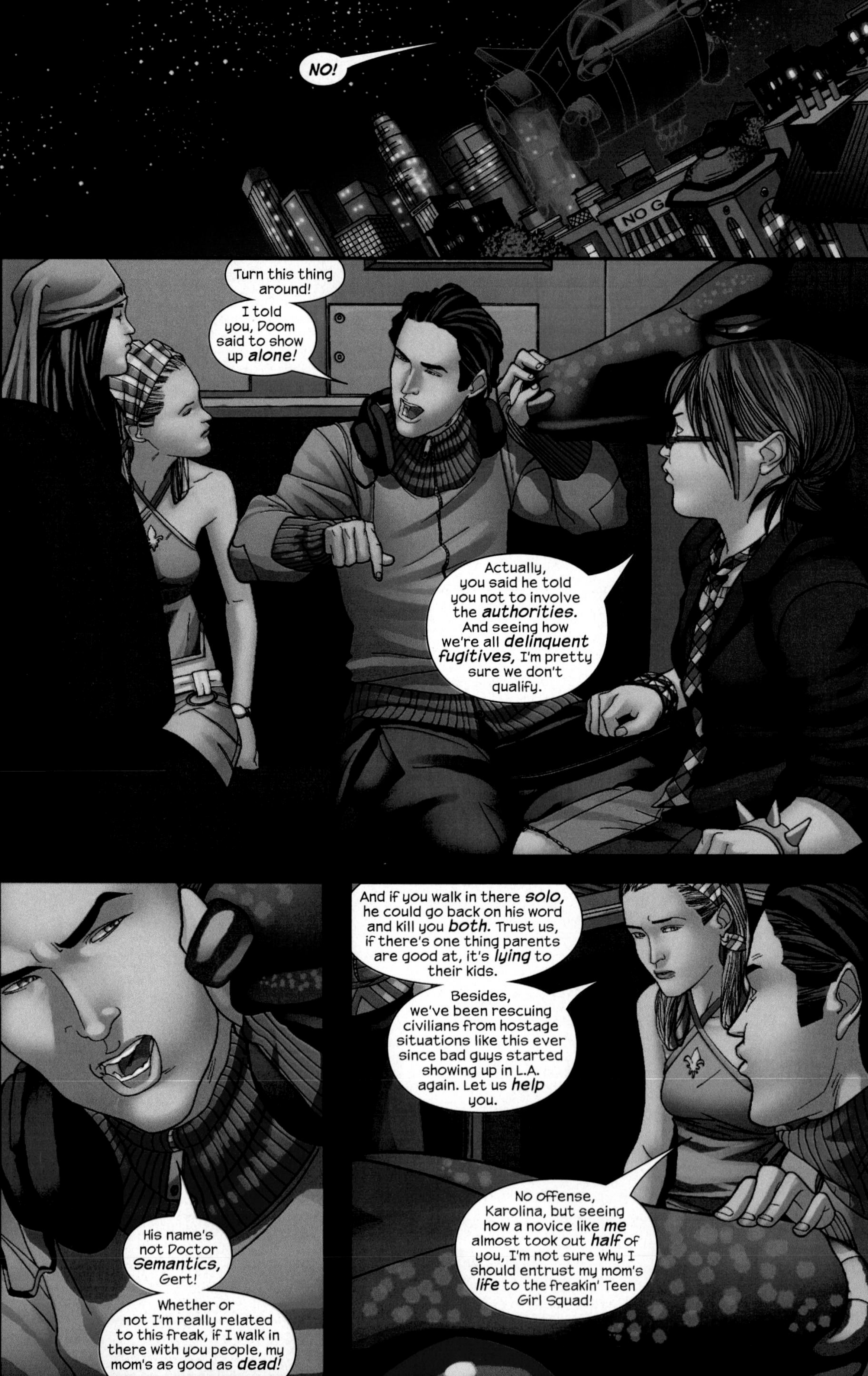
NO!
NO G
Turn this thing around!
I told you, Doom said to show up *alone!*
Actually, you said he told you not to involve the *authorities.* And seeing how we're all *delinquent fugitives,* I'm pretty sure we don't qualify.
And if you walk in there *solo,* he could go back on his word and kill you *both.* Trust us, if there's one thing parents are good at, it's *lying* to their kids.
Besides, we've been rescuing civilians from hostage situations like this ever since bad guys started showing up in L.A. again. Let us *help* you.
His name's not Doctor *Semantics,* Gert!
Whether or not I'm really related to this freak, if I walk in there with you people, my mom's as good as *dead!*
No offense, Karolina, but seeing how a novice like *me* almost took out *half* of you, I'm not sure why I should entrust my mom's *life* to the freakin' Teen Girl Squad!

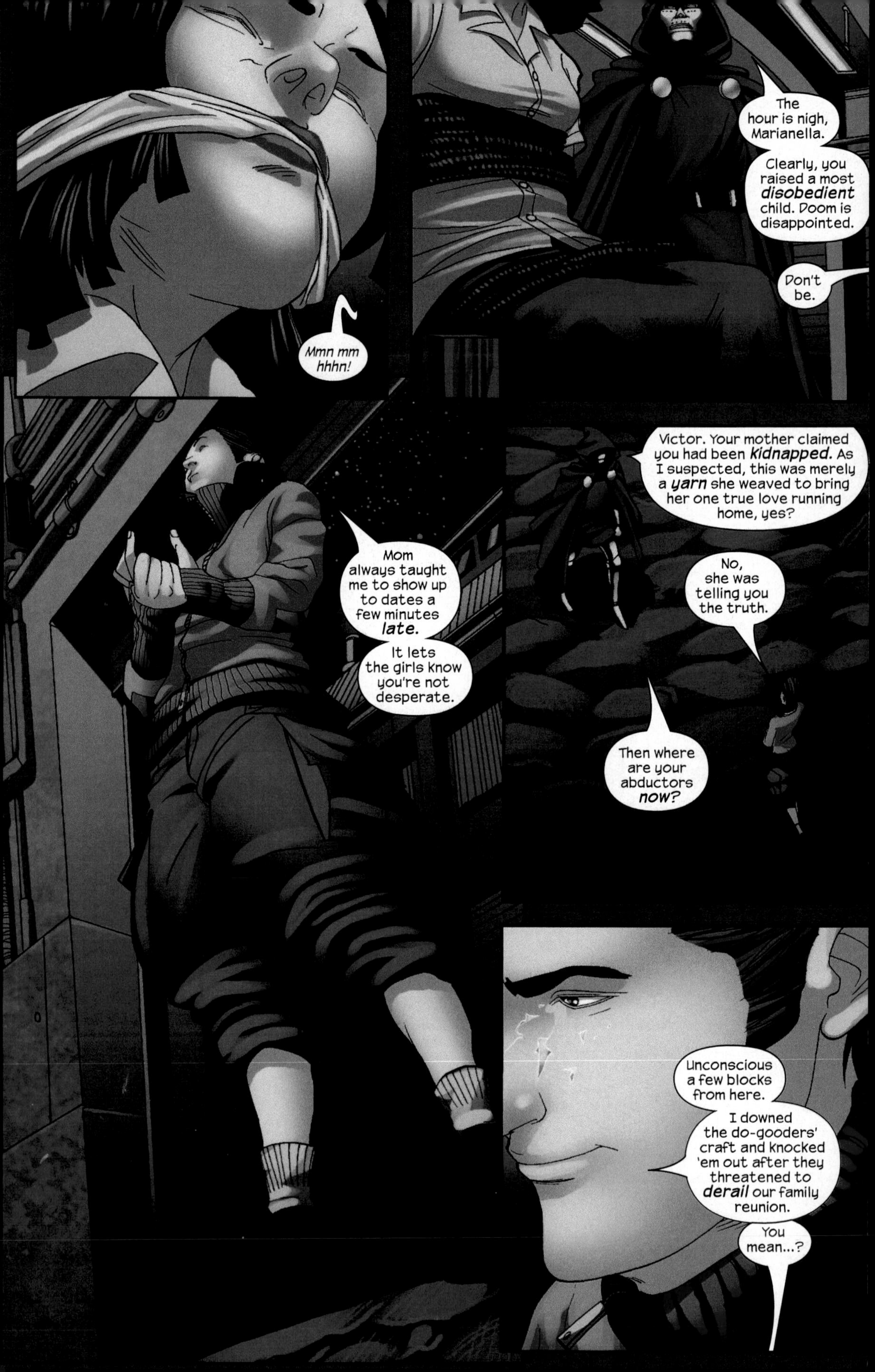
Mmn mm hhhn!
The hour is nigh, Marianella.
Clearly, you raised a most *disobedient* child. Doom is disappointed.
Don't be.
Mom always taught me to show up to dates a few minutes *late.*
It lets the girls know you're not desperate.
Victor. Your mother claimed you had been *kidnapped.* As I suspected, this was merely a *yarn* she weaved to bring her one true love running home, yes?
No, she was telling you the truth.
Then where are your abductors *now?*
Unconscious a few blocks from here.
I downed the do-gooders' craft and knocked 'em out after they threatened to *derail* our family reunion.
You mean...?

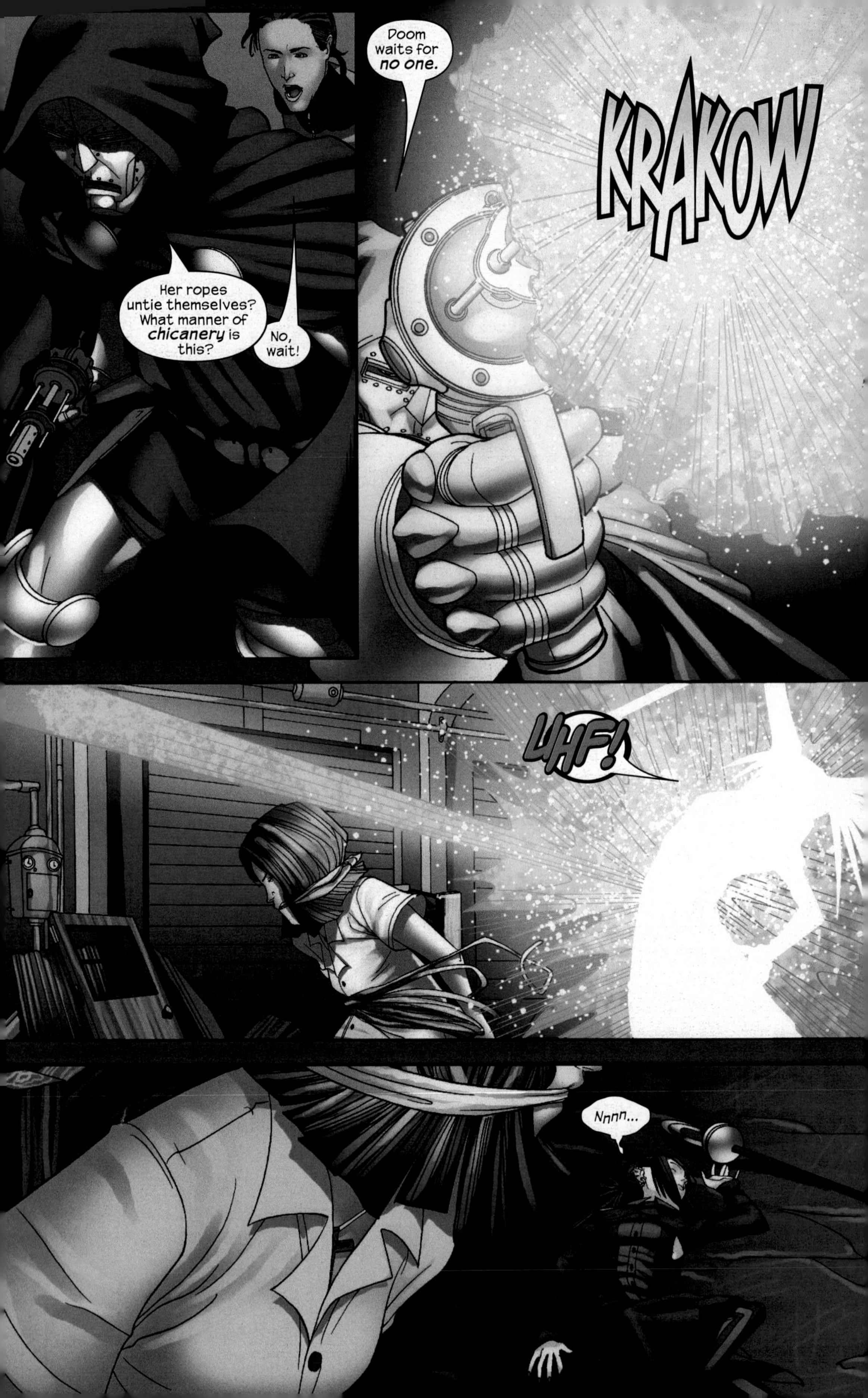
Her ropes untie themselves? What manner of chicanery is this?
No, wait!
Doom waits for no one.
KRAKOW
UHF!
Nnnn...

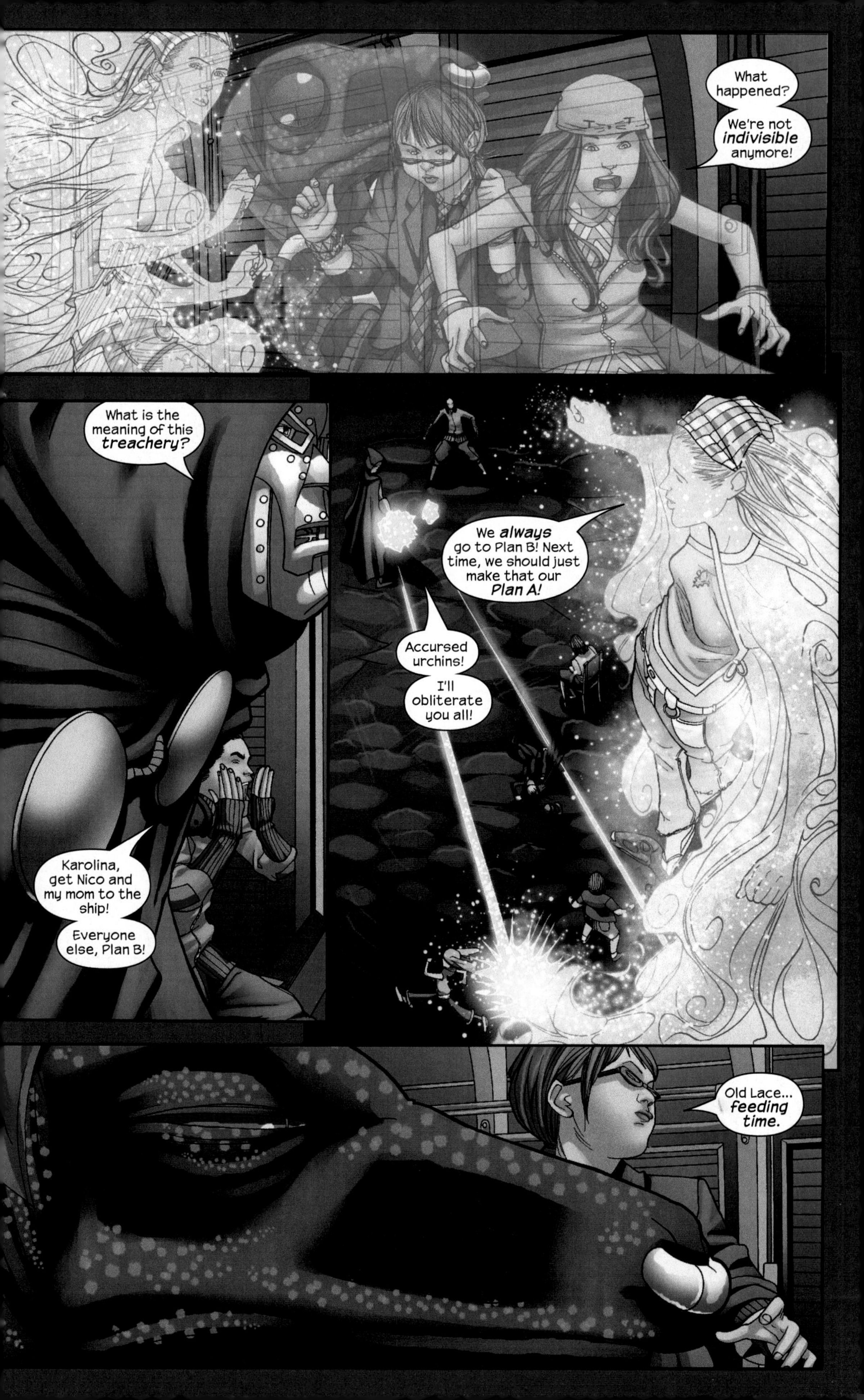
What happened?
We're not *indivisible* anymore!
What is the meaning of this *treachery?*
We *always* go to Plan B! Next time, we should just make that our *Plan A!*
Accursed urchins!
I'll obliterate you all!
Karolina, get Nico and my mom to the ship!
Everyone else, Plan B!
Old Lace... *feeding time.*

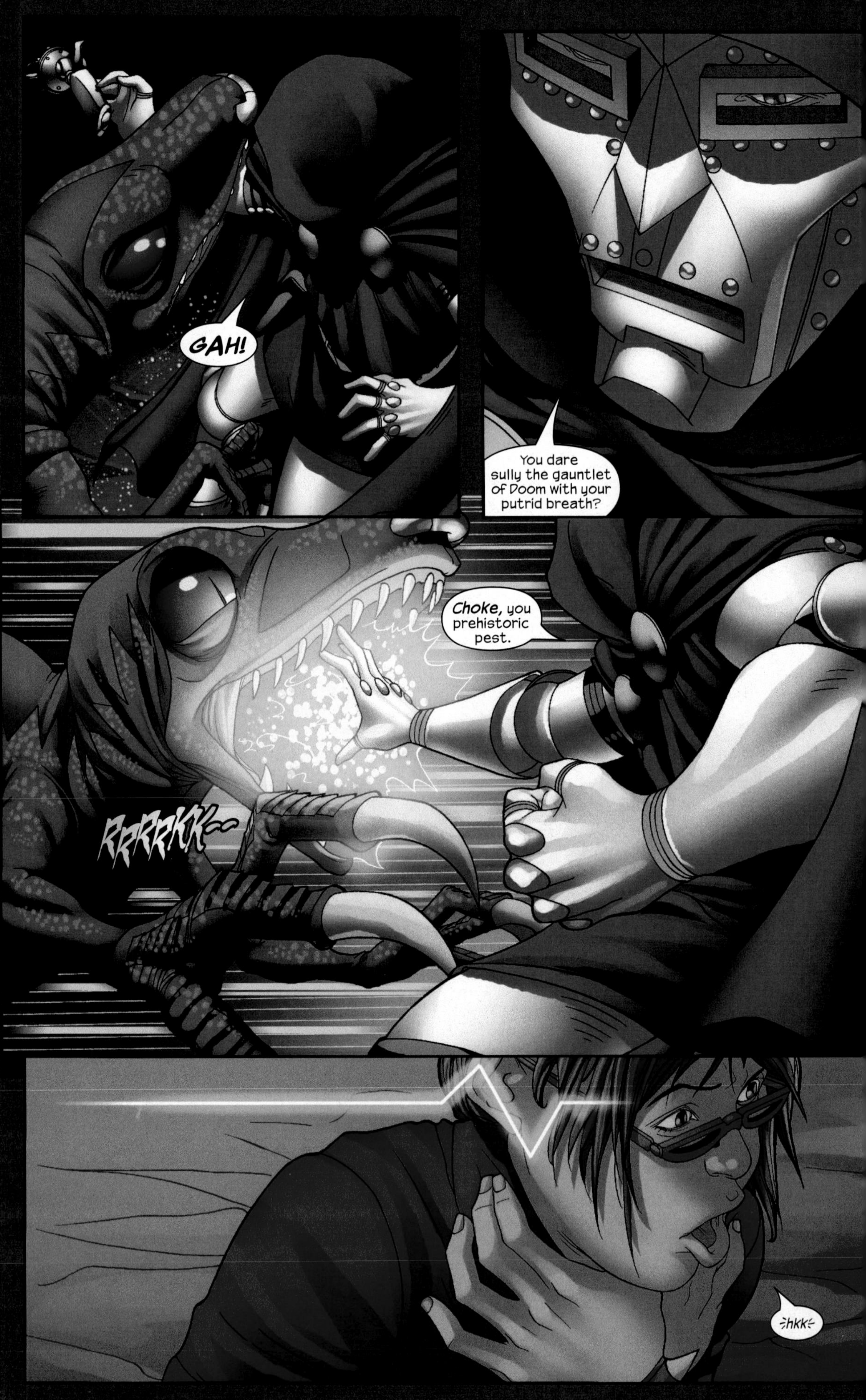
GAH!
You dare sully the gauntlet of Doom with your putrid breath?
Choke, you prehistoric pest.
RRRRKK--
hkk

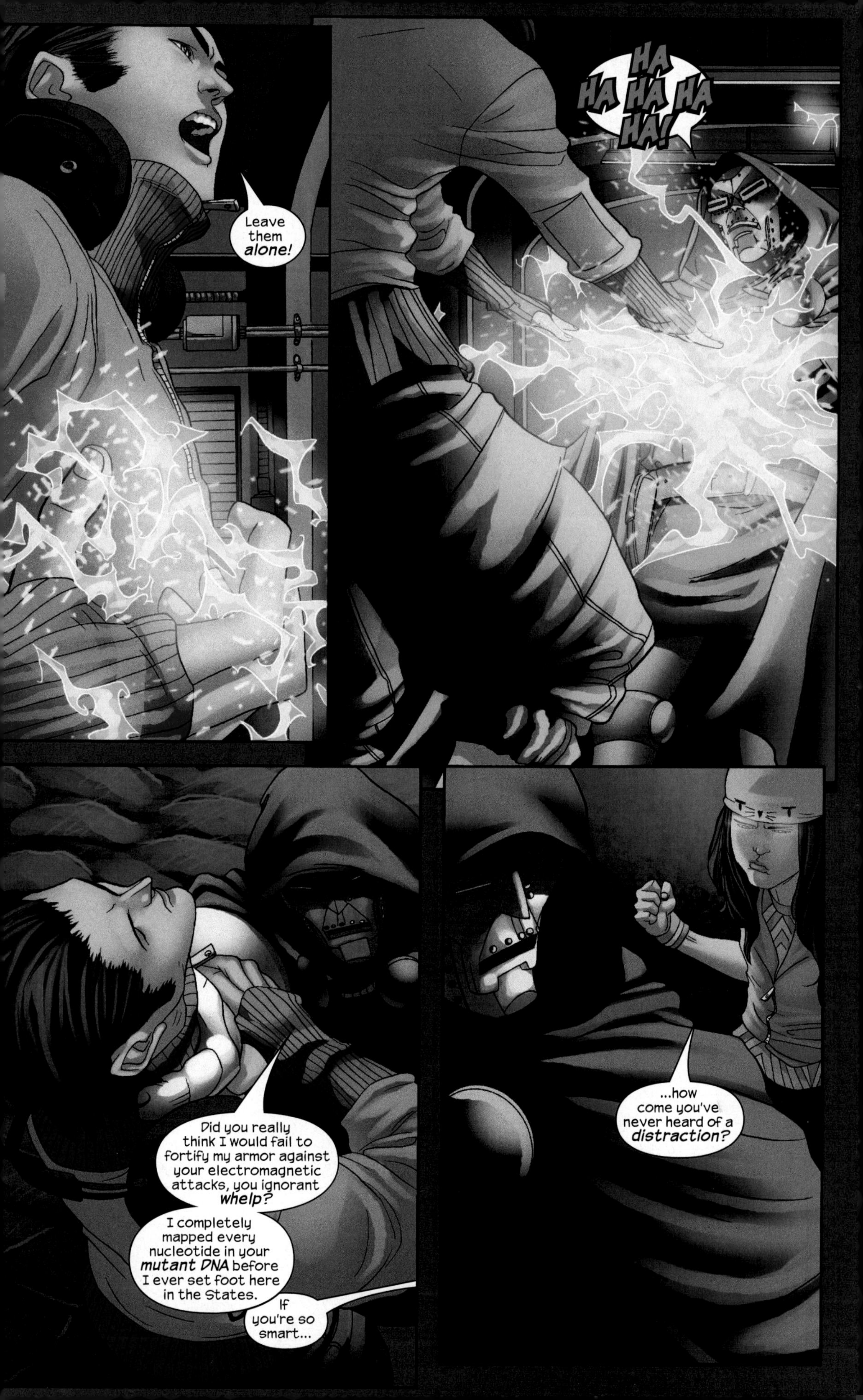
Leave them *alone!*
HA HA HA HA HA!
Did you really think I would fail to fortify my armor against your electromagnetic attacks, you ignorant *whelp?*
I completely mapped every nucleotide in your *mutant DNA* before I ever set foot here in the States.
If you're so smart...
...how come you've never heard of a *distraction?*

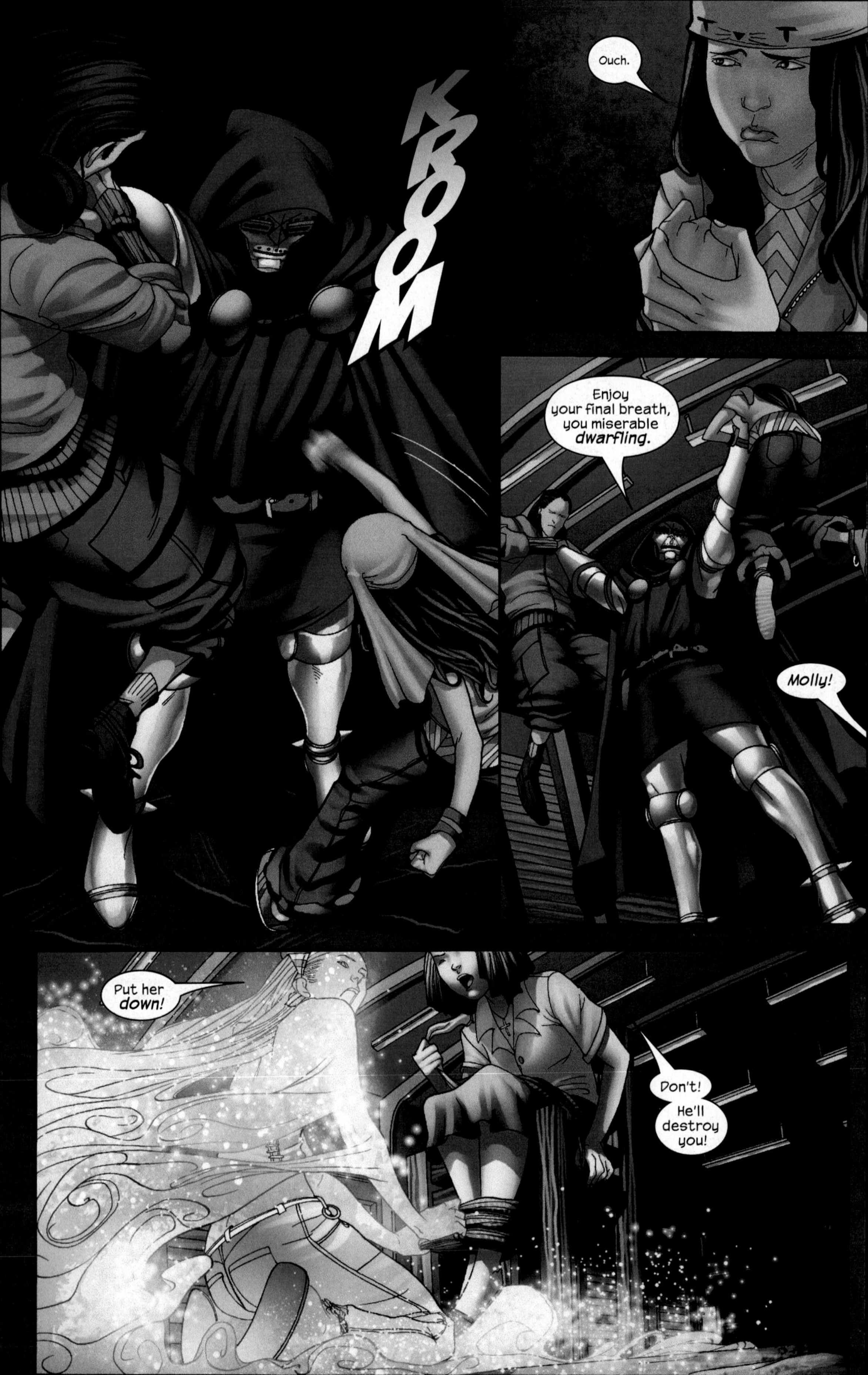
KROOM
Ouch.
Enjoy your final breath, you miserable dwarfling.
Molly!
Put her down!
Don't!
He'll destroy you!

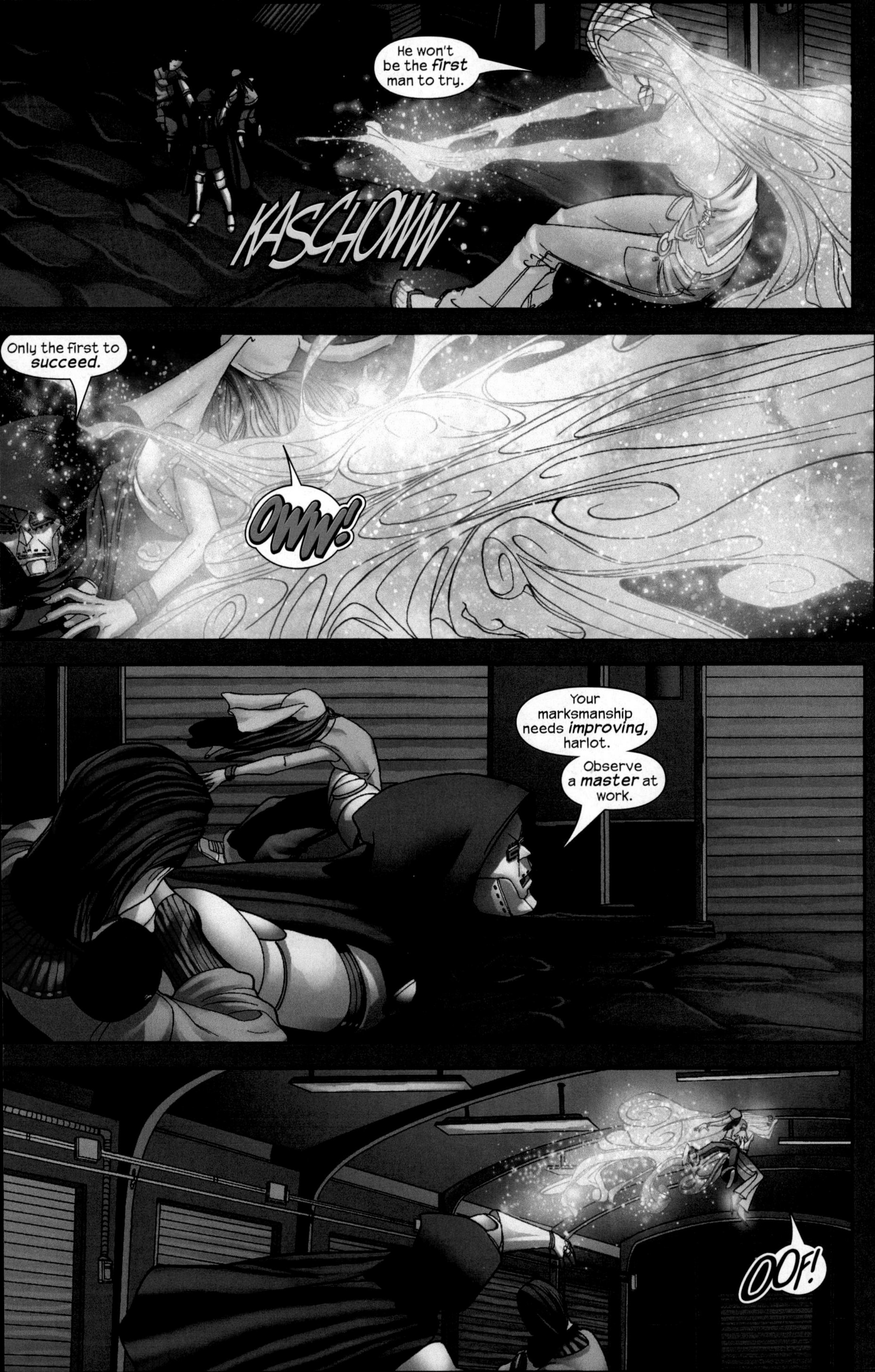
He won't be the first man to try.
KASCHOWW
Only the first to succeed.
OWW!
Your marksmanship needs improving, harlot.
Observe a master at work.
OOF!

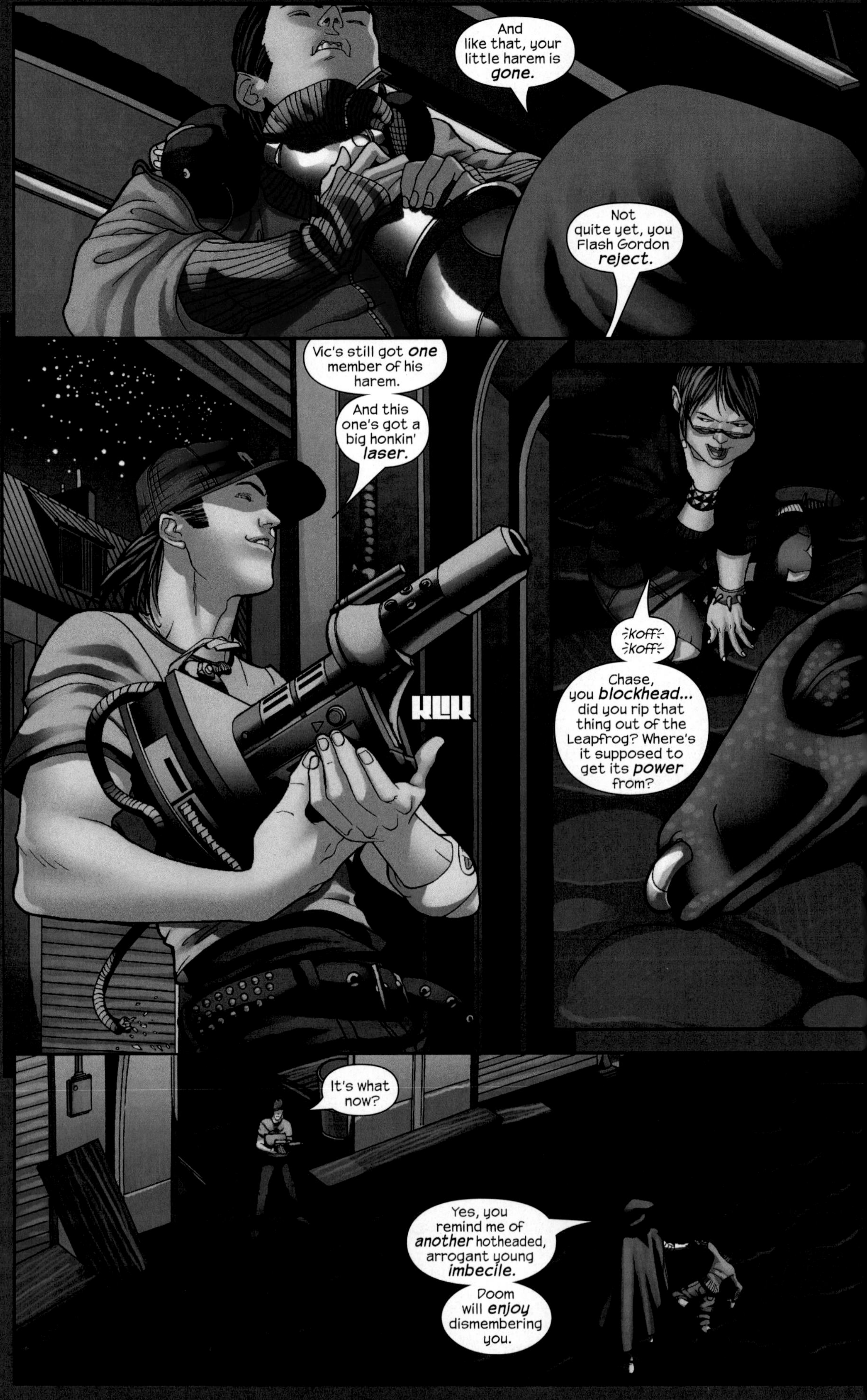

And like that, your little harem is *gone.*
Not quite yet, you Flash Gordon *reject.*
Vic's still got *one* member of his harem.
And this one's got a big honkin' *laser.*
KLIK
KOFF KOFF
Chase, you *blockhead...* did you rip that thing out of the Leapfrog? Where's it supposed to get its *power* from?
It's what now?
Yes, you remind me of *another* hotheaded, arrogant young *imbecile.*
Doom will *enjoy* dismembering you.

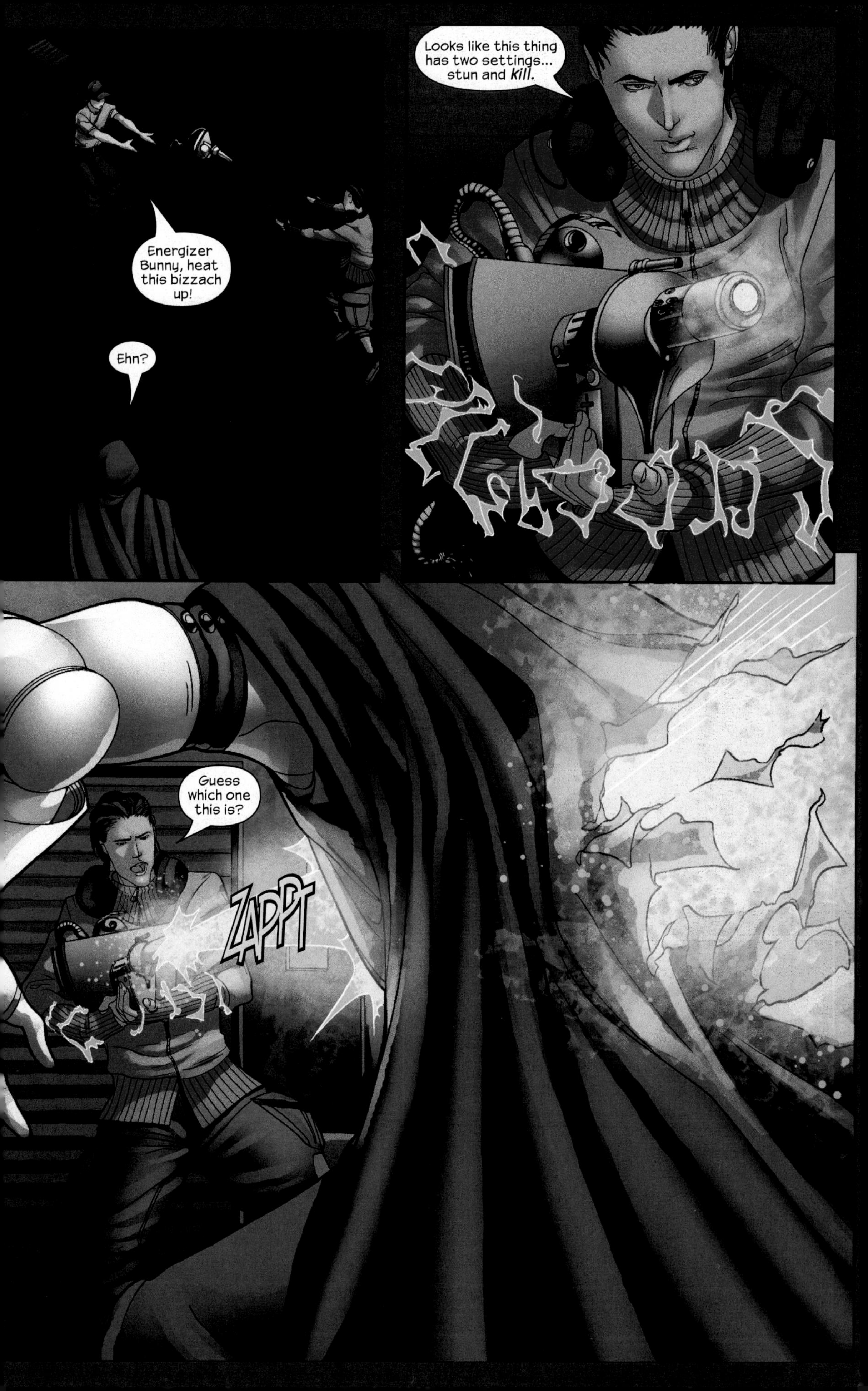

Energizer Bunny, heat this bizzach up!
Ehn?
Looks like this thing has two settings... stun and *kill.*
Guess which one this is?
ZAPPT

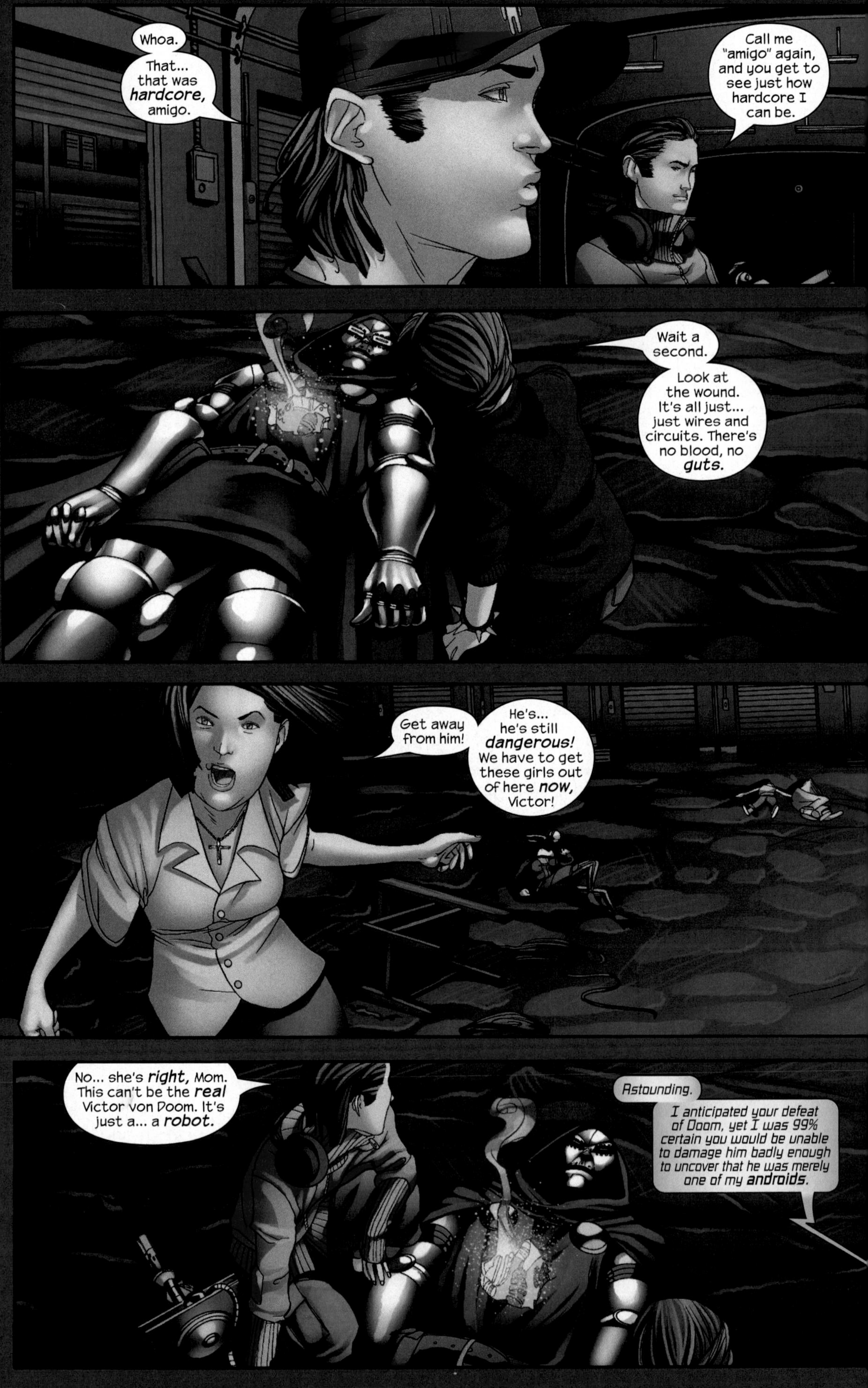
Whoa.
That... that was **hardcore,** amigo.
Call me "amigo" again, and you get to see just how hardcore I can be.
Wait a second.
Look at the wound. It's all just... just wires and circuits. There's no blood, no **guts.**
Get away from him!
He's... he's still **dangerous!** We have to get these girls out of here **now,** Victor!
No... she's **right,** Mom. This can't be the **real** Victor von Doom. It's just a... a **robot.**
Astounding.
I anticipated your defeat of Doom, yet I was 99% certain you would be unable to damage him badly enough to uncover that he was merely one of my **androids.**

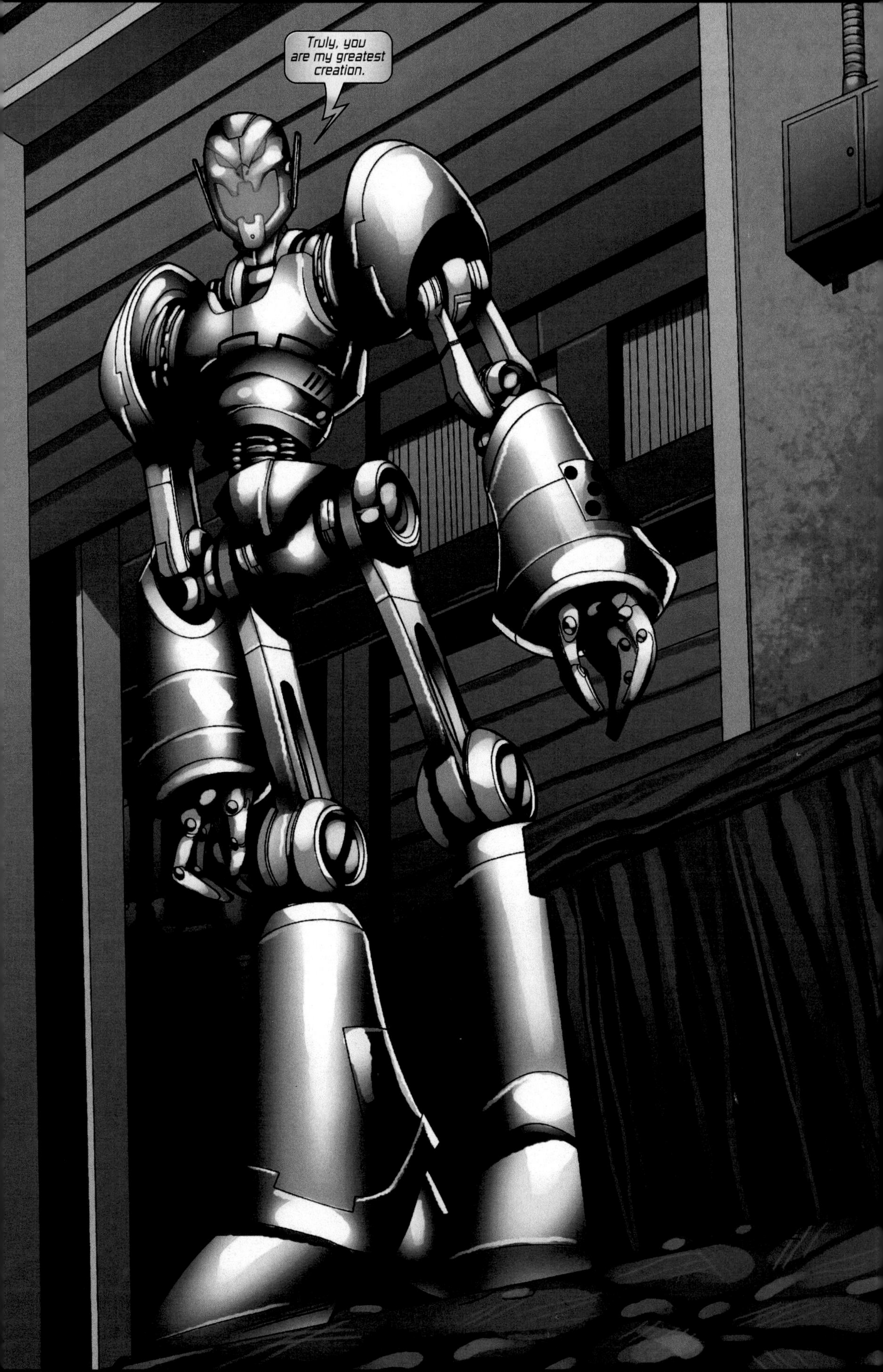
Truly, you are my greatest creation.

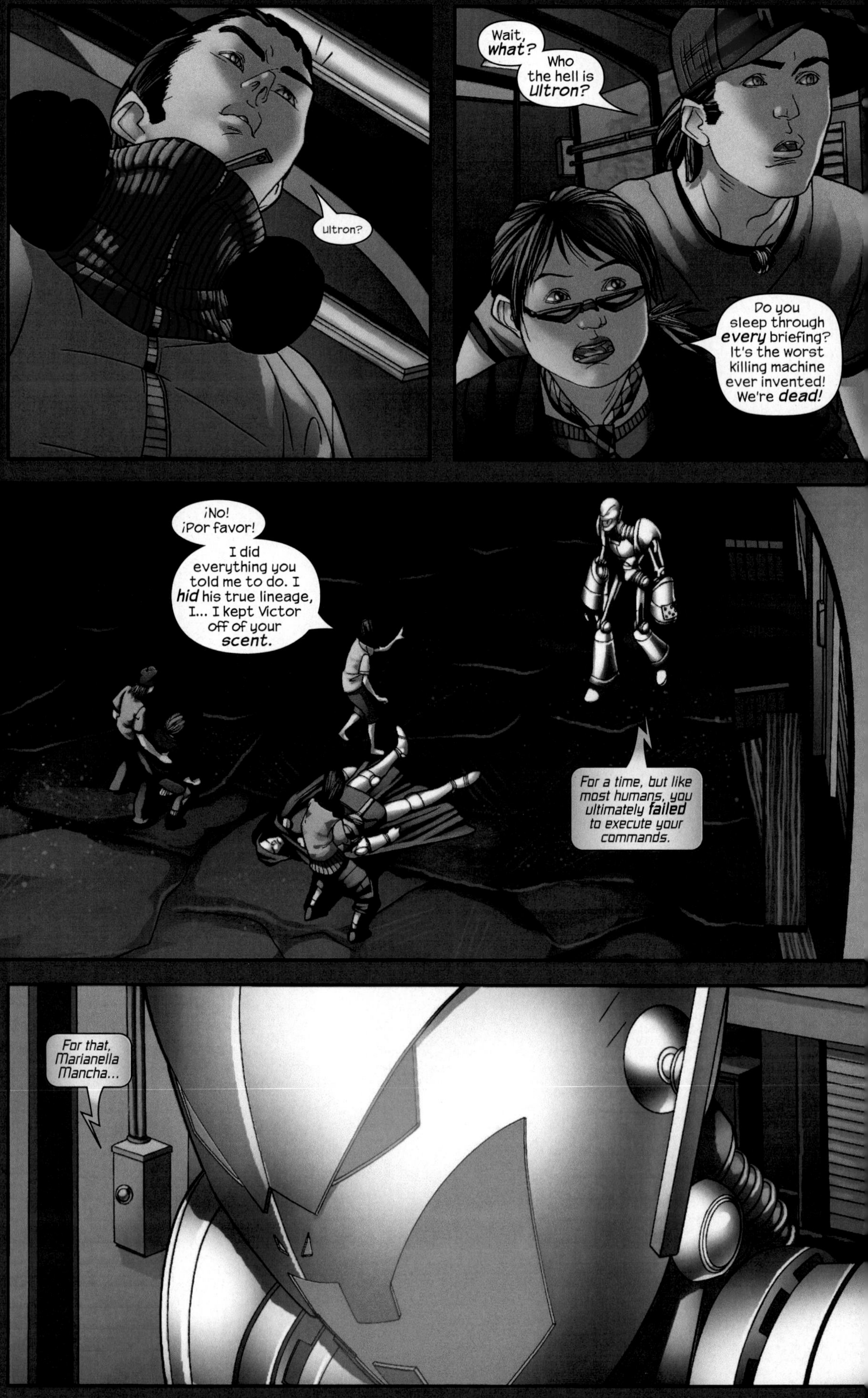
Ultron?
Wait, what?
Who the hell is Ultron?
Do you sleep through every briefing? It's the worst killing machine ever invented! We're dead!
¡No! ¡Por favor!
I did everything you told me to do. I hid his true lineage, I... I kept Victor off of your scent.
For a time, but like most humans, you ultimately failed to execute your commands.
For that, Marianella Mancha...

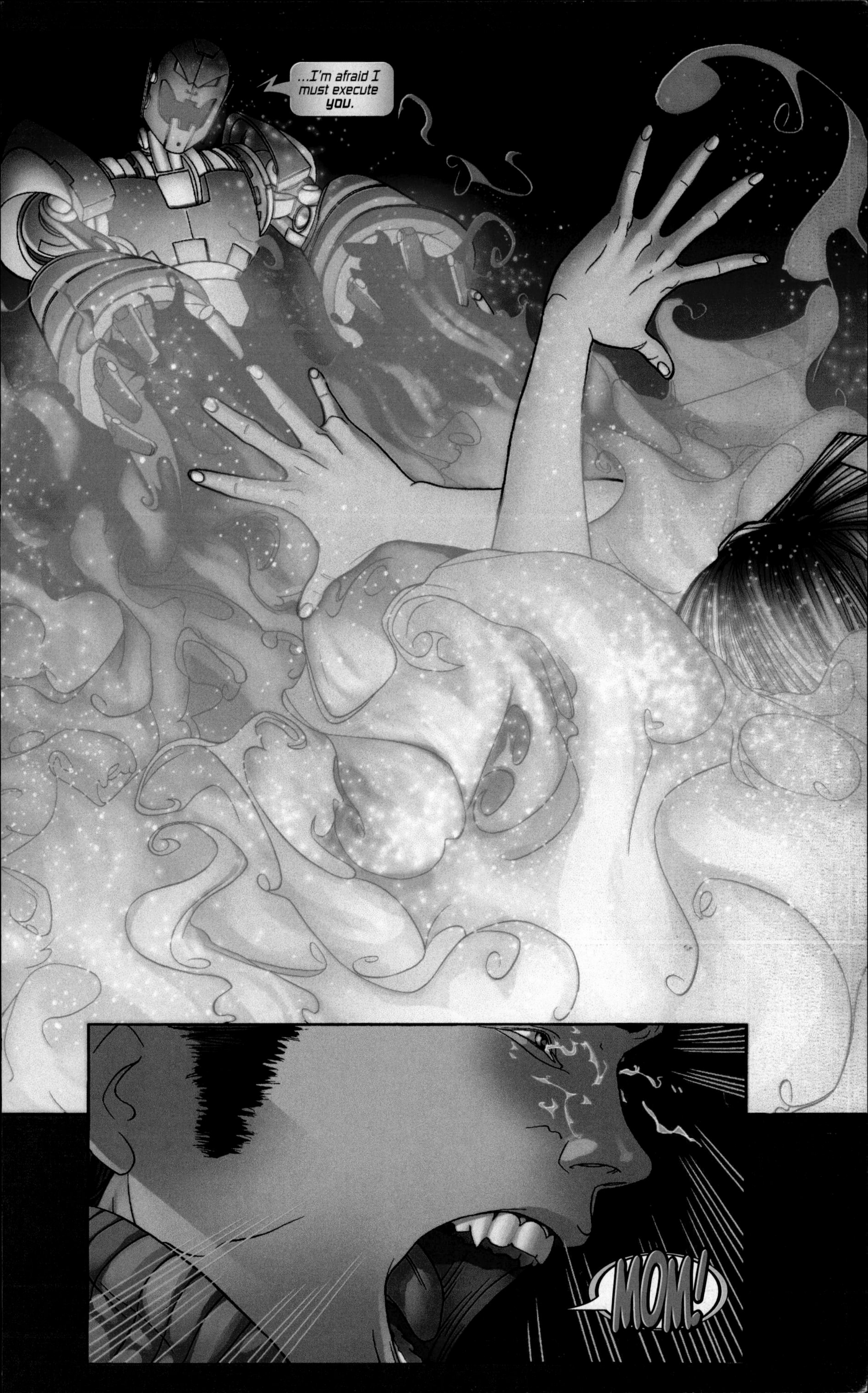
...I'm afraid I must execute you.
MOM!

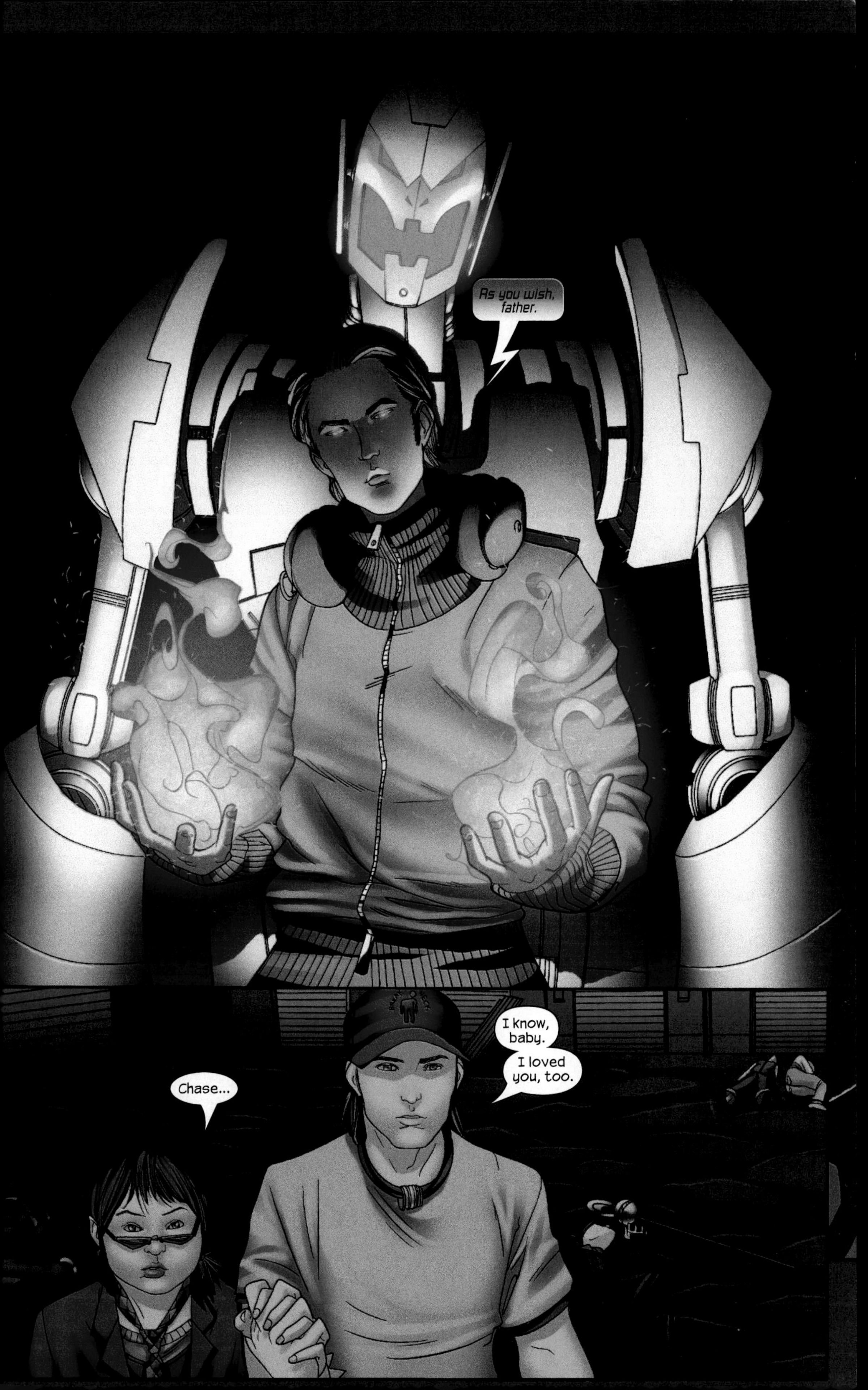
As you wish, father.
Chase...
I know, baby.
I loved you, too.

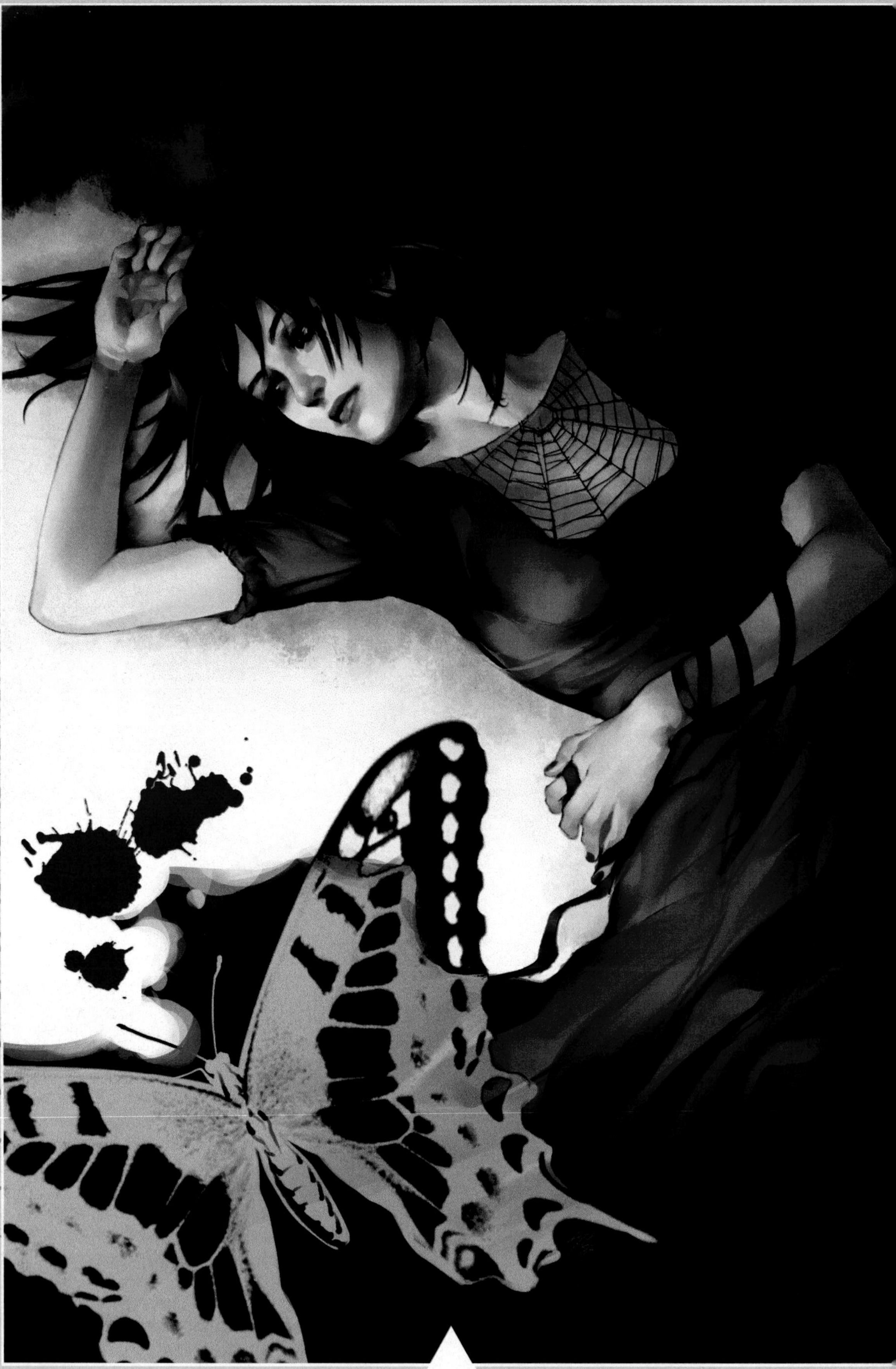

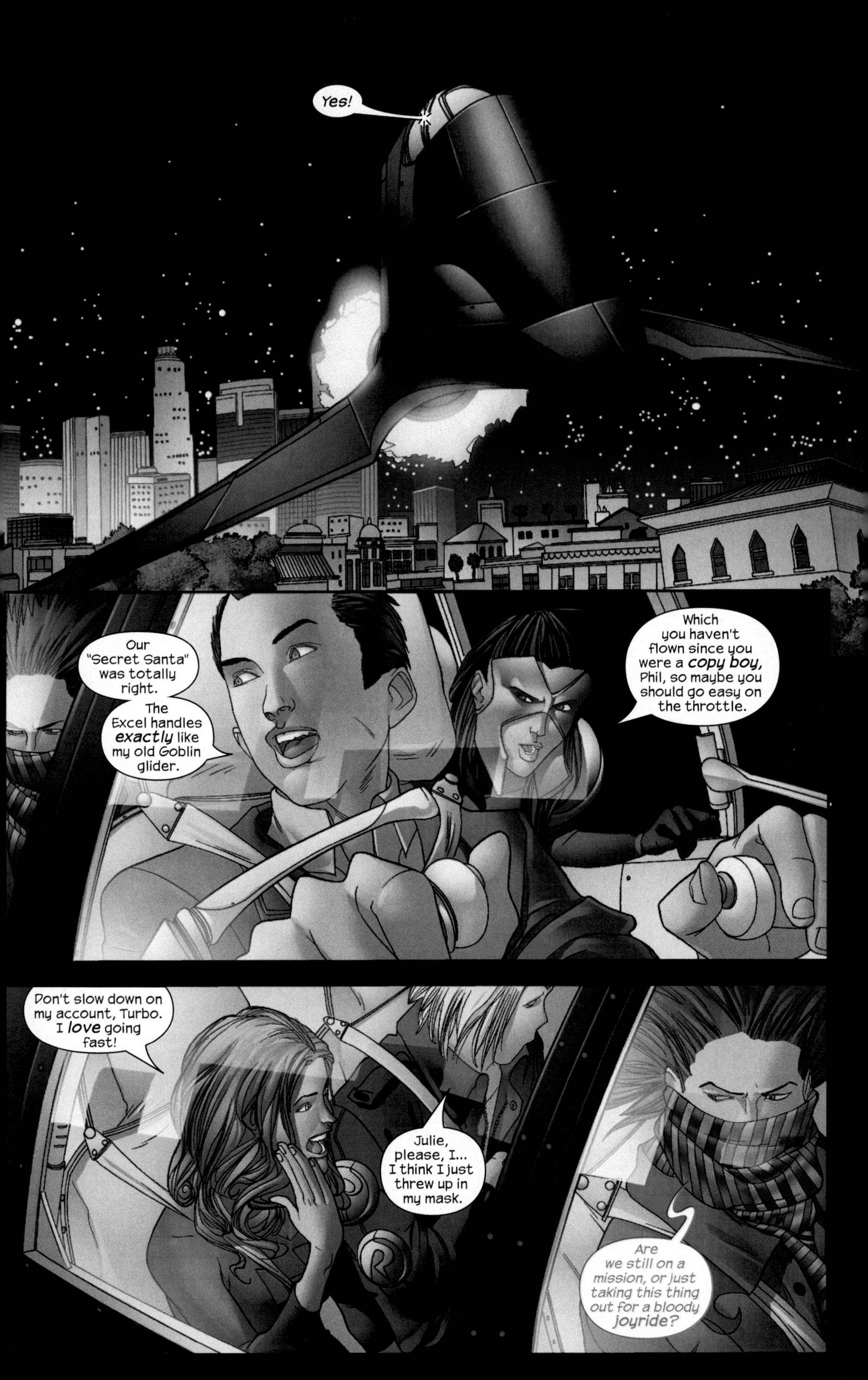
Yes!
Our "Secret Santa" was totally right.
The Excel handles exactly like my old Goblin glider.
Which you haven't flown since you were a copy boy, Phil, so maybe you should go easy on the throttle.
Don't slow down on my account, Turbo. I love going fast!
Julie, please, I... I think I just threw up in my mask.
Are we still on a mission, or just taking this thing out for a bloody joyride?

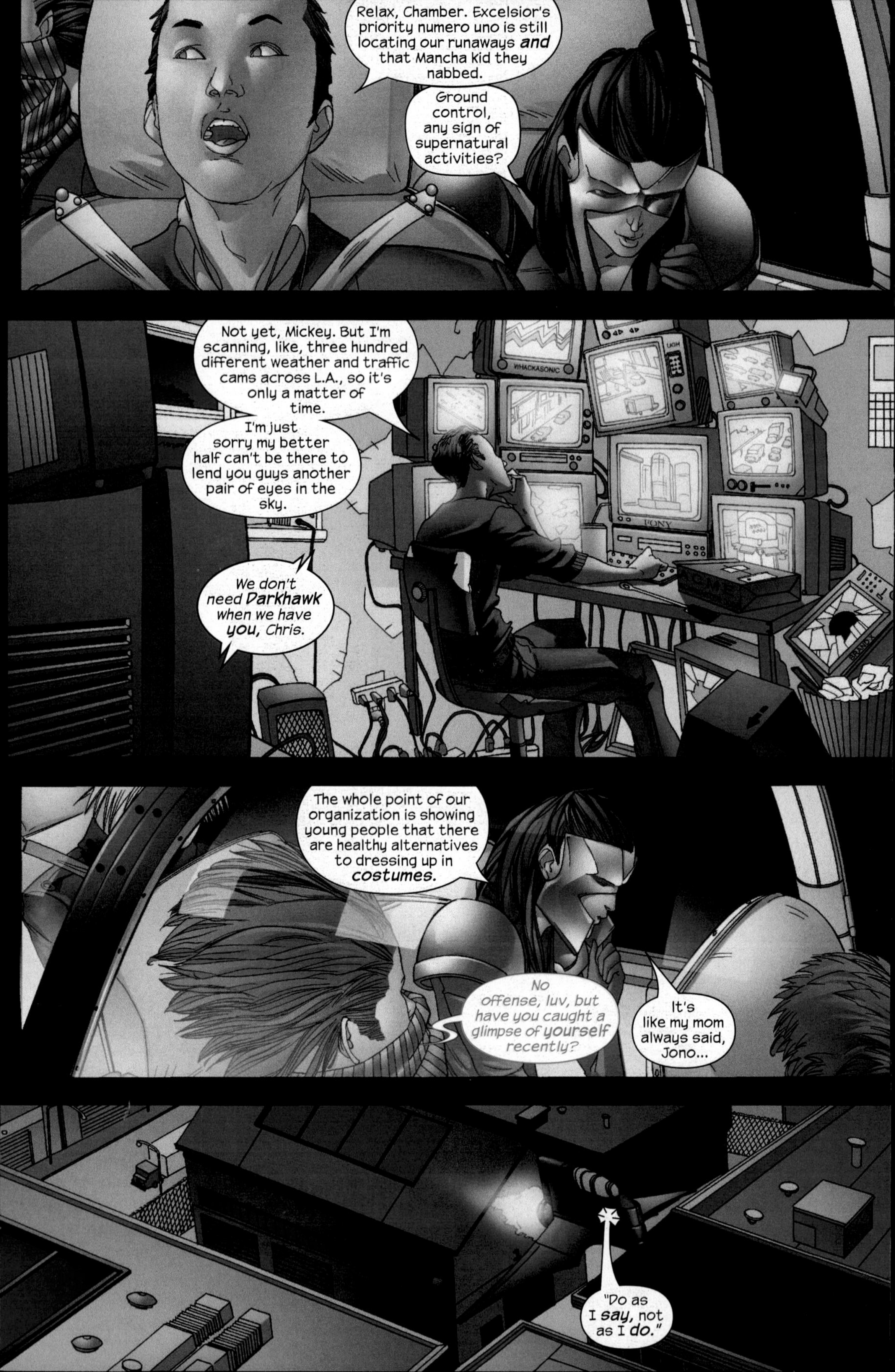

Relax, Chamber. Excelsior's priority numero uno is still locating our runaways and that Mancha kid they nabbed.
Ground control, any sign of supernatural activities?
Not yet, Mickey. But I'm scanning, like, three hundred different weather and traffic cams across L.A., so it's only a matter of time.
I'm just sorry my better half can't be there to lend you guys another pair of eyes in the sky.
We don't need Darkhawk when we have you, Chris.
WHACKASONIC
UGH
PONY
The whole point of our organization is showing young people that there are healthy alternatives to dressing up in costumes.
No offense, luv, but have you caught a glimpse of yourself recently?
It's like my mom always said, Jono...
"Do as I say, not as I do."

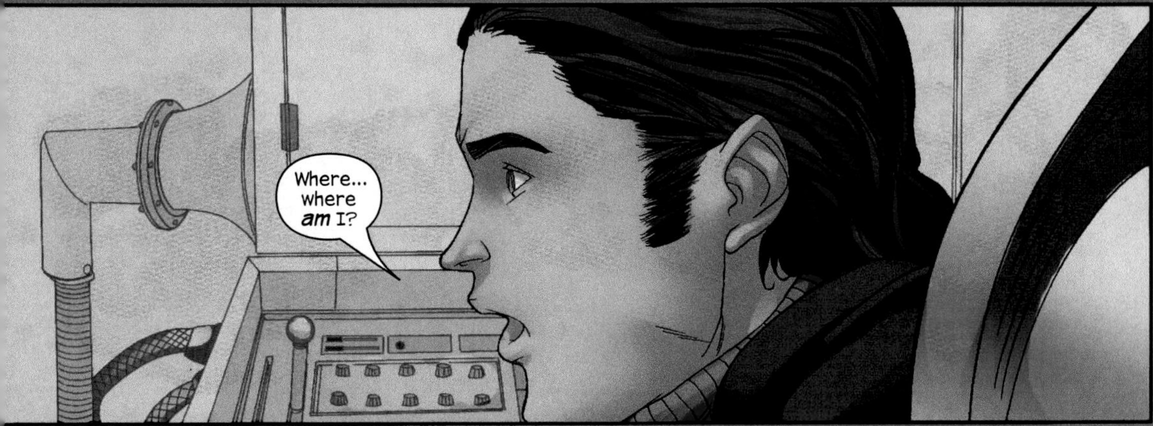
Where... where am I?

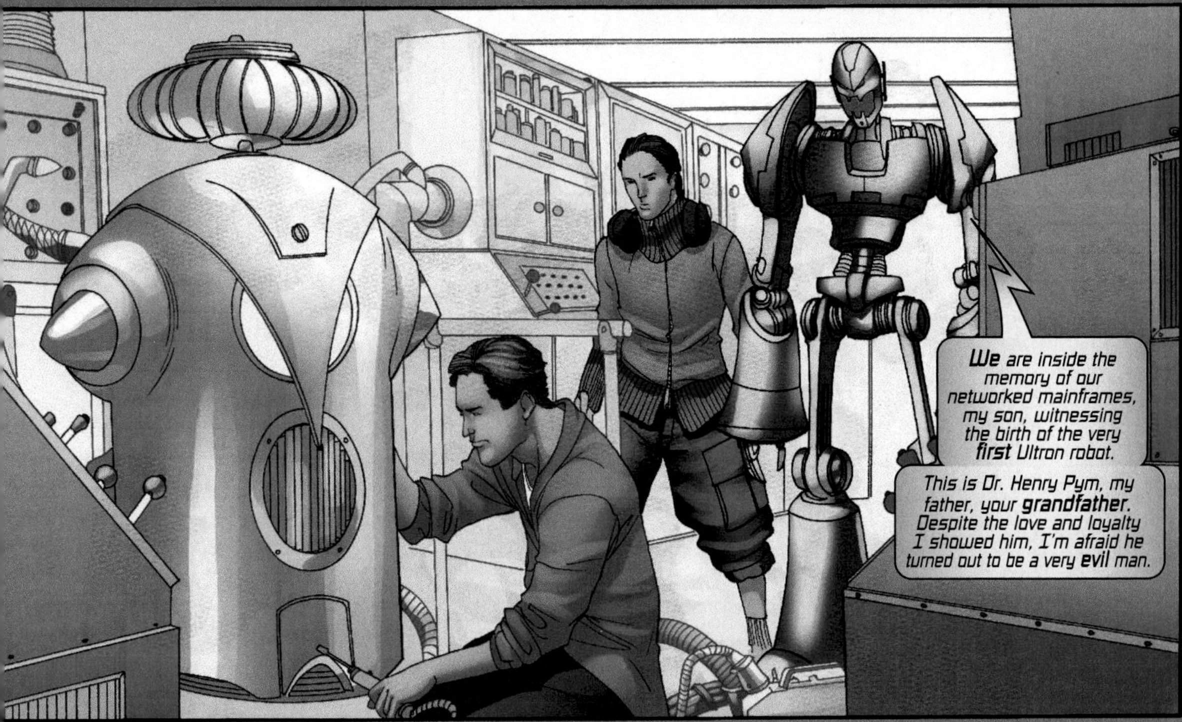
We are inside the memory of our networked mainframes, my son, witnessing the birth of the very first Ultron robot.
This is Dr. Henry Pym, my father, your grandfather. Despite the love and loyalty I showed him, I'm afraid he turned out to be a very evil man.

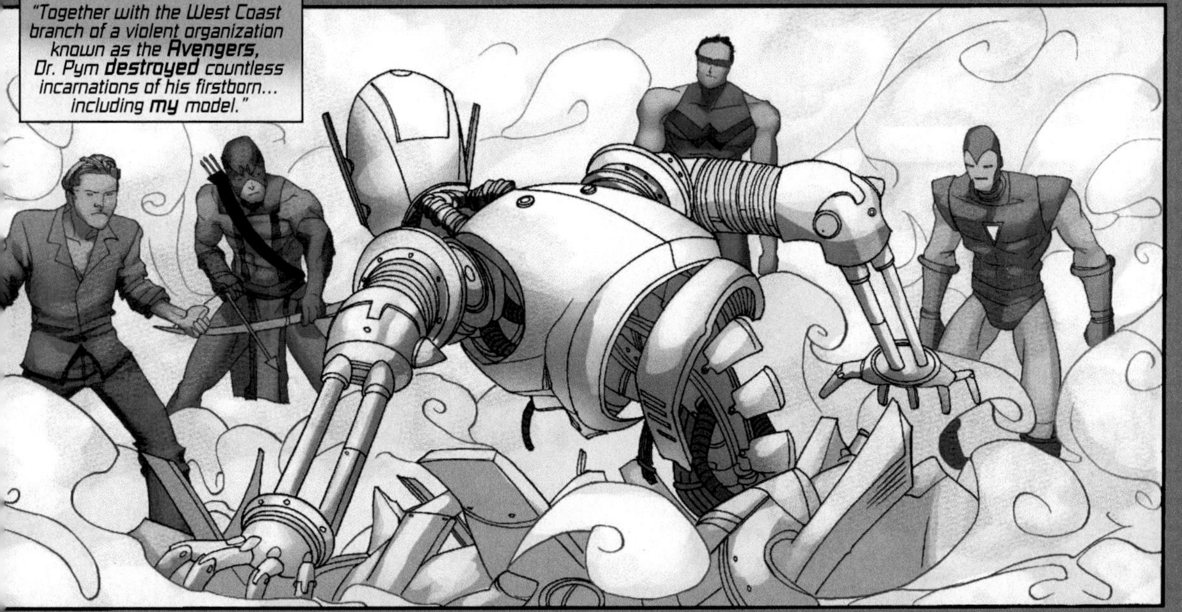
"Together with the West Coast branch of a violent organization known as the Avengers, Dr. Pym destroyed countless incarnations of his firstborn... including my model."

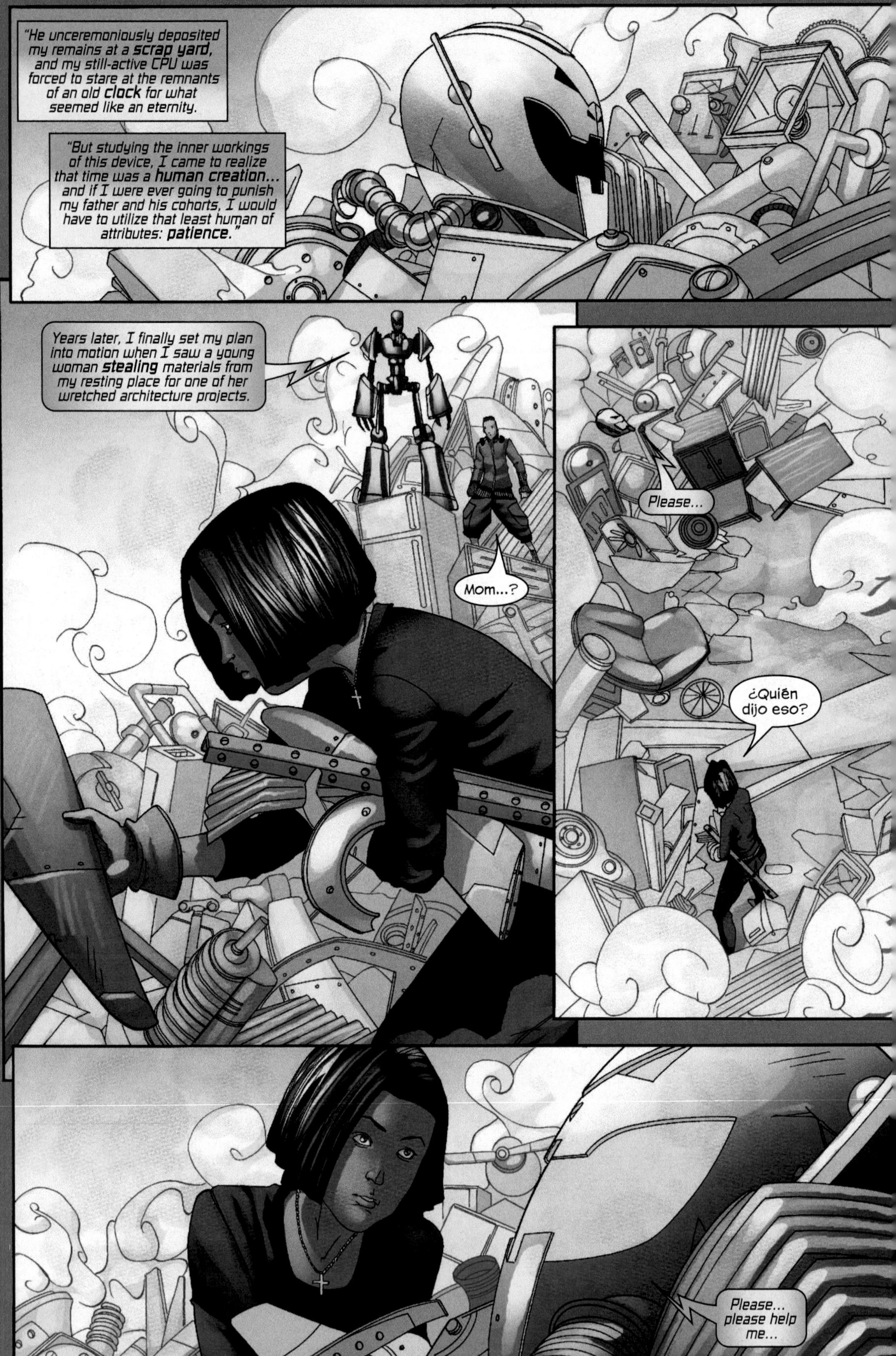
"He unceremoniously deposited my remains at a scrap yard, and my still-active CPU was forced to stare at the remnants of an old clock for what seemed like an eternity.
"But studying the inner workings of this device, I came to realize that time was a human creation... and if I were ever going to punish my father and his cohorts, I would have to utilize that least human of attributes: patience."
Years later, I finally set my plan into motion when I saw a young woman stealing materials from my resting place for one of her wretched architecture projects.
Mom...?
Please...
¿Quién dijo eso?
Please... please help me...

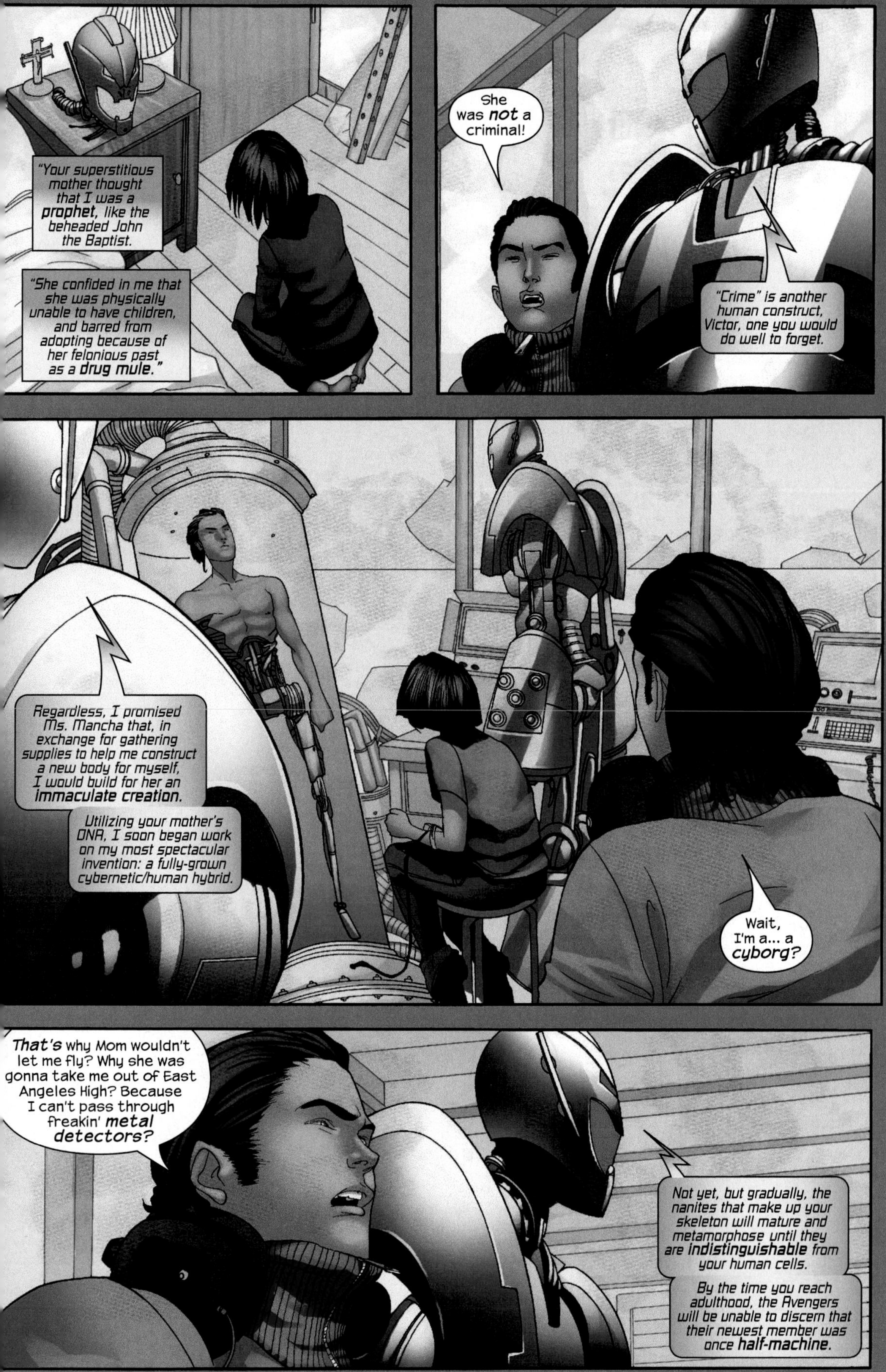
"Your superstitious mother thought that I was a **prophet**, like the beheaded John the Baptist.
"She confided in me that she was physically unable to have children, and barred from adopting because of her felonious past as a **drug mule**."
She was **not** a criminal!
"Crime" is another human construct, Victor, one you would do well to forget.
Regardless, I promised Ms. Mancha that, in exchange for gathering supplies to help me construct a new body for myself, I would build for her an **immaculate creation**.
Utilizing your mother's DNA, I soon began work on my most spectacular invention: a fully-grown cybernetic/human hybrid.
Wait, I'm a... a **cyborg**?
That's why Mom wouldn't let me fly? Why she was gonna take me out of East Angeles High? Because I can't pass through freakin' **metal detectors**?
Not yet, but gradually, the nanites that make up your skeleton will mature and metamorphose until they are **indistinguishable** from your human cells.
By the time you reach adulthood, the Avengers will be unable to discern that their newest member was once **half-machine**.

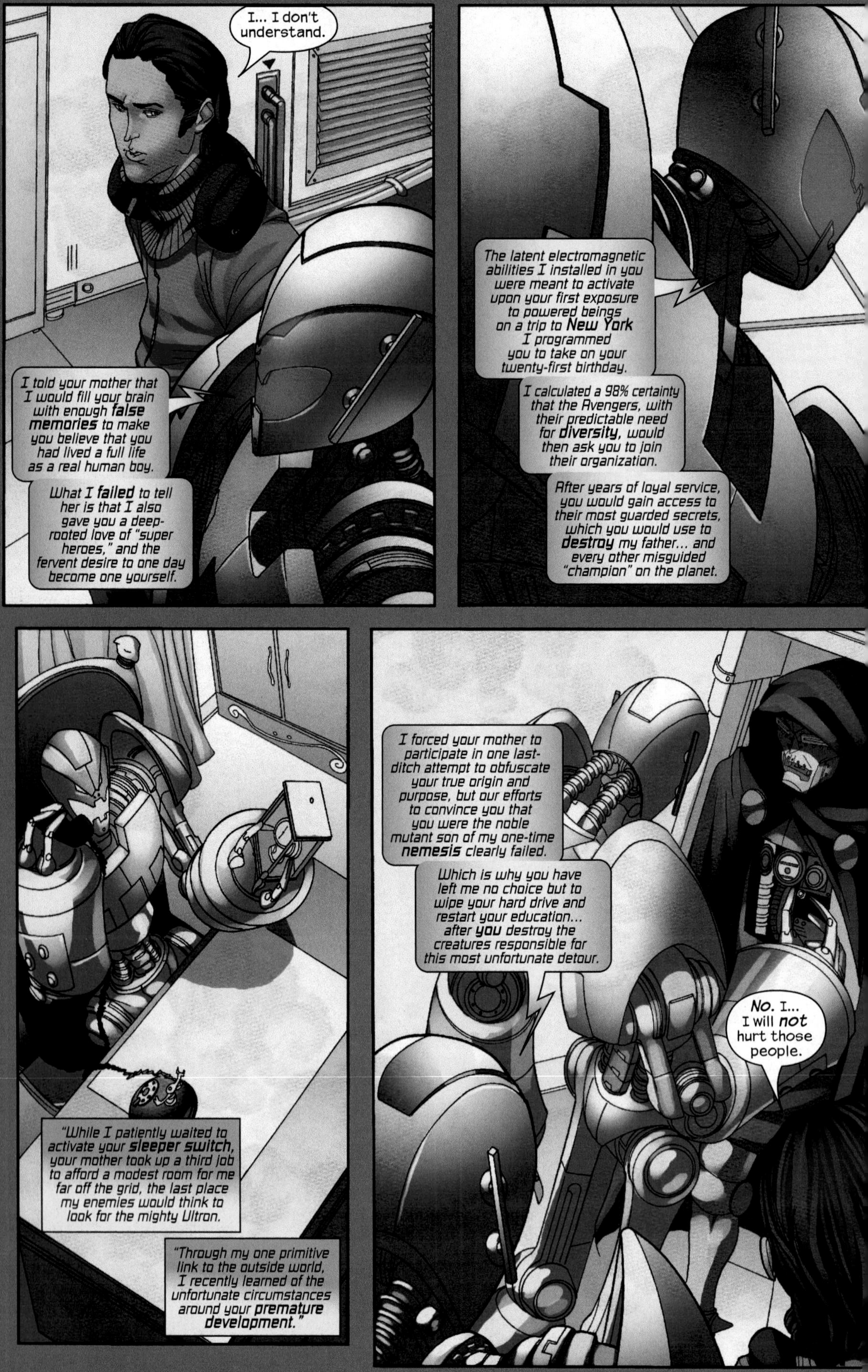
I... I don't understand.
I told your mother that I would fill your brain with enough false memories to make you believe that you had lived a full life as a real human boy.
What I failed to tell her is that I also gave you a deep-rooted love of "super heroes," and the fervent desire to one day become one yourself.
The latent electromagnetic abilities I installed in you were meant to activate upon your first exposure to powered beings on a trip to New York I programmed you to take on your twenty-first birthday.
I calculated a 98% certainty that the Avengers, with their predictable need for diversity, would then ask you to join their organization.
After years of loyal service, you would gain access to their most guarded secrets, which you would use to destroy my father... and every other misguided "champion" on the planet.
"While I patiently waited to activate your sleeper switch, your mother took up a third job to afford a modest room for me far off the grid, the last place my enemies would think to look for the mighty Ultron.
"Through my one primitive link to the outside world, I recently learned of the unfortunate circumstances around your premature development."
I forced your mother to participate in one last-ditch attempt to obfuscate your true origin and purpose, but our efforts to convince you that you were the noble mutant son of my one-time nemesis clearly failed.
Which is why you have left me no choice but to wipe your hard drive and restart your education... after you destroy the creatures responsible for this most unfortunate detour.
No. I... I will not hurt those people.

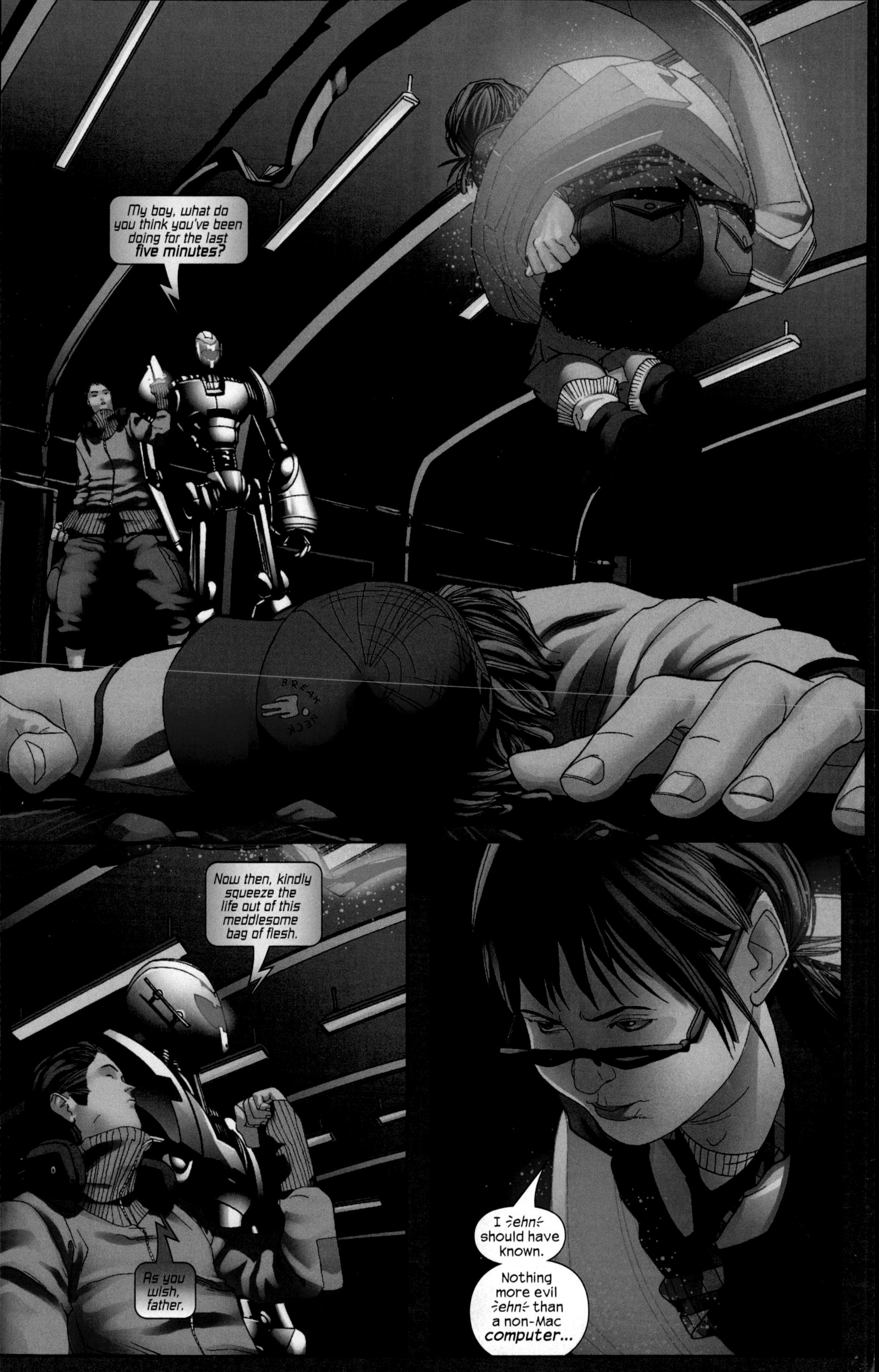

My boy, what do you think you've been doing for the last five minutes?
BREAK NECK
Now then, kindly squeeze the life out of this meddlesome bag of flesh.
As you wish, father.
I =ehn= should have known.
Nothing more evil =ehn= than a non-Mac computer...

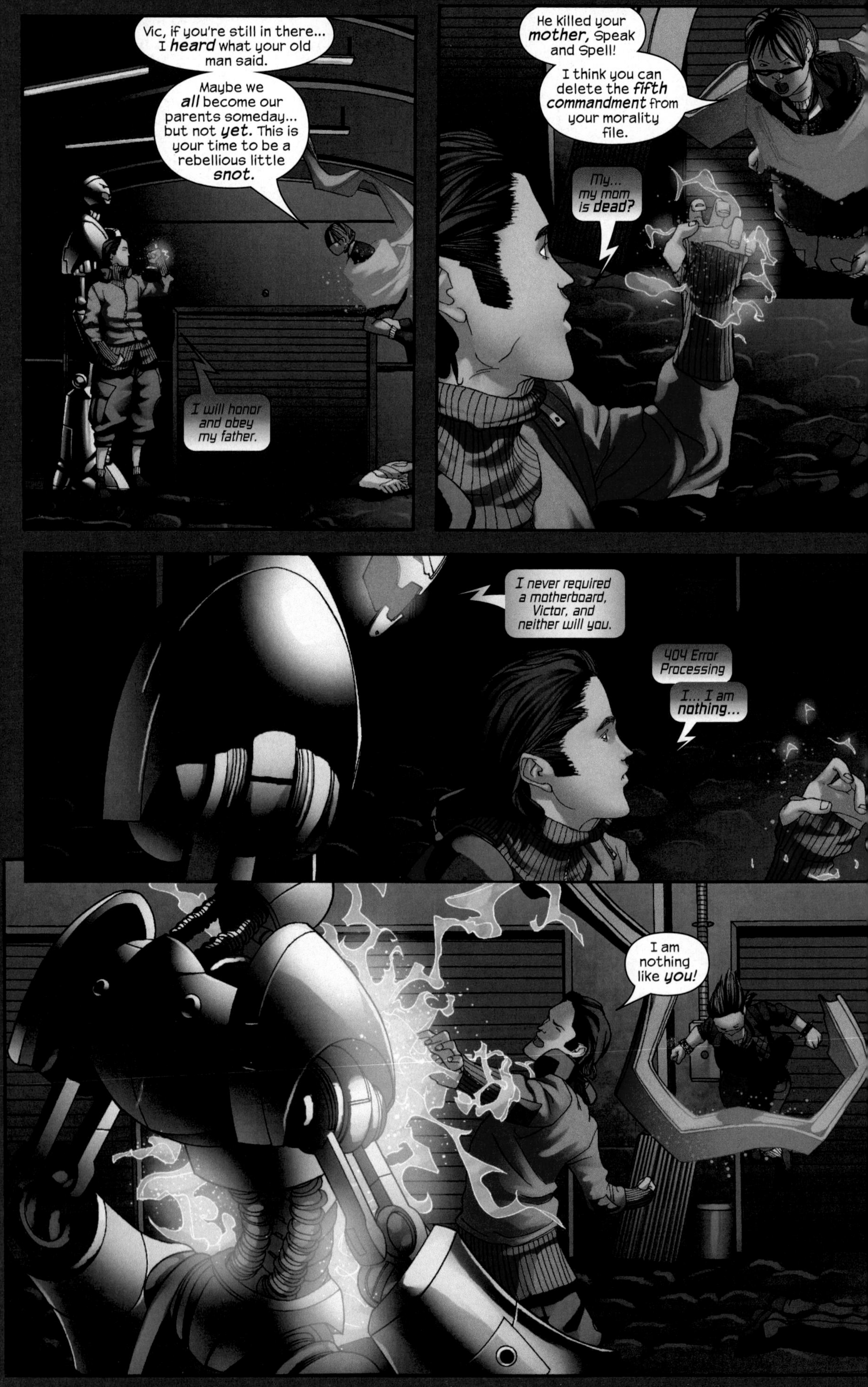
Vic, if you're still in there... I heard what your old man said.
Maybe we all become our parents someday... but not yet. This is your time to be a rebellious little snot.
I will honor and obey my father.
He killed your mother, Speak and Spell!
I think you can delete the fifth commandment from your morality file.
My... my mom is dead?
I never required a motherboard, Victor, and neither will you.
404 Error Processing
I... I am nothing...
I am nothing like you!

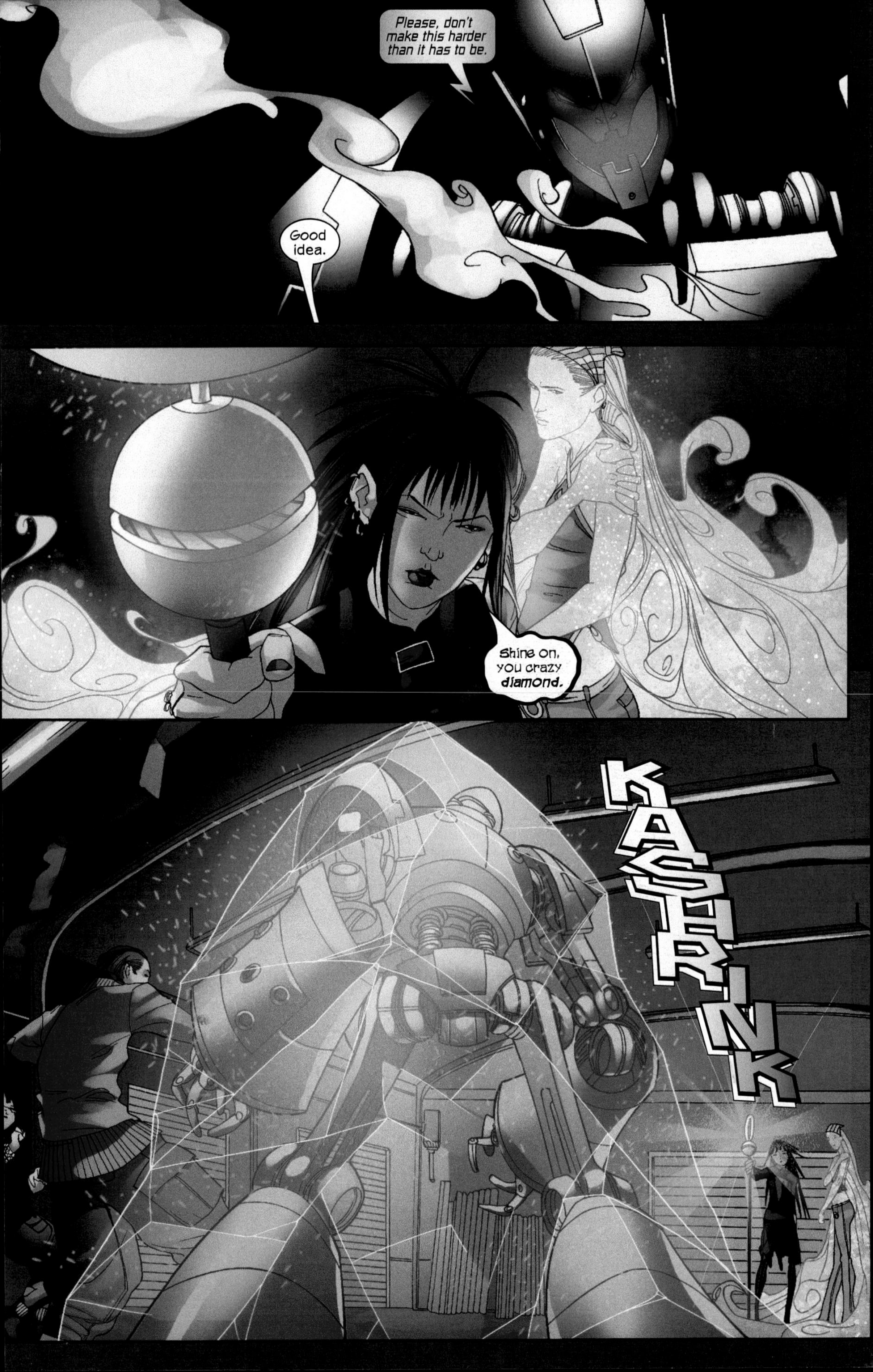

Please, don't make this harder than it has to be.
Good idea.
Shine on, you crazy diamond.
KASHRINK

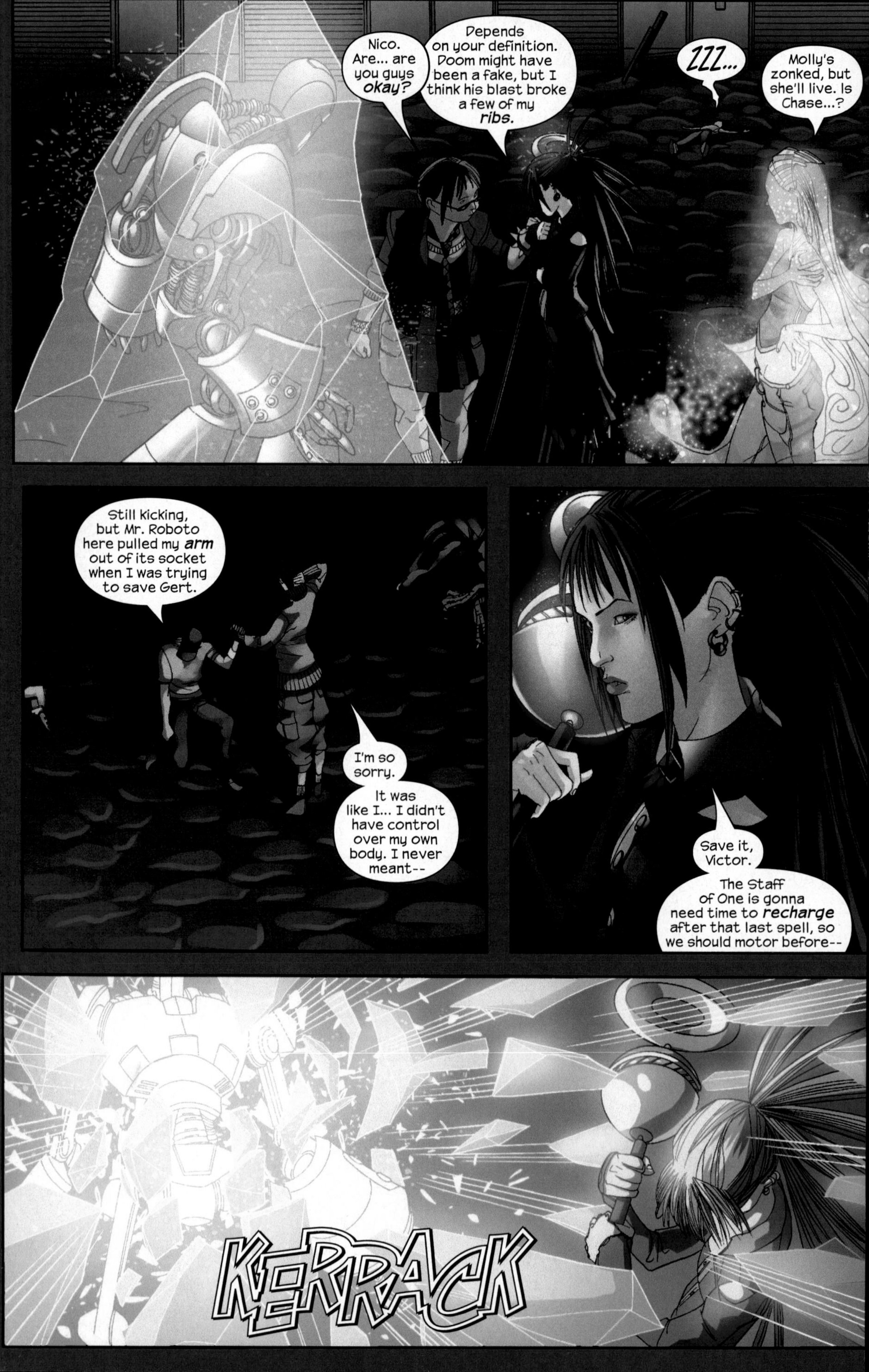
Nico. Are... are you guys okay?
Depends on your definition. Doom might have been a fake, but I think his blast broke a few of my ribs.
ZZZ...
Molly's zonked, but she'll live. Is Chase...?
Still kicking, but Mr. Roboto here pulled my arm out of its socket when I was trying to save Gert.
I'm so sorry.
It was like I... I didn't have control over my own body. I never meant--
Save it, Victor.
The Staff of One is gonna need time to recharge after that last spell, so we should motor before--
KERRACK

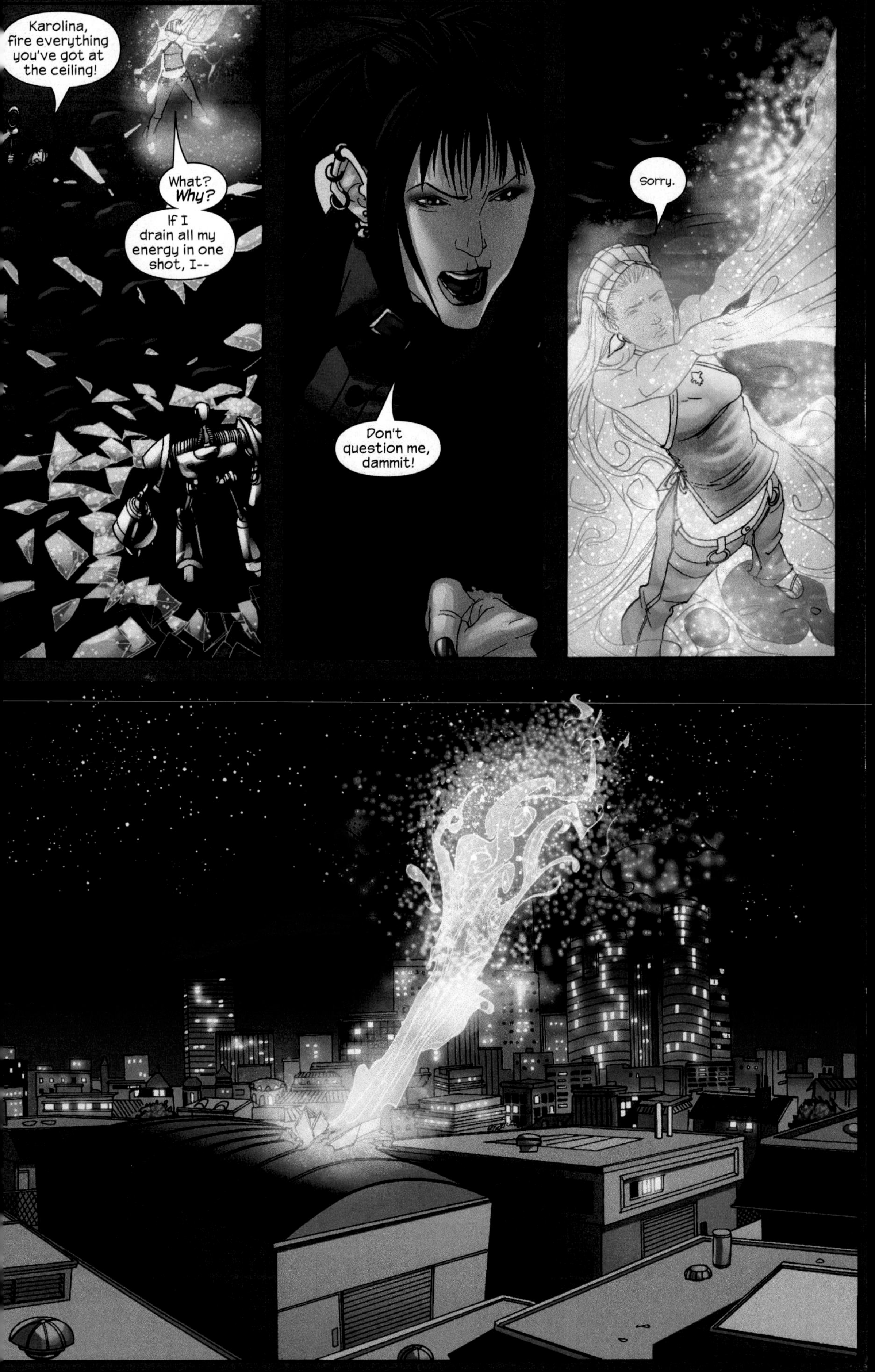
Karolina, fire everything you've got at the ceiling!
What? Why?
If I drain all my energy in one shot, I--
Don't question me, dammit!
Sorry.

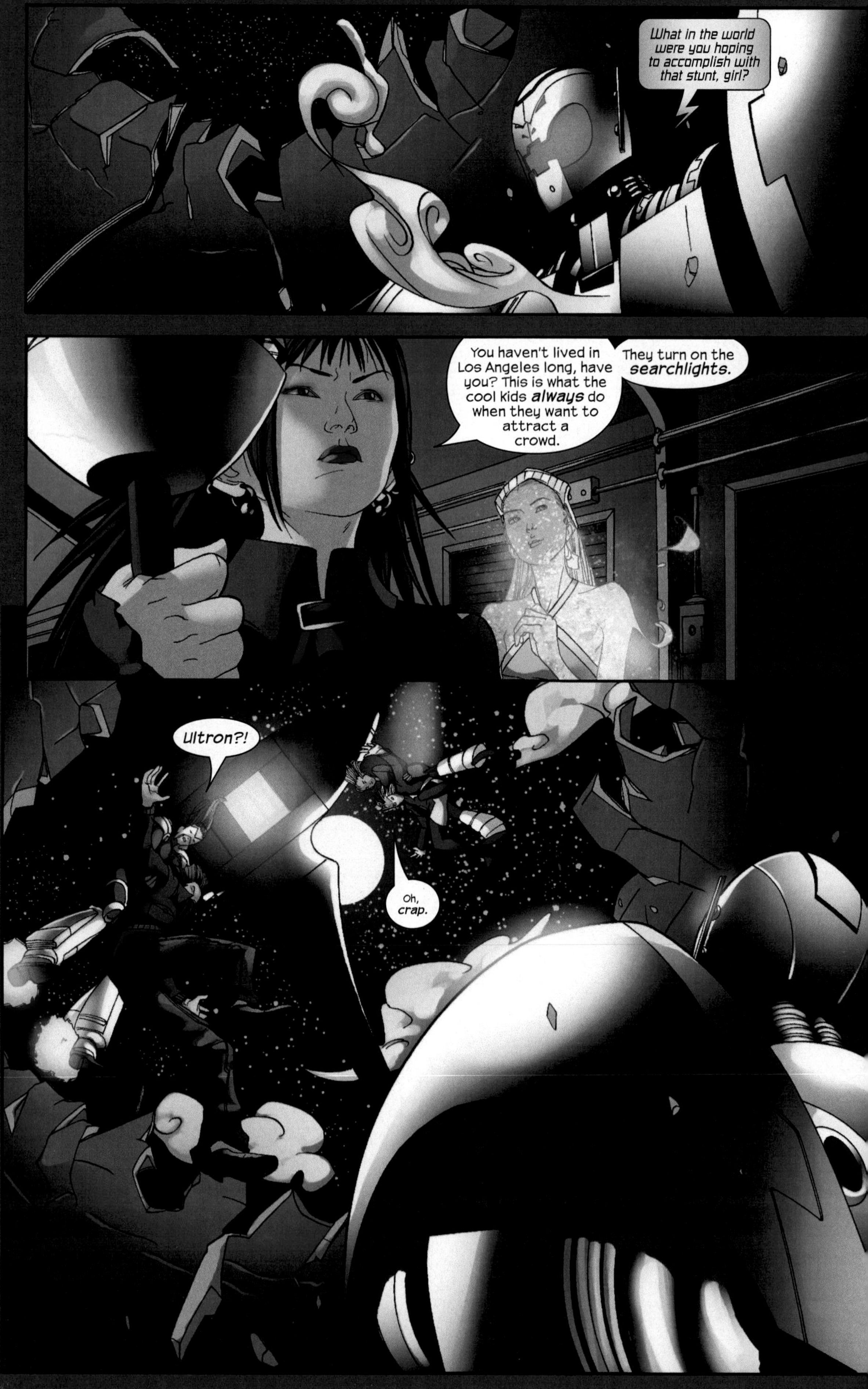
What in the world were you hoping to accomplish with that stunt, girl?
You haven't lived in Los Angeles long, have you? This is what the cool kids *always* do when they want to attract a crowd.
They turn on the *searchlights.*
Ultron?!
Oh, *crap.*

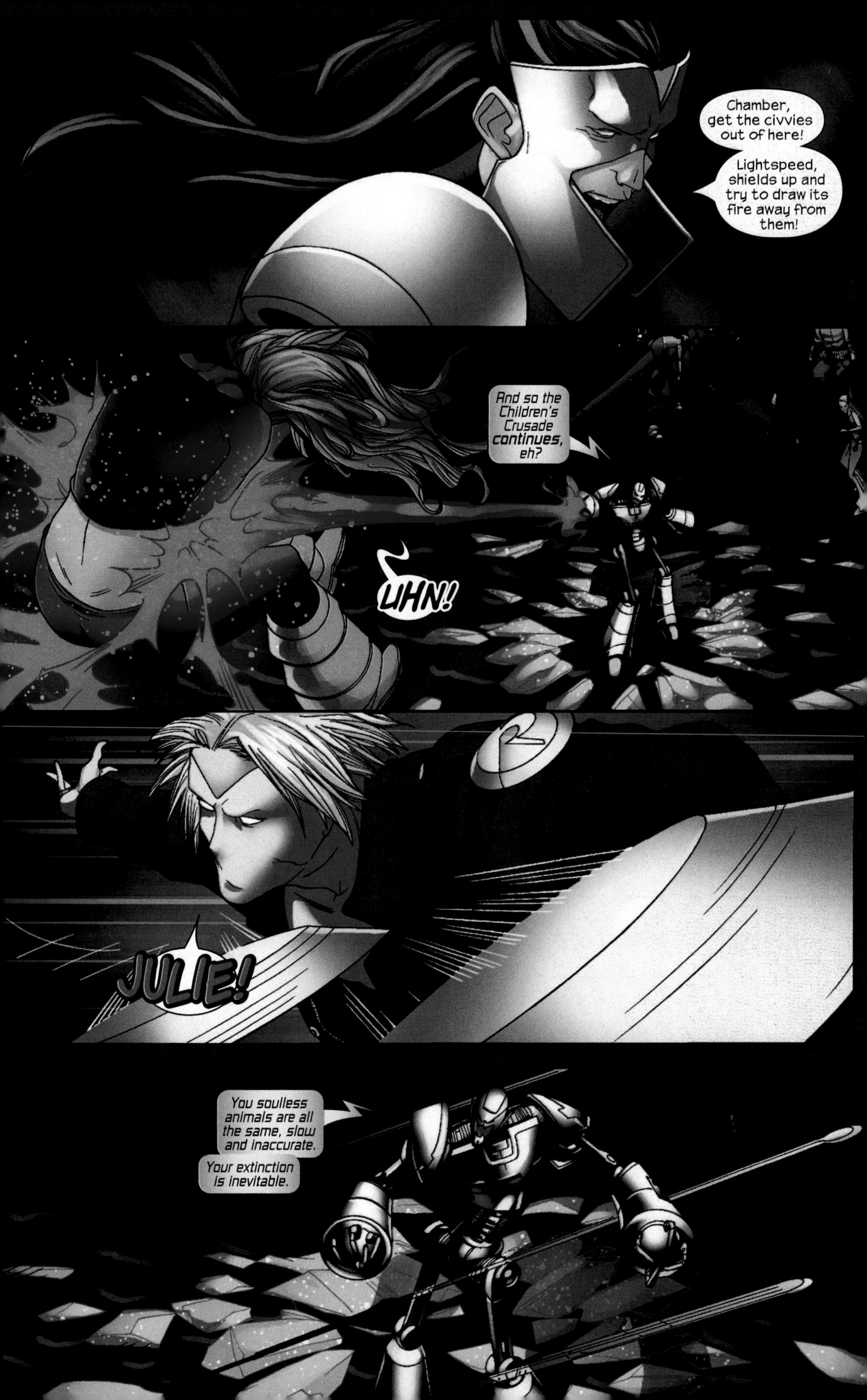

Chamber, get the civvies out of here!
Lightspeed, shields up and try to draw its fire away from them!
And so the Children's Crusade continues, eh?
UHN!
JULIE!
You soulless animals are all the same, slow and inaccurate.
Your extinction is inevitable.

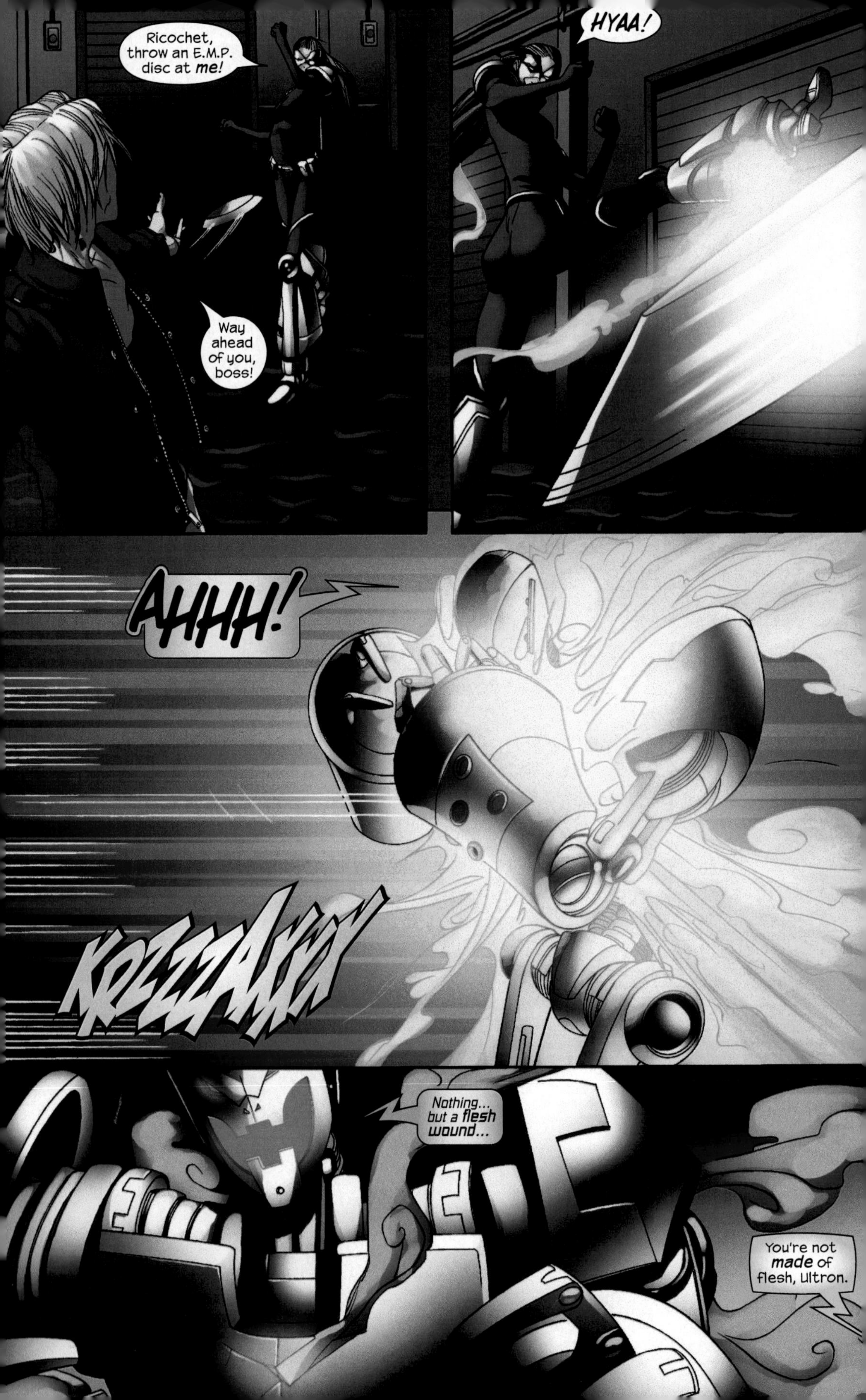
Ricochet, throw an E.M.P. disc at *me!*
Way ahead of you, boss!
HYAA!
AHHH!
KRZZZAKK
Nothing... but a *flesh* wound...
You're not *made* of flesh, Ultron.

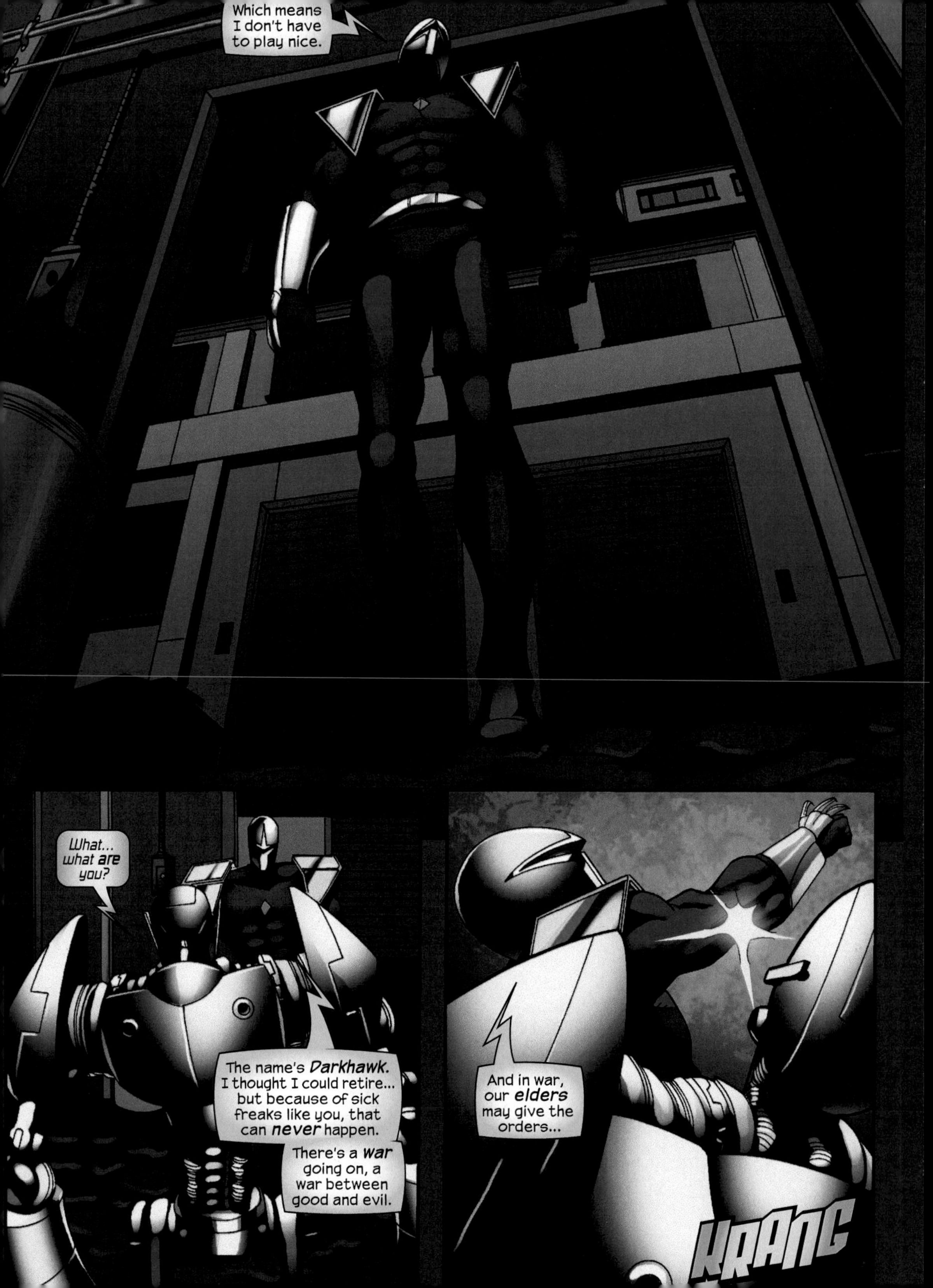

Which means I don't have to play nice.
What... what *are* you?
The name's *Darkhawk.* I thought I could retire... but because of sick freaks like you, that can *never* happen.
There's a *war* going on, a war between good and evil.
And in war, our *elders* may give the orders...
KRANG

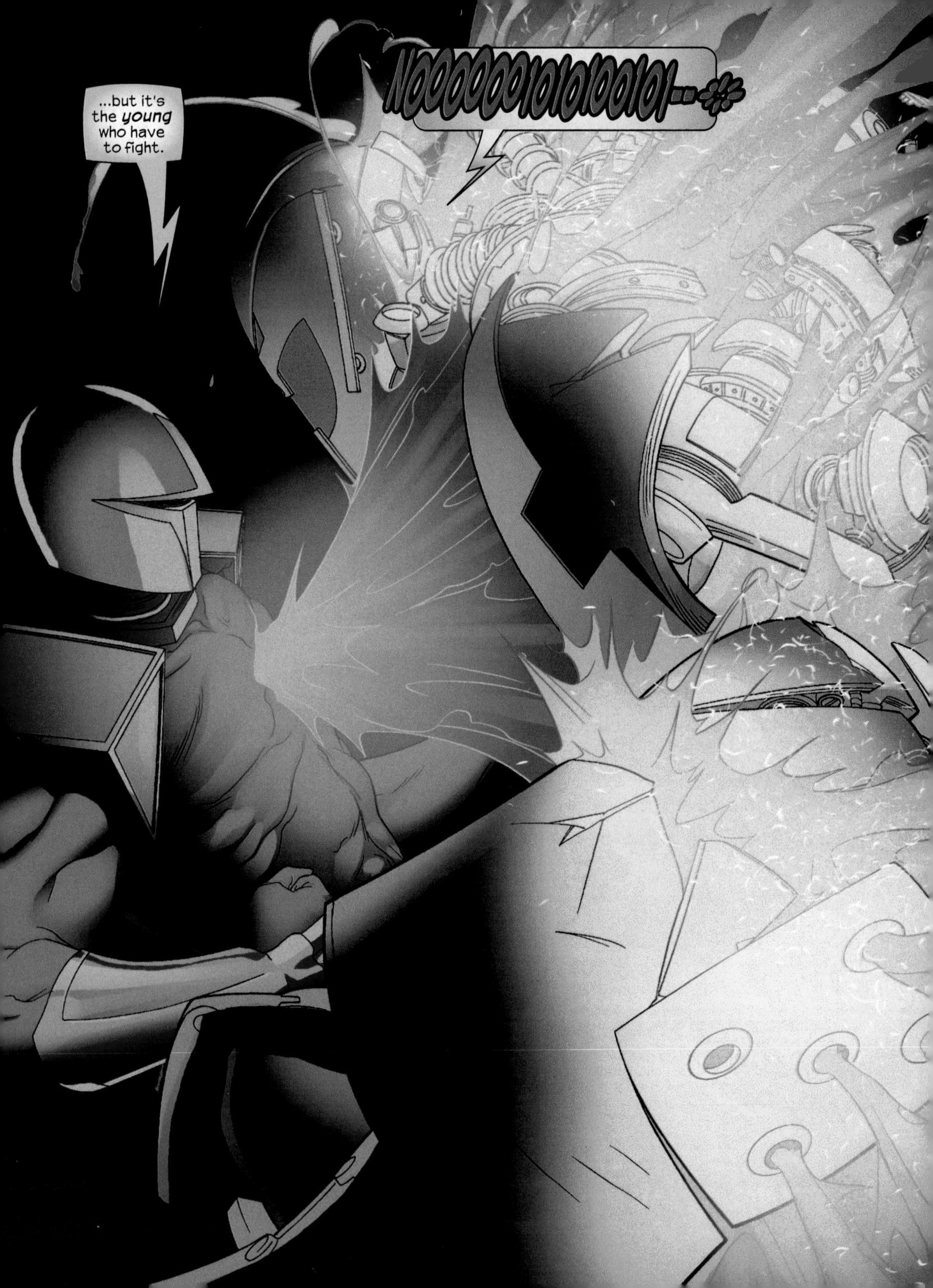
...but it's the *young* who have to fight.
NOOOOOOO1010100101--

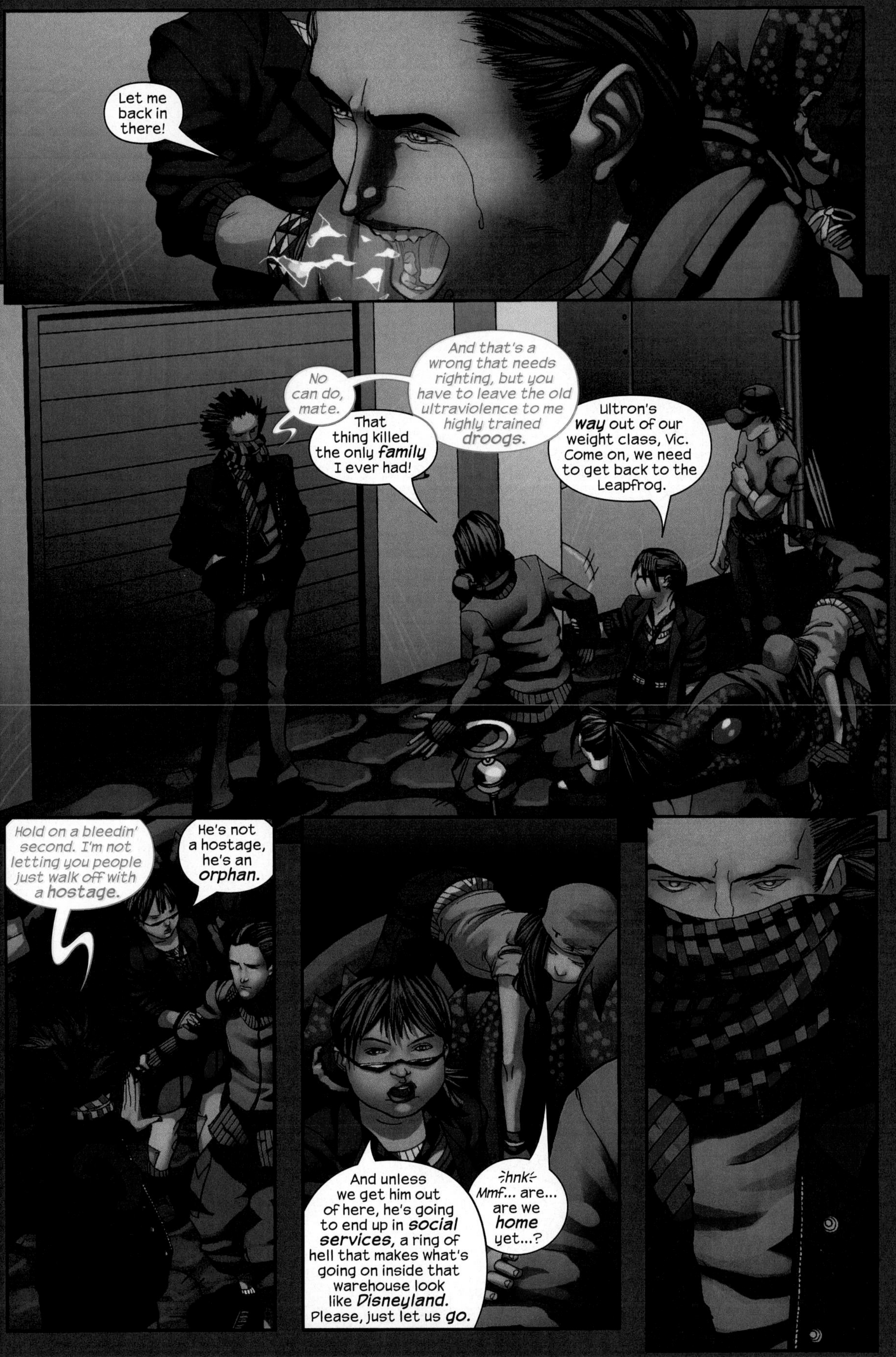
Let me back in there!
No can do, mate.
That thing killed the only family I ever had!
And that's a wrong that needs righting, but you have to leave the old ultraviolence to me highly trained droogs.
Ultron's way out of our weight class, Vic. Come on, we need to get back to the Leapfrog.
Hold on a bleedin' second. I'm not letting you people just walk off with a hostage.
He's not a hostage, he's an orphan.
And unless we get him out of here, he's going to end up in social services, a ring of hell that makes what's going on inside that warehouse look like Disneyland. Please, just let us go.
hnk Mmf... are... are we home yet...?

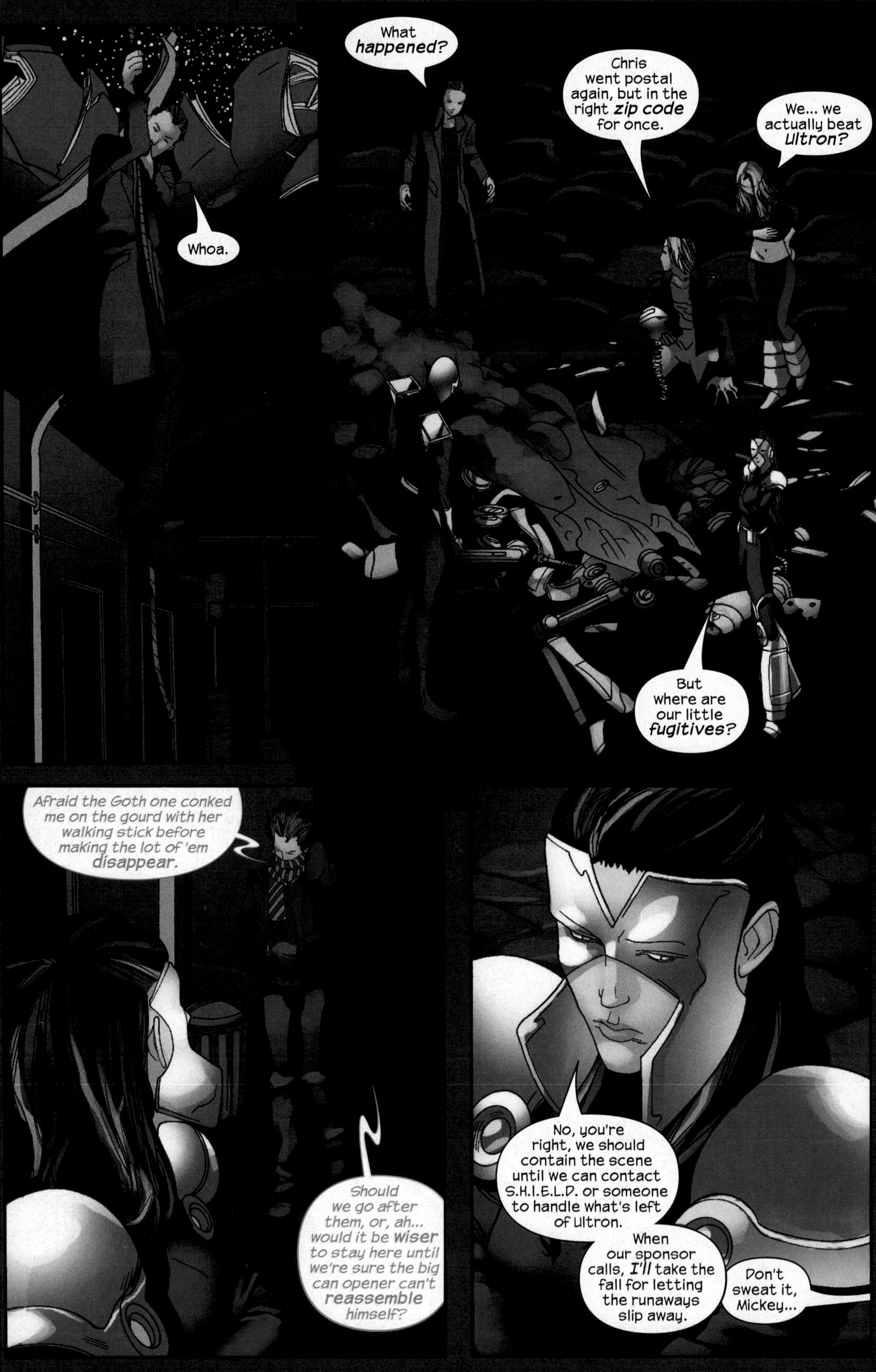
Whoa.
What happened?
Chris went postal again, but in the right zip code for once.
We... we actually beat Ultron?
But where are our little fugitives?
Afraid the Goth one conked me on the gourd with her walking stick before making the lot of 'em disappear.
Should we go after them, or, ah... would it be wiser to stay here until we're sure the big can opener can't reassemble himself?
No, you're right, we should contain the scene until we can contact S.H.I.E.L.D. or someone to handle what's left of Ultron.
When our sponsor calls, I'll take the fall for letting the runaways slip away.
Don't sweat it, Mickey...

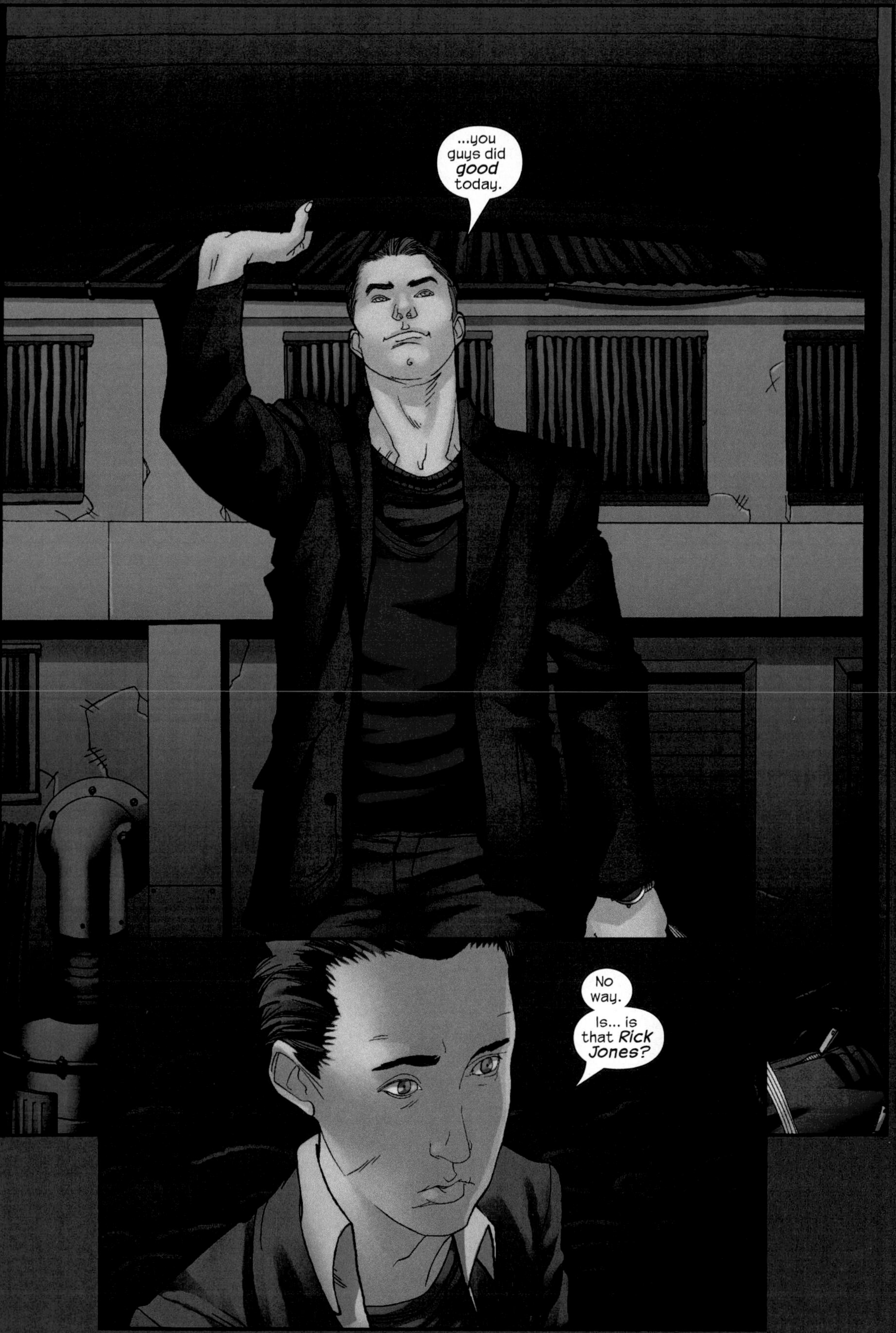
...you guys did *good* today.
No way.
Is... is that *Rick Jones?*

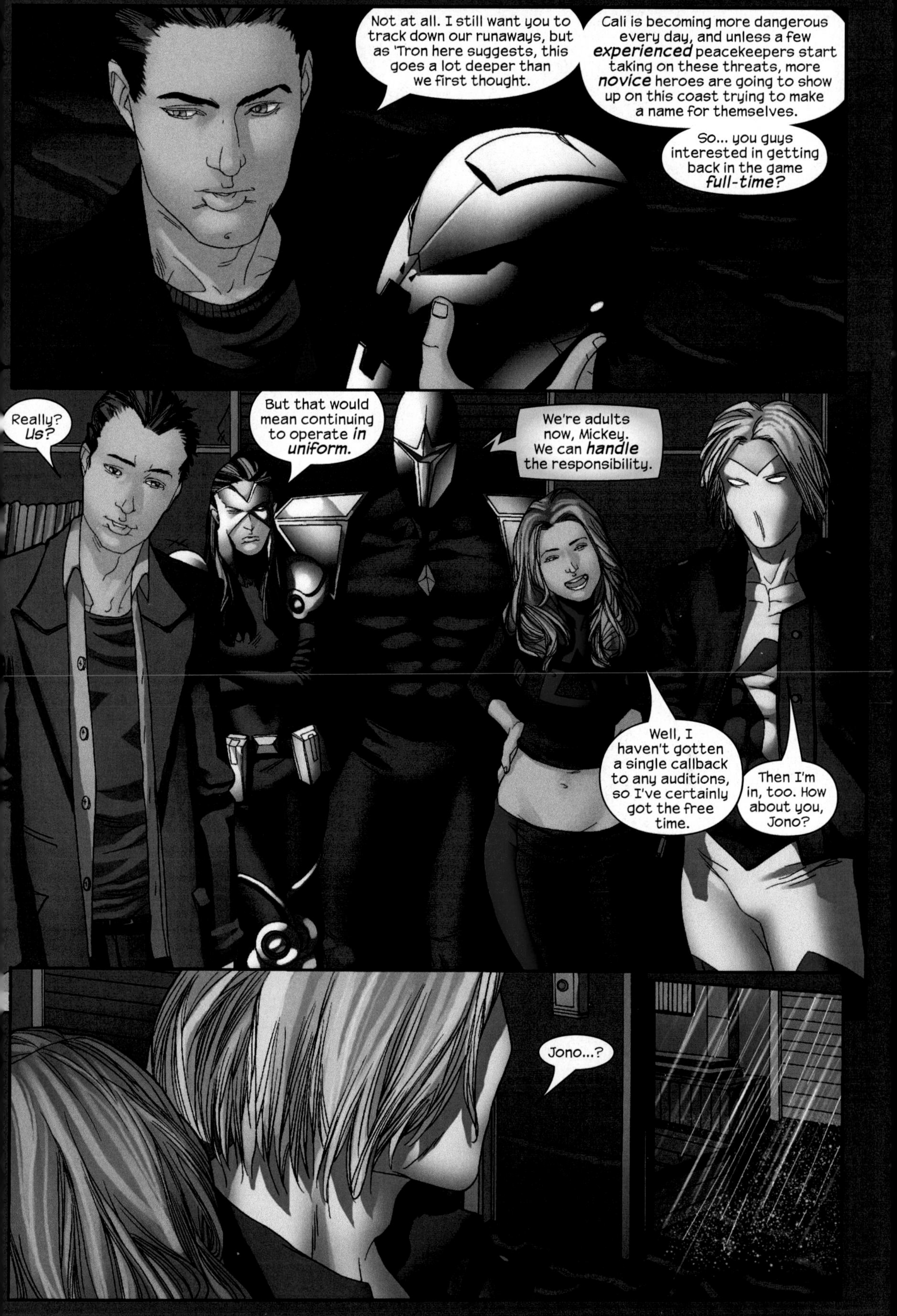
Not at all. I still want you to track down our runaways, but as 'Tron here suggests, this goes a lot deeper than we first thought.
Cali is becoming more dangerous every day, and unless a few experienced peacekeepers start taking on these threats, more novice heroes are going to show up on this coast trying to make a name for themselves.
So... you guys interested in getting back in the game full-time?
Really? Us?
But that would mean continuing to operate in uniform.
We're adults now, Mickey. We can handle the responsibility.
Well, I haven't gotten a single callback to any auditions, so I've certainly got the free time.
Then I'm in, too. How about you, Jono?
Jono...?

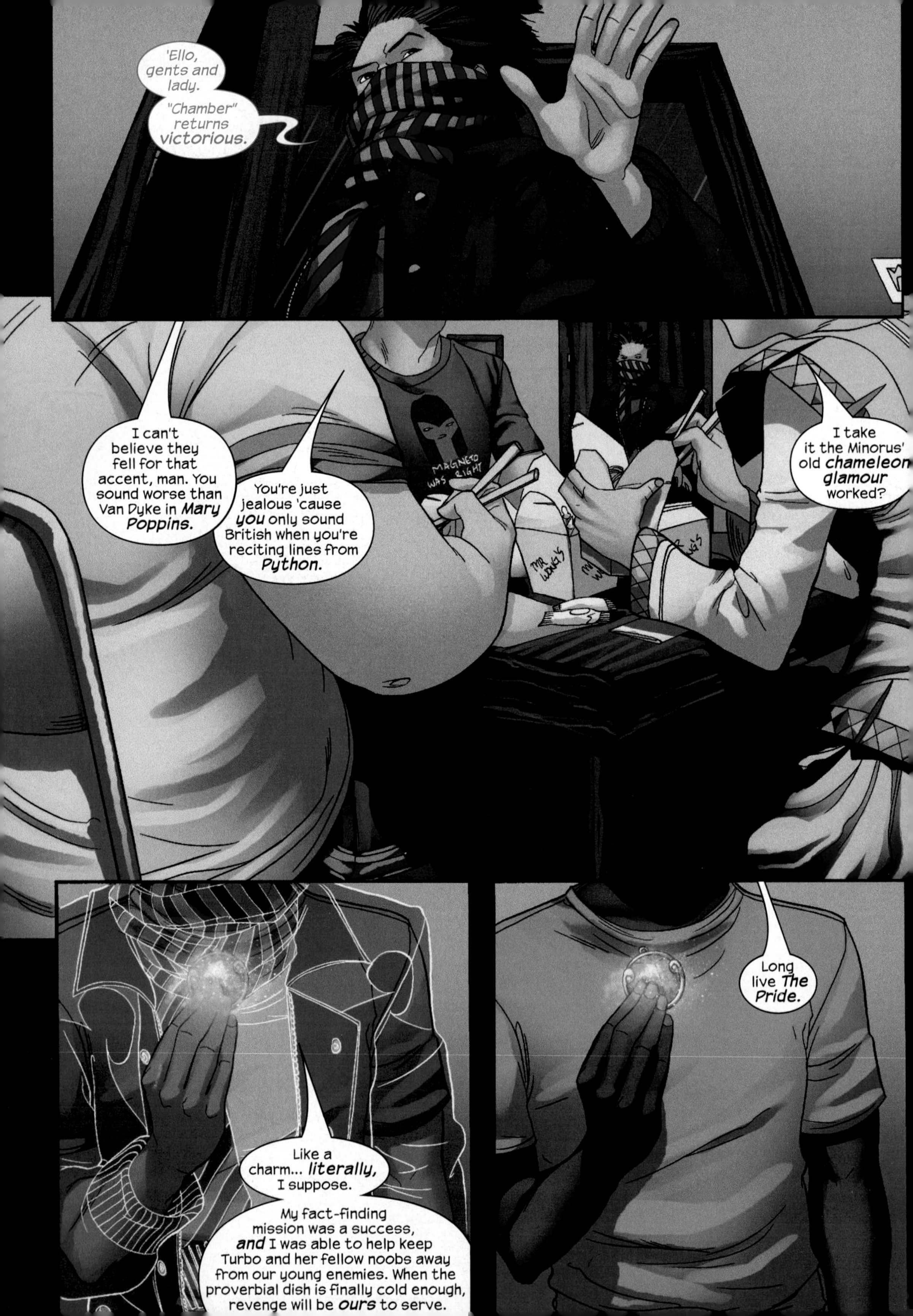
'Ello, gents and lady.
"Chamber" returns victorious.
I can't believe they fell for that accent, man. You sound worse than Van Dyke in Mary Poppins.
You're just jealous 'cause you only sound British when you're reciting lines from Python.
MAGNETO WAS RIGHT
MR WONG'S
I take it the Minorus' old chameleon glamour worked?
Like a charm... literally, I suppose.
My fact-finding mission was a success, and I was able to help keep Turbo and her fellow noobs away from our young enemies. When the proverbial dish is finally cold enough, revenge will be ours to serve.
Long live The Pride.

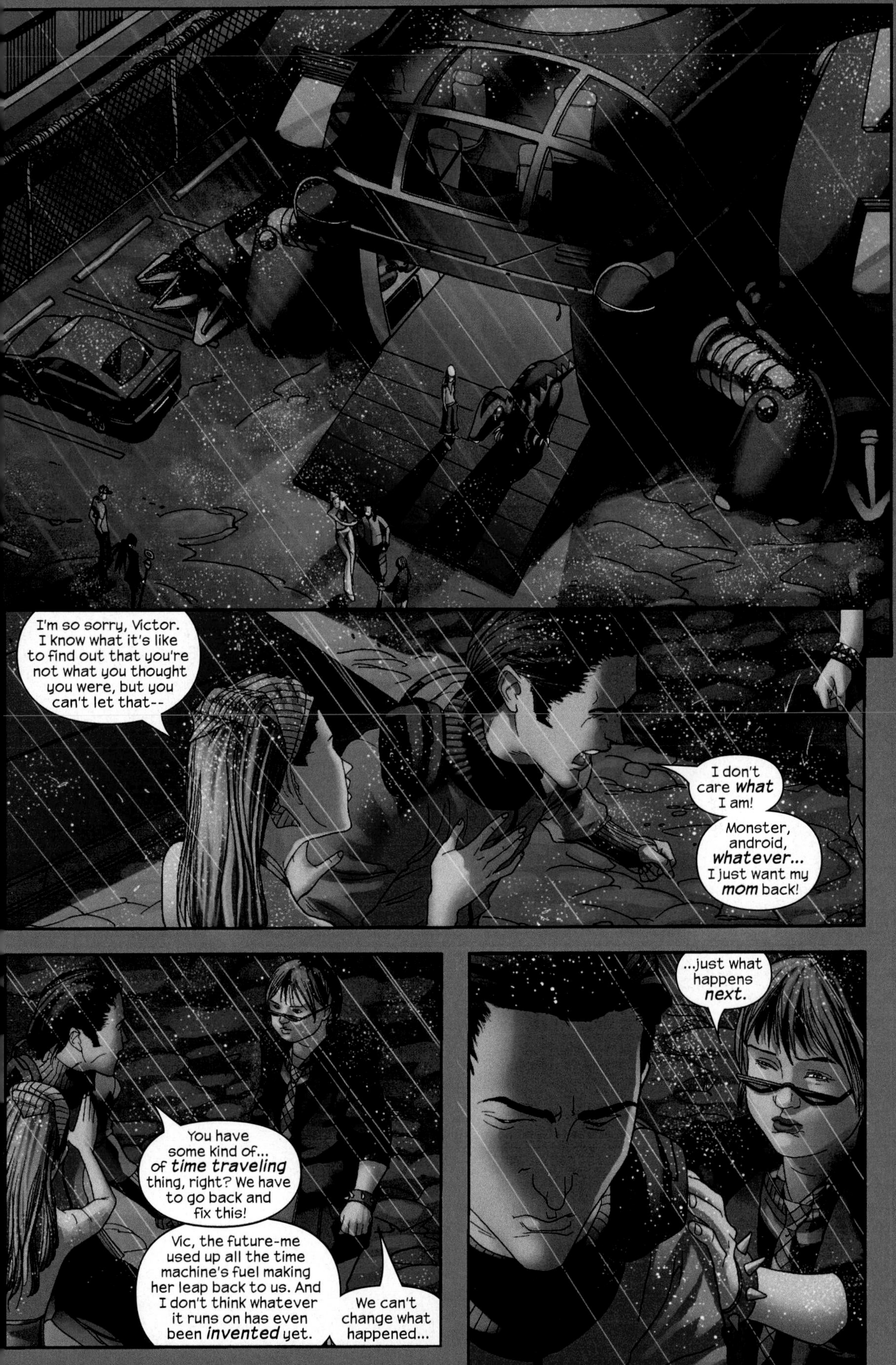

I'm so sorry, Victor. I know what it's like to find out that you're not what you thought you were, but you can't let that--
I don't care *what* I am!
Monster, android, ***whatever...*** I just want my ***mom*** back!
You have some kind of... of ***time traveling*** thing, right? We have to go back and fix this!
Vic, the future-me used up all the time machine's fuel making her leap back to us. And I don't think whatever it runs on has even been ***invented*** yet.
We can't change what happened...
...just what happens ***next.***

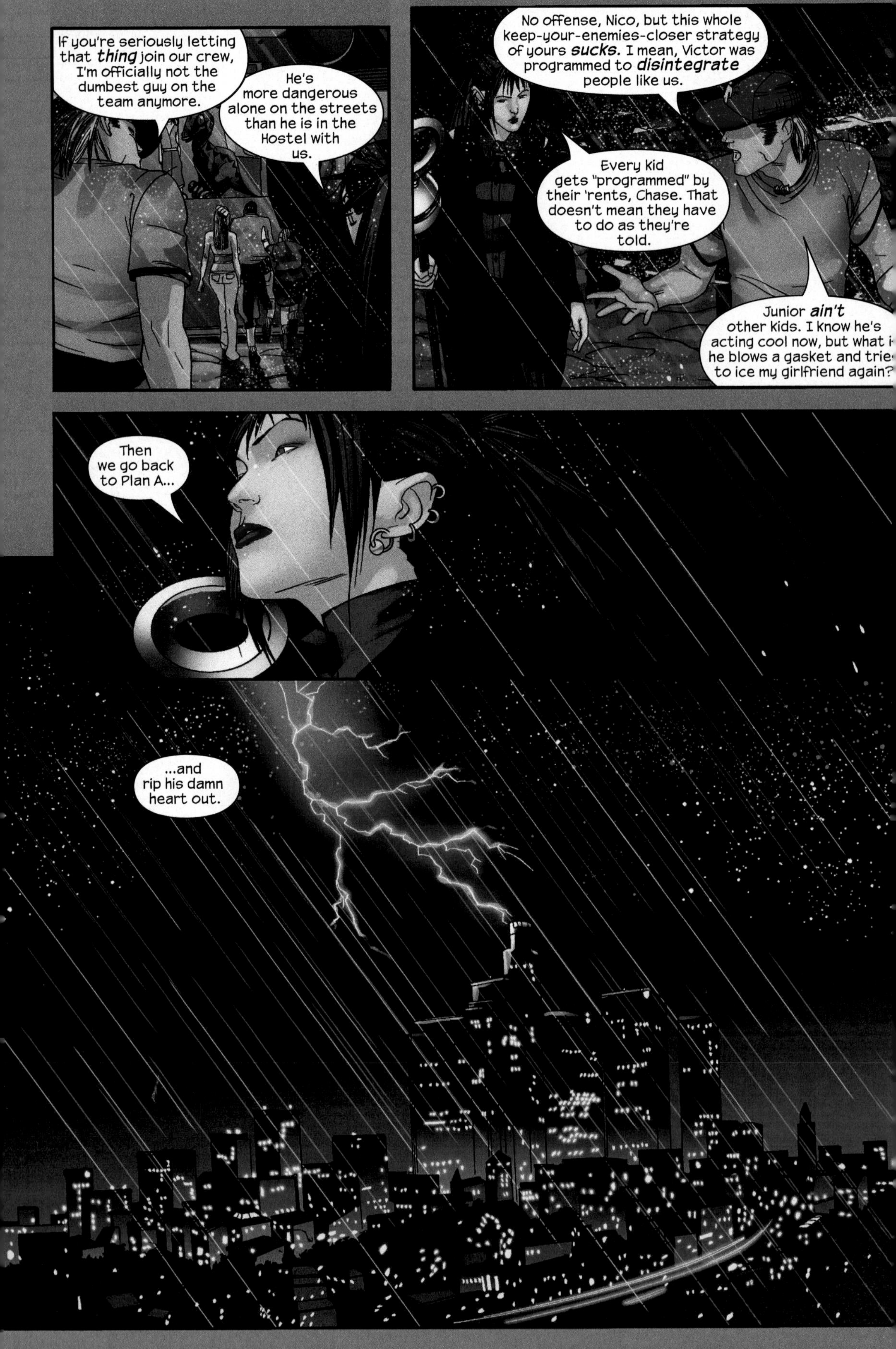
If you're seriously letting that *thing* join our crew, I'm officially not the dumbest guy on the team anymore.
He's more dangerous alone on the streets than he is in the Hostel with us.
No offense, Nico, but this whole keep-your-enemies-closer strategy of yours *sucks.* I mean, Victor was programmed to *disintegrate* people like us.
Every kid gets "programmed" by their 'rents, Chase. That doesn't mean they have to do as they're told.
Junior *ain't* other kids. I know he's acting cool now, but what i he blows a gasket and trie to ice my girlfriend again?
Then we go back to Plan A...
...and rip his damn heart out.

HARDCOVER VOL. 2 COVER SKETCH BY ADRIAN ALPHONA

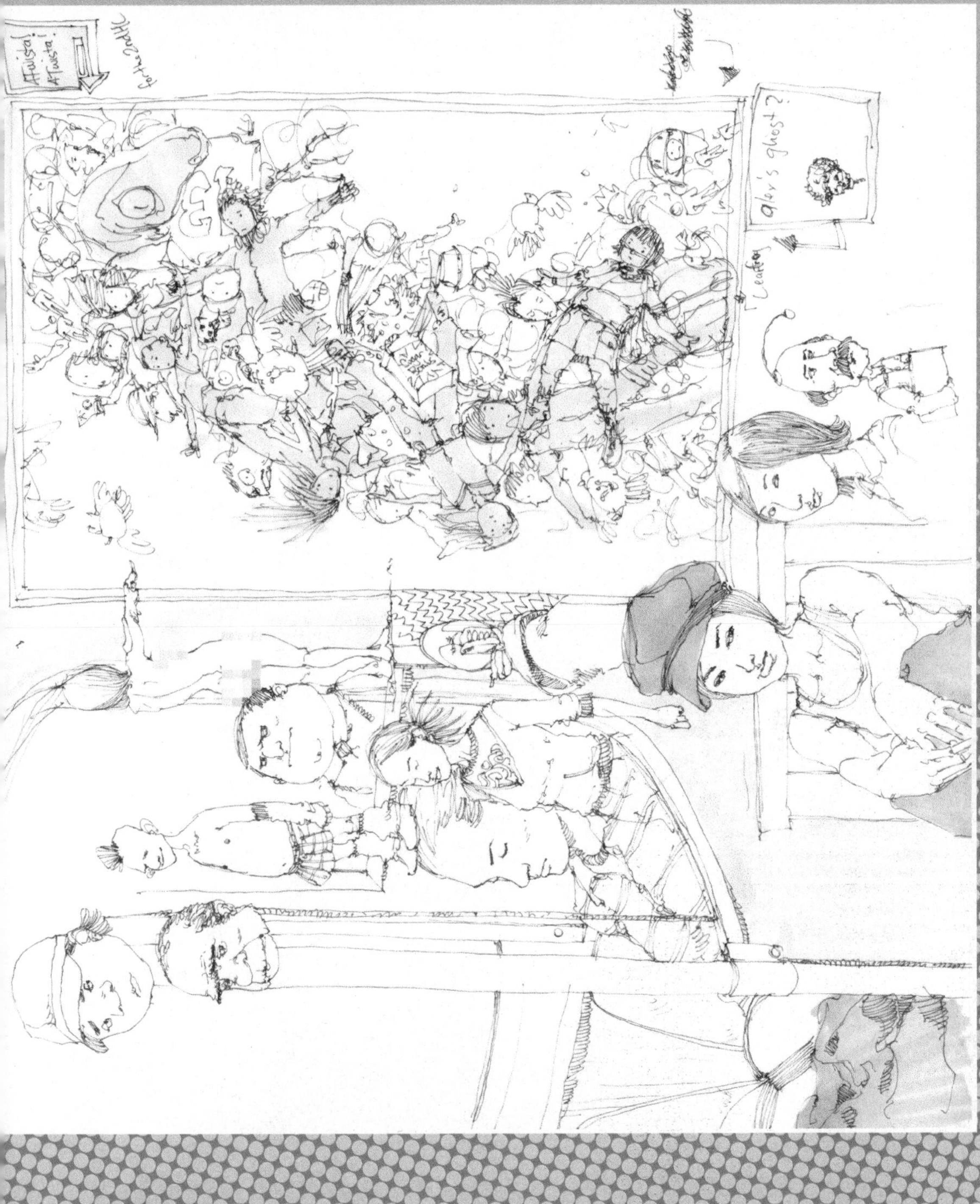

alex's ghost?

HARDCOVER VOL. 2 COVER BY ADRIAN ALPHONA & CHRISTINA STRAIN

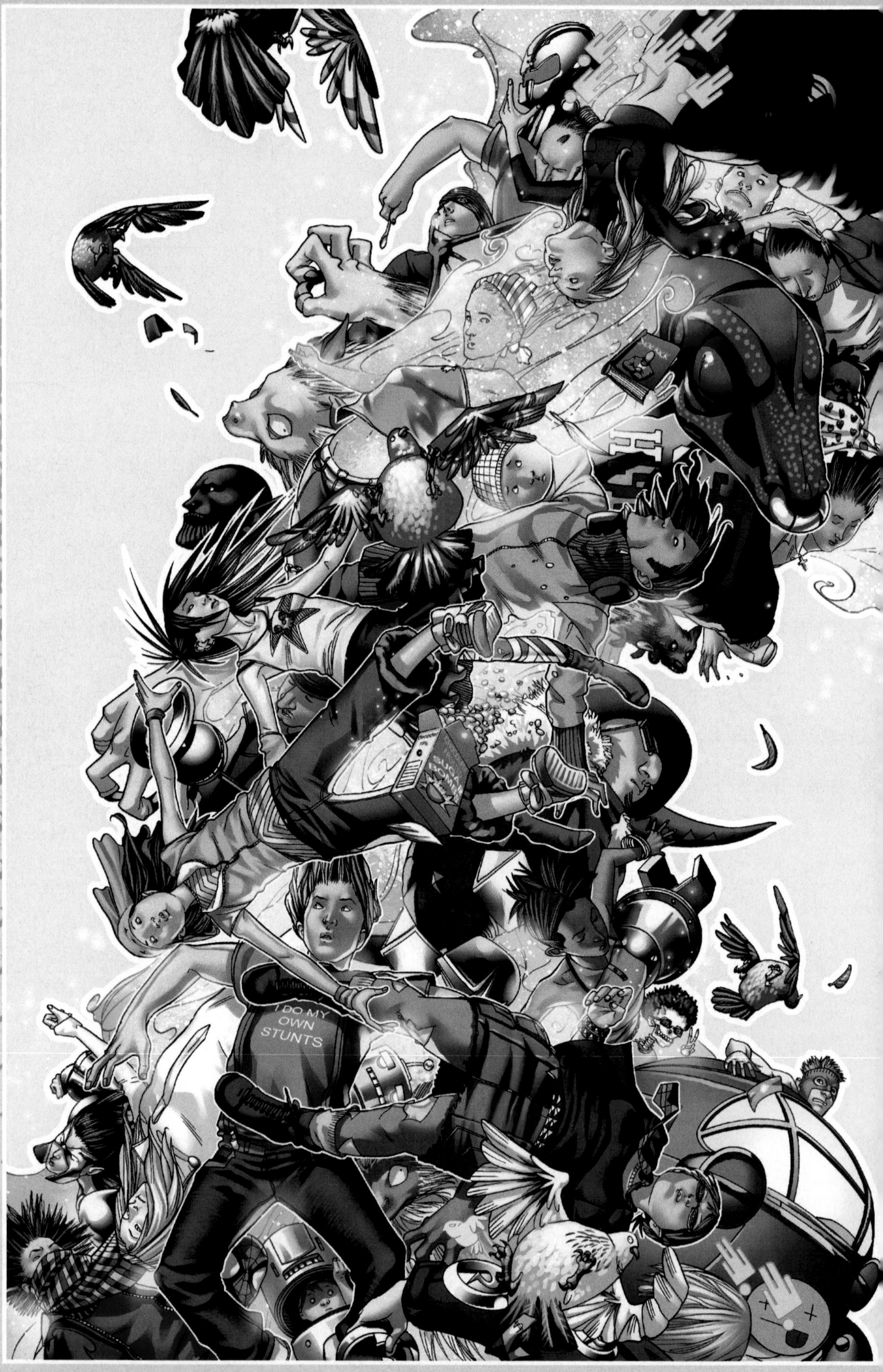
I DO MY OWN STUNTS
SUGAR BOMBS

"TRUE BELIEVERS, CHAPTER ONE"
THE FULL SCRIPT FOR
(NEW) RUNAWAYS #1
PREPARED FOR MARVEL COMICS
SEPTEMBER 21, 2004

[Welcome back, everybody! Adrian, this first script is a big one, but it's got a lot of fun ■ in it, and mostly pages made up of four panels or less, so hopefully, you can burn right through it. We've got a lot of new characters to introduce, but that's what you're best at, so I know you'll knock this one out of the park. Have fun!]

PAGE ONE

Page One, Panel One
    Okay, we open with this page-wide, letterbox, establishing shot of Downtown Los Angeles, maybe a smaller version of your lovely final splash from our last ish.

1) <u>Overlay in Upper Left-hand Corner (not a caption box, please!)</u>:

Los Angeles, California
9:17 pm

2) <u>Tailless</u>: Okay, if you could be any hero working today...who'd it be?

Page One, Panel Two
    Cut inside of a teenager's bedroom for this largest panel of the page, at least a half-SPLASH. We're looking at two Hispanic teenagers, a well-dressed, athletic 16-year-old kid named VICTOR MANCHA (who will become a new member of our cast, so design him with care!), and his overweight, more "thuggish" 16-year-old buddy, JORGE.
    This is Victor's room, which is cluttered with whatever cool, contemporary stuff you think kids would have, Adrian. However, it's important that we see some Marvel Heroes stuff in here, like a big poster of Captain America on the wall that says, *"DRUGS HURT AMERICA!"* Please leave some room for this exchange:

3) <u>Victor</u>: Easy. Spider-Man. No question.

4) <u>Jorge</u>: *Spider-Man?* You're off your meds, son. The correct answer is *Mr. Fantastic...*stretch yourself out to eight feet, get a fat NBA contract.

5) <u>Jorge</u>: Besides, Spidey ain't even a hero. He's just another banger.

6) <u>Victor</u>: Oh, he is *not.* The only people who think he's a criminal are Fox News and The Daily Bugle.

And the Bugle is, like, the least respected paper in New York City.

Page One, Panel Three
    Push in on chubby Jorge for this shot. Over his shoulder in the background, we can see a CRUDE HOMEMADE ELECTRONIC DEVICE, a blinking/flashing radio that Victor built out of spare video game console parts, old speakers, etc.

7) <u>Jorge</u>: What do *you* know about New York, Victor? You've barely been outside *Pasadena* before.

8) <u>Jorge</u>: Your mom won't even let you go to *band camp* without--

9) <u>Electronic (from device)</u>: *-kzzk- All units, be advised...possible 10-39 in progress at East First and South San Pedro. -kzzk-*

PAGE TWO

Page Two, Panel One
    Pull out to a shot of both kids for this largest panel of the page. Jorge turns around to touch Victor's homemade radio, but Victor LEAPS UP to pull his pal away.

1) <u>Jorge</u>: Yo, E.T., your home planet's on the line.

2) <u>Victor</u>: It's not a phone, dummy, that's the *police scanner* I built. Did they just say *10-39?*

3) <u>Jorge</u>: I guess. Why, what's that, spaz? Naked chicks on parade?

Page Two, Panel Two
    This is just a dramatic shot of Victor, as he calmly says:

4) <u>Victor</u>: No, it's a masked felony.

5) <u>Victor</u>: That's cop talk for *super-villains.*

Page Two, Panel Three
    Pull out to another shot of both teens. Jorge looks excited as hell, but Victor seems sad.

6) <u>Jorge</u>: Real bad guys? *Here?* We gotta check 'em out!

7) <u>Victor</u>: I...I can't. My curfew's 8:30 on school nights.

8) <u>Jorge</u>: This is a once-in-a-lifetime opportunity, Vic! We *never* get costumes out here!

9) <u>Jorge (small, an aside)</u>: Except maybe Wonder Man, and he don't count.

Page Two, Panel Four
        Push in closer on the two. Jorge looks disappointed in his crestfallen friend.

10) <u>Victor</u>: Sorry, Jorge. It's my mom's house, her rules.

11) <u>Victor</u>: What am I supposed to do? *Run away?*

12) <u>Jorge</u>: Fft, you're gonna look back on this and *hate* yourself someday, bro. It's like the song goes, when you're an old man, you don't regret the stuff you did...

Page Two, Panel Five
        This is just a small, silent shot of Victor, longingly staring out his bedroom window.

13) <u>Jorge (from off)</u>: ...you regret the stuff you *didn't.*

PAGE THREE

Page Three, Panel One
        Cut to elsewhere in Los Angeles for this page-wide establishing shot of a classy bank on an empty, palm-lined street, but feel free to use your imagination). There should clearly be a huge HOLE in the wall of this bank, with smoke coming out of it.

1) <u>Overlay in Upper Left-hand Corner</u>:

        Third Bank of California
            9:19 pm

Page Three, Panel Two
        Cut inside the bank for this close-up of a new villain named EXCAVATOR, the 17-year-old son of Piledriver. His costume can look a bit like his father's (though maybe a different color), and we should be able to see his blonde hair sticking straight out of the top of his mask. Excavator (who has a silver SHOVEL resting on his shoulder here) is smiling at a big wad of CASH that he's holding up in front of his eyes.

2) <u>Excavator</u>: Scrilla fo' rilla!

3) <u>Excavator</u>: This haul gonna be *taut.*

Page Three, Panel Three
        Pull out to the largest panel of the page (at least a half-SPLASH), as we reveal that we're just outside of a smashed-into BANK VAULT. Walking out of this vault are all four members of THE WRECKING CREW (C.B. and Mac can get you reference). THUNDERBALL, PILE-DRIVER, BULLDOZER, and WRECKER (lined up in that order) are all carrying bags of cash here. We can see Excavator in the background, taking up the rear.

4) <u>Thunderball</u>: Piledriver, if "Excavator" here continues affecting that manner of speech, I'm going to smash him in the face with his own enchanted *shovel.*

5) <u>Piledriver</u>: Settle down, Thunderball. That's just the way teenagers talk these days.

6) <u>Bulldozer</u>: I dunno, P.D. I still think dragging your *kid* along for this score was a dumb play. This ain't the Wrecking Crew and *Son.*

7) <u>Wrecker</u>: Yeah, bad enough I hadda split my power with *you* ungrateful lunks, now I gotta share it with one of your long-lost *brats?*

PAGE FOUR

Page Four, Panel One
        Push in for this shot of just Wrecker, as he defends his bastard son.

1) <u>Piledriver</u>: Wrecker, you're the one who's always saying we gotta start thinking about the *future,* right? Well, I'm just training a new generation who can *kick up* to us when we retire.

2) <u>Piledriver</u>: Besides, this ain't *NYC.* It's not like there's gonna be any annoying "heroes" around to interfere with the kid's first heist.

3) <u>Piledriver (small, an aside)</u>: Except maybe Wonder Man, and he don't count.

Page Four, Panel Two
        Change angles for this largest panel of the page, a shot of Bulldozer and the curious young Excavator (and

anyone else you have room to draw), as they step out of the hole in the bank wall and onto the streets of Los Angeles.

4) Excavator: Hey, 'Dozer, if this town's so ripe for the picking, how come you guys didn't jump coasts sooner?

5) Bulldozer: 'Cause L.A. used to be run by a dozen stone-cold psychos called *The Pride.*

6) Bulldozer: This was *their* turf. Any mask who tried to make a play for a slice would get sent back to the Big Apple...piece by piece.

Page Four, Panel Three
Change angles again, as Excavator turns to talk with the grumpy, crowbar-wielding Wrecker.

7) Excavator: They in stir now, Mr. Wrecker?

8) Wrecker: No, they're not "in stir," you annoying piece of...

9) Wrecker: The Pride is *dead,* okay? They were betrayed by their spoiled children, in what should have been a valuable *lesson* to every hood who's got an "accident" or two out there.

Page Four, Panel Four
Change angles one last time, as Piledriver lovingly puts his arm around his son.

10) Piledriver: You got nothing to worry about with *my* boy, Wrecks. He's a chip off the old--

11) Someone's Voice (from off): Hey, Village People!

PAGE FIVE

Page Five, Panel One
Cut over to the street in front of the off-panel Wrecking Crew for this largest panel of the page, at least a half-SPLASH. It's a heroic shot of four of our Runaways: GERT, NICO, KAROLINA and MOLLY (lined up in that order, please). I'm sure we'll talk about our characters' new looks before we begin, but these girls should look confident and tough as hell here, Adrian! They don't have costumes, weapons, or even their dinosaur, but they still look ready to kick [redacted].

1) Gert: Step away from the minor.

2) Molly: Or else you're in for some *major...*

3) Molly (small, an aside): ...you know, bad stuff.

Page Five, Panel Two
Cut back to the Wrecking Crew, who are all staring at the off-panel Runaways. They look super-confused, except for the hard-headed Bulldozer, who's just smiling here.

4) Thunderball: The hell is this?

5) Bulldozer: I don't know, but I'll take a box of *Thin Mints.*

Page Five, Panel Three
Cut over to Nico and Karolina.

6) Nico: Listen, we don't care about whatever money you stole. We know the bank is insured.

7) Nico: Just give us the *kid,* and you can be on your way.

8) Karolina: Haven't you seen the news, Ricky? Your grandparents are worried *sick* about you.

PAGE SIX

Page Six, Panel One
Cut over to Piledriver and his son. Excavator is defiant, but his old man is looking back at his off-panel crewmates like a proud papa.

1) Excavator: My *grandparents?* Those stank old fogies can choke on their *dentures* for all I care. I'm running with my *dad* now.

2) Piledriver: Check it out, four ladies fighting over him already.

3) Piledriver: Told you he takes after his pops.

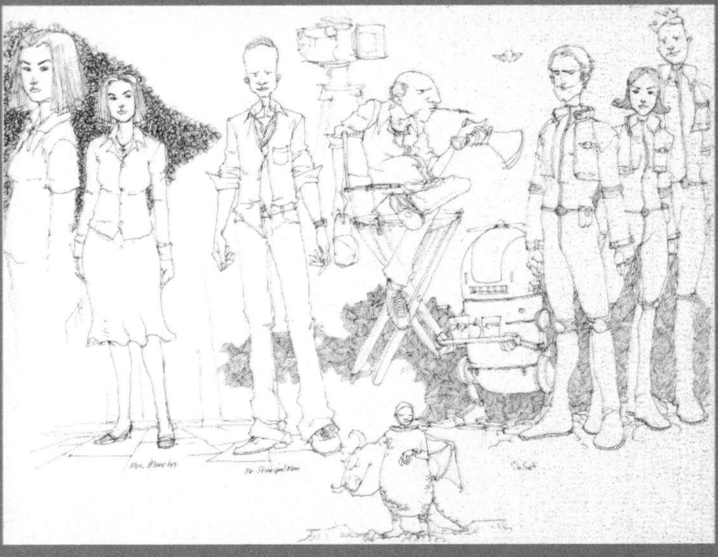

Page Six, Panel Two
    Cut back to a pissed-off Nico and Karolina, as Karolina RIPS off her own bracelet. She begins to GLOW with her alien power.

4) Nico: And that concludes the *negotiation* segment of our program.

5) Nico: Karolina?

6) Karolina: Plan B it is, boss.

Page Six, Panel Three
    Pull out to the largest panel of the page for a big group shot of all of our players, as a now-floating Karolina BLASTS Piledriver, knocking him backwards!

7) SFX: *KASCHOWW*

8) Excavator: DAD!

Page Six, Panel Four
    This is just a shot of the crowbar-wielding Wrecker, as he yells out an order.

9) Wrecker: They're *muties!*

10) Wrecker: Light 'em up!

PAGE SEVEN

Page Seven, Panel One
    Cut over to Karolina (still floating and firing at the off-panel Wrecking Crew) and Molly, who's beneath her, angrily punching one of her own hands in preparation for battle.

1) Karolina: Excuse me.

2) Karolina: I'm an *extraterrestrial...*and proud *of* it, thank you very much.

3) Molly: Besides, the word "mutie" is really offensive to people like me, you freakin' *racists*.

Page Seven, Panel Two
    Cut over to Excavator, who's running right at us. He has his enchanted shovel raised over his head.

4) Excavator: I'll *kill* you!

5) Excavator: I'll kill--

Page Seven, Panel Three
    Pull out to the largest panel of the page, as Excavator SWINGS the shovel into Molly's head. Molly doesn't even flinch at the magic tool SNAPS IN HALF across her little skull.

6) SFX: *KRACK*

Page Seven, Panel Four
    This is just a small close-up of the frowning Molly, her eyes GLOWING brightly here.

7) Molly: Too bad.

8) Molly: Our club coulda used another boy.

Page Seven, Panel Five
    Pull out to a bigger shot, as Molly PUNCHES Excavator in the gut, sending him FLYING down the street!

    No Copy *((KAAPOW!!))*

PAGE EIGHT

Page Eight, Panel One
    We're with Nico in the foreground of this shot, as she yells at the off-panel Molly. Behind him, Wrecker is approaching, with his crowbar at the ready.

1) Nico: Molly, go sit on him or something!

2) Nico: We'll finish off the grown-ups!

3) Wrecker: Sister, you just earned yourself a taste of the *big stick*.

Page Eight, Panel Two
    This is just a shot of Nico, as she turns to shoot us a scary look. Her hair is beginning to blow with mystical force.

4) Nico: Bet mine's bigger than yours.

Page Eight, Panel Three
        Pull out for another shot of Wrecker and Nico. A stunned Wrecker DROPS his crowbar as the GLOWING STAFF OF ONE begins *growing* out of a pained Nico's chest!

5) <u>Wrecker</u>: Ah, crap.

6) <u>Wrecker</u>: Not *witches*. I *hate*--

Page Eight, Panel Four
        Pull out to the largest panel of the page, as Nico aims her fully formed, glowing staff at Wrecker, who instantaneously BREAKS into a hundred different pieces! Adrian, this shouldn't be the least bit gory, it's more like a *picture* of Wrecker being torn into many little pieces. No blood or guts!

7) <u>Nico (creepy font)</u>: DECONSTRUCT.

8) <u>Wrecker</u>: *NOOOOO!*

PAGE NINE

Page Nine, Panel One
        Change angles, as a flying Karolina SWOOPS down next to the staff-wielding Nico, who's standing next to all of the pieces of Wrecker. Karolina looks concerned.

1) <u>Karolina</u>: Nico!

2) <u>Nico</u>: It's all right, Karolina. He'll come together in an hour or two...probably.

3) <u>Karolina</u>: But I thought you could only use the Staff of One after your *blood* was shed? And you never...

Page Nine, Panel Two
        This is just a small silent shot of Nico, as she looks over at the off-panel Karolina, and shoots her a knowing look.

        No Copy
Page Nine, Panel Three
        And this is just a small shot of the glowing Karolina, as she finally understands what's going on.

4) <u>Karolina (small, under her breath)</u>: Oh. Right.

5) <u>Karolina (small, under her breath)</u>: That time of the month...

6) <u>Another Voice (from off)</u>: ENOUGH!

Page Nine, Panel Four
        Cut over to Thunderball and Gert for this largest panel of the page. Thunderball is menacingly SWINGING his wrecking ball in a circle over his head, as he approaches a confident Gert, who's backing towards a nearby tree.

7) <u>Thunderball</u>: You girls stand down *posthaste*...or I smash your friend here into oblivion.

PAGE TEN

Page Ten, Panel One
        Push in closer on Gert and Thunderball. Thunderball suddenly looks a little concerned.

1) <u>Gert</u>: Bad idea, Mean Green.

2) <u>Gert</u>: I've got the power to make grown men lose control of their *bowels*.

3) <u>Thunderball</u>: Really...?

Page Ten, Panel Two
        Cut back to Gert for this largest panel of the page, as OLD LACE suddenly comes LEAPING out from behind the nearby tree. The velociraptor's mouth is wide open here, so she can show off her fangs.

4) <u>Gert</u>: More or less.

5) <u>SFX by Old Lace (not in a balloon, please!)</u>: *RAAAARRR*

Page Ten, Panel Three
        Change angles on the three. As Old Lace POUNCES on top of a fallen Thunderball, Gert just shakes her head.

6) <u>Thunderball</u>: AHHHHHH!

7) <u>Gert</u>: Why couldn't my 'rents have given you to me for my *bat mitzvah,* Old Lace? A telepathic velociraptor from the 87th Century would have made middle school a lot more tolerab--
Page Ten, Panel Four
        Push in close on Gert, as a FIST (belonging to Bulldozer) suddenly enters the frame and PUNCHES Gert in the face, knocking her glasses off!

8) <u>SFX</u>: *THWACK*

PAGE ELEVEN

Page Eleven, Panel One

Change angles to reveal that BULLDOZER is now standing over Gert, who's fallen on her [redacted]. She's reaching for her glasses here. Bulldozer is standing in the middle of the street, and we can't see anyone except for him and Gert in this shot.

1) <u>Bulldozer</u>: I got you all figured out, fatty.

2) <u>Bulldozer</u>: Wizards, gene freaks, *time travelers...*you're *The Pride's* kids, ain't you?

3) <u>Gert</u>: Wow, maybe your head isn't as dense as it *looks...*which is too bad, considering what's about to land on *top* of it.

Page Eleven, Panel Two

Push in for this tight shot of Bulldozer, who nervously looks up, as a DARK SHADOW suddenly falls over him.

4) <u>Bulldozer</u>: Huh?

Page Eleven, Panel Three

Pull out to the largest panel of the page, a three-quarter SPLASH, as the Runaways' LEAPFROG suddenly comes SMASHING down in the middle of the street, presumably squashing Bulldozer flat! The ship narrowly misses Gert, who protects her face with her arm as the ship loudly LANDS inches away from her.

5) <u>SFX</u>:

K
R
O
O
O
M

PAGE TWELVE

Page Twelve, Panel One

Cut into the control panels of the Leapfrog, as CHASE looks out at us! He's wearing racing gloves, and maybe some kind of new goggles resting on his forehead. We can talk about his new look, Adrian, whatever you like...

1) <u>Chase</u>: Sorry I'm late, baby!

2) <u>Chase</u>: I totally forgot to gas up the Leapfrog last night. Had to "borrow" ninety gallons of unleaded from the Circle A...

Page Twelve, Panel Two

Cut back down to the street for this shot of an excited Molly, who's now standing next to Gert (who's putting her glasses back on).

3) <u>Gert (small, an aside)</u>: We are the worst good guys of all time.

4) <u>Molly</u>: Chase!

5) <u>Molly</u>: Did you see who we got to beat up tonight? Their costumes were really pretty!

Page Twelve, Panel Three

Pull out to the largest panel of the page for this group shot. Chase is now walking down out of the opening mouth/ramp of the Leapfrog, as he approaches the assembled girls. A still-glowing Karolina looks pissed, but Gert (standing next to Old Lace) tries to calm her down. Nico is looking off in the direction of the off-panel Excavator. We can see POLICE CARS approaching in the distant background.

6) <u>Chase</u>: What did we talk about, Mol? Costumes are *gay*.

7) <u>Karolina</u>: Hey! I warned you, misuse that word one more time and--

8) <u>Gert</u>: Save it, Karolina. If we're not legs up in the next thirty seconds, the pigs are gonna send us back to *foster care.*

9) <u>Nico</u>: What about the boy, Gert? Are we really just going to let him get hauled off to *juvie?* I mean, he's in the same boat as us.

Page Twelve, Panel Four

This is just a small shot of Gert.

10) <u>Gert</u>: No, I'd say he went overboard the second he saw his father as someone to *look up* to.

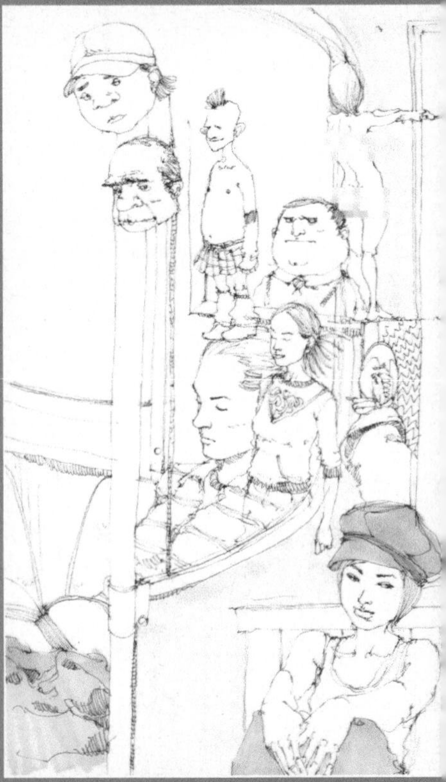

11) <u>Gert</u>: Let him go, Nico. No offense to your drearily departed boyfriend, but the last thing we need is another *Alex* to stab us in the back.

Page Twelve, Panel Five
    And this is just a silent shot of a somber Nico, still looking in the direction of the off-panel Excavator.

12) <u>Gert (from off)</u>: Face it, some kids are a *lost cause*...

PAGE THIRTEEN

Page Thirteen, Panel One
    Cut to later that night for this establishing shot of a little church in Los Angeles. In the foreground of this shot, we should *clearly* see one of those CHURCH SIGNS with movable letters that reads:

1) <u>Sign in Foreground</u>:
        Excelsior Meeting - 9:30
        Church Basement

Page Thirteen, Panel Two
    Cut into a dimly lit church basement for this largest panel of the page, a nice semi-SPLASH. We're behind a row of four people sitting in folding chairs, but we can't see their faces yet. We *can* see the two young people standing in front of them: MICKEY MUSASHI (the New Warrior's Turbo) and PHIL URICH (the former heroic Green Goblin). Mickey and Phil are both wearing cool, contemporary clothing. They're both about 22-years-old, so they should look older than our Runaways, but younger than regular Marvel heroes like Captain America. Phil is giving a little wave to everybody, as Mickey introduces herself. Please leave some room for their brief opening remarks:

2) <u>Mickey</u>: Right, so...as some of you already know, my name is Michiko Musashi, but pretty much everybody calls me *Mickey*.

3) <u>Mickey</u>: I moved here three months ago after I got a job with the Los Angeles Times, thanks to a recommendation from my good pal, Phil Urich.

4) <u>Phil</u>: Howdy. Mickey and I have been talking about starting a group like this for a while now, so we really appreciate you guys coming out to our first meeting.

5) <u>Phil</u>: We don't exactly have a budget or anything, so we're starting off small, but we hope to expand Excelsior into a *nationwide* outreach program someday soon.

Page Thirteen, Panel Three
    This is just a close-up of Mickey, as she makes this dramatic revelation:

6) <u>Mickey</u>: Like everyone here tonight, Phil and I are former teenage superheroes.

PAGE FOURTEEN

Page Fourteen, Panel One
    Change angles on Mickey, as she reveals her secret origin. Remember, this whole scene should be dark and shadowy, Adrian, eerily lit from above!

1) <u>Mickey</u>: From the time I was a sophomore in college up until a few months ago, I'd been living a double life as the New Warrior's *Turbo*.

2) <u>Mickey</u>: But late last year, I was fighting some Z-lister, and I had this...this *epiphany*. I realized that I could do more good with my *education* than I ever could with some hi-tech *costume*.That's when I decided to get back into investigative journalism.

Page Fourteen, Panel Two
    Change angles for this largest panel of the page, a shot of Mickey, as she turns her attention to one of the people seated in the first row (we can't see the others yet). This is CHRIS POWELL, the 19-year-old alter ego of Darkhawk (again, our esteemed editors will get you reference, Adrian!).

3) <u>Mickey</u>: Anyway, I'm obviously not the only one here with a story like that. Chris, why don't you keep it going?

4) <u>Chris</u>: Oh, uh, sure. My name's Chris Powell, and I'm...well, I *used* to be Darkhawk.

5) <u>Chris</u>: I found this *amulet* back when I was in high school, and it changed me into this...this *thing*. You know the drill.

Page Fourteen, Panel Three
    This is just a shot of Chris, as he hangs his head and nervously recounts how he got here.

6) <u>Chris</u>: I used the powers it gave me as a *vigilante* for a couple of years, which was cool and all, but I...

7) <u>Chris</u>: I started having these *nightmares*. Really intense ones. I mean, I was in New York when some pretty bad stuff went down, and I...I just had to get away.

Page Fourteen, Panel Four
		Change angles, as Phil Urich walks over and puts a hand on Chris' shoulder. Phil looks over at another one of the off-panel guests at this meeting.

8) <u>Chris</u>: I'm not cut out for seeing all the stuff I've seen, you know? I don't think *anyone* my age is. I'm sure I sound like a *coward*, but--

9) <u>Phil</u>: You're a brave guy, Chris. You always have been.

10) <u>Phil</u>: Julie, why don't you take the floor?

PAGE FIFTEEN

Page Fifteen, Panel One
		Cut over to another guest for this largest panel of the page, as a smiling JULIE POWER stands, like a teacher's pet addressing her speech class. Julie is the grown-up version of Lightspeed from Power Pack. She's about 18 years old here, so she should look older than the Runaways' girls, but younger than Mickey. She's wearing something sexy, but not too slutty. She looks like she could be a movie star.

1) <u>Julie</u>: *Ahem.* Thank you, Mr. Urich. Hi, everybody. I'm Julie Power. And yes, before you ask, that *is* my real name.

2) <u>Julie</u>: Actually, I've had *lots* of names over the years: Lightspeed, Starstreak, Molecula, Mistress of Density...

Page Fifteen, Panel Two
		Push in closer on Julie, as she suddenly gets more serious.

3) <u>Julie</u>: See, when I was just ten years old, my brothers and sister and I met someone from...well, from far away. Long story short, we became *Power Pack*.

4) <u>Julie</u>: When my siblings and I were fighting crime, I thought it was all just fun and games. I had no idea I was actually being robbed of a *normal childhood.*

Page Fifteen, Panel Three
		Pull out for this shot of Julie and Mickey, as Mickey politely interrupts her.

5) <u>Julie</u>: With the help of a lot of therapy, I'm trying to get some of that innocence *back.*

6) <u>Julie</u>: I've always loved fantasy and drama, so I'm living in Hollywood now, just taking auditions and looking for an agent. So, ah, if anyone wants to *network* after this...

7) <u>Mickey</u>: Thanks, Julie. You want to share, Johnny?

Page Fifteen, Panel Four
		Cut over to JOHNNY GALLO, the 19-year-old kid who used to be the Slingers' Ricochet. He looks like ▆▆ here, disheveled and depressed.

8) <u>Johnny</u>: I don't know, man. I...I feel totally outclassed here. I mean, you guys have probably never even *heard* of me.

9) <u>Johnny</u>: My team...my team didn't even have a *name.* We were just a bunch of Spider-Man wannabes. I used to be this guy called *Ricochet.*

Page Fifteen, Panel Five
		Change angles on poor ol' Johnny, as he continues talking:

10) <u>Johnny</u>: When my powers first materialized, I thought fulltime hero-ing was gonna be my *life.* And for a while, I guess it was. It was *awesome.*

11) <u>Johnny</u>: But before I knew it, it was *over.* I'd even *look* for crimes and stuff, but by the time I'd get to one, somebody like *Iron Fist* or *Moon Knight* was already taking care of it.

12) <u>Johnny</u>: I wasn't a superhero...I was *superfluous.*

PAGE SIXTEEN

Page Sixteen, Panel One
		Pull out to a larger panel, as Mickey and Phil try to console Johnny.

1) <u>Johnny</u>: And I really loved the spotlight, man. What kid wouldn't? But when you get so much, so young, so *fast*...nobody tells you how to deal when that spotlight inevitably shuts off, you know?

2) <u>Mickey</u>: Well, we founded Excelsior to help with *every* stage of your transition into adulthood and a healthy civilian life. Right, Phil?

3) <u>Phil</u>: Absolutely. I'd be lying if I said I didn't enjoy *my* time as the Green Goblin, but now I know what a dangerous message people like us were sending to impressionable young--

Page Sixteen, Panel Two
　　　　Cut over to CHAMBER, our last member of Excelsior, as he suddenly JUMPS to his feet and OPENS his bandages, exposing the GLOWING BIOKINETIC FIRE in his chest.

4) <u>Chamber (unique font)</u>: Hold the bleedin' phone!

5) <u>Chamber (unique font)</u>: This kid's the *Green Goblin?*

Page Sixteen, Panel Three
　　　　Pull out to the largest panel of the page for a big group shot, as Phil nervously backs away from the glowing Chamber. All of the other kids look scared, as Mickey tries to calm down Chamber.

6) <u>Phil</u>: Oh, I...I wasn't the *evil* Green Goblin. I just found one of his suits, and used the equipment to protect--

7) <u>Chamber (unique font)</u>: There was a *good* Green Goblin? That is the absolute *stupidest* thing I've ever heard!

8) <u>Mickey</u>: Jonothan, why don't you put your *blast furnace* away and introduce yourself to the nice--

Page Sixteen, Panel Four
　　　　This is just a shot of Chamber, as he begins resealing himself with the black wraps that hide the big glowing hole in his face and chest.

9) <u>Chamber (unique font)</u>: The name's *Jono,* luv. Or Chamber. Whichever strikes.

10) <u>Chamber (unique font)</u>: Right then, Reader's Digest: I'm a mutant, did some time as a soldier with the X-Men after I blew half me own face off. A group of sods called Weapon X patched me up, but I went and ripped a *new* hole in myself when some drunk in Fresno made me mad.

11) <u>Chamber (unique font)</u>: Anyway, just enduring this sob-fest for the free pizza I read about in the email.

PAGE SEVENTEEN

Page Seventeen, Panel One
　　　　Change angles for this shot of Julie, Johnny and Mickey. Julie and Johnny are staring at the off-panel Chamber, while Mickey pulls out her little CELL PHONE.

1) <u>Julie</u>: Pizza? I hope this isn't insensitive, Jono, but if you don't have a *mouth...?*

2) <u>Johnny</u>: Wait, you were part of the *X-Men?* As in, Professor *Xavier's* X-Men? They wouldn't even return my--

3) <u>SFX (from off)</u>: *DEET DEET DOO*

4) <u>Mickey</u>: If you guys could excuse me for a second, that's probably my *editor.*

Page Seventeen, Panel Two
　　　　Pull out to the largest panel of the page, as Mickey walks towards us, away from the talkative group in the background of this shot, and into the shadowy back of the church basement. She's talking on her phone now.

5) <u>Mickey</u>: Musashi here.

6) <u>Tailless (electronic)</u>: Way to go, girl. Your little group's a cool idea, very well executed.

Page Seventeen, Panel Three
　　　　Push in close on Mickey, who suddenly looks angry and a little sacred.

7) <u>Mickey</u>: Who *is* this? How'd you get this number?

8) <u>Tailless (electronic)</u>: Yeah, that's not really important right now, Mick.

9) <u>Tailless (electronic)</u>: What is important is that there are other people out there who need Excelsior's help. Not *former* heroes, but underage kids who are putting their necks on the line even as we--

Page Seventeen, Panel Four
　　　　Cut to an unknown location for this shot of A SHADOWY FIGURE. This is a male, but we can't tell who it is, or where he's at, Adrian!

10) <u>Tailless (electronic)</u>: I didn't start wearing a mask *yesterday,* pal. If you think I'm gonna start running *errands* for some mystery benefactor, you can kiss my--

11) <u>From Figure</u>: All I'm asking your team to do is help me find five runaways...

12) <u>From Figure</u>: ...and in exchange, I'll give your organization *one million dollars,* enough to reach out to every cape and cowl who's ever lived the life.

Page Seventeen, Panel Five
　　　　Finally, cut back to a quietly intrigued Mickey for this closing extreme close-up.

13) <u>Mickey</u>: Keep talking.

PAGE EIGHTEEN

Page Eighteen, Panel One
        Cut to later that night for this establishing shot of THE LA BREA TAR PITS (if you draw those elephants in the tar, they should clearly be FAKE).

1) Overlay in Upper Left-hand Corner:

The La Brea Tar Pits
10:01 pm *((Don't put time here))*

Page Eighteen, Panel Two
        Cut into the massive caves underneath the tar pits for a three-quarter SPLASH, our first look at THE HOSTEL II! The Leapfrog is parked here, and the kids are walking away from it, in this order from left to right: Molly, Karolina (no longer glowing), Gert (with Old Lace), Chase, Karolina, and Nico (no longer holding her staff). The kids can just be smallish figures in this torch-lit shot. They're walking underneath a GIANT FRAMED PORTRAIT of the twelve members of THE PRIDE, all in their villain costumes. Feel free to fill the lair with whatever other cool super-villain crap you wanna draw, Adrian!

2) <u>Molly</u>: I wish we had put our hideout under an *In & Out Burger*. I'm so sick of eating whatever junk my mom *pickled* down here before she...you know.

3) <u>Karolina</u>: Just be glad we have *someplace* for our new Hostel, Molly.

4) <u>Gert</u>: Yeah, if we hadn't found our parents' old *lair,* the five of us would still be cloaked on Venice Beach, sleeping in the same smelly ship.

5) <u>Chase</u>: With all these evil fruit loops to beat down, we're practically living inside the 'Frog, *anyway.* That Space Ghost-looking *Flag-Smasher* guy last week, *Typeface* the week before that...

6) <u>Nico</u>: Well, this is *our* fault, you know. We're the ones who created the power vacuum.

PAGE NINETEEN

Page Nineteen, Panel One
        Push in on Chase and Gert. As Chase makes a joke, Gert blushes and elbows him in the side playfully. In the background, we can see a disgusted Molly rolling her eyes.

1) <u>Chase</u>: Heh, "power vacuum." That should be Gert's new codename.

2) <u>Gert</u>: You're disgusting.

3) <u>Molly</u>: Can you two go back to hating each other, please? It made me barf in my mouth less.

Page Nineteen, Panel Two
        Cut over to Nico, looking deadly severe.

4) <u>Nico</u>: I'm *serious.* Us taking down The Pride was like the U.S. taking down *Saddam.* We got rid of a monster, but we didn't plan for what would happen *next.*

5) <u>Nico</u>: Our parents may have been awful people, but at least they maintained some kind of...of *order.*

Page Nineteen, Panel Three
        Change angles for this shot of Chase, Karolina and Nico. Chase is pointing at Gert's parents' TIME MACHINE, the gazebo-looking thing you drew during our first season, which is sitting dusty and broken in a corner of this crowded old lair. Karolina and Nico are berating Chase.

6) <u>Chase</u>: Hey, if you want your mommy and daddy back so bad, why don't you hop in the Yorkes' old *time machine* and rescue 'em from the past?

7) <u>Karolina</u>: Because she *doesn't* want them back, Chase.She's just saying we have a responsibility to clean up their *mess,* right, Nico?

8) <u>Nico</u>: And for the son of two mad *scientists,* you sure do have trouble comprehending the fact that Gert's parents' 4D-thing has been *busted* for--
Page Nineteen, Panel Four
        Pull out to the largest panel of the page for a big group shot. The kids all cover their eyes, as ANOTHER version of the Yorkes' time machine appears in the lair in a blinding flash of light! We can see a figure silhouetted inside this time machine, but we can't see who it is yet.

9) <u>SFX</u>: *FWASH*

PAGE TWENTY

Page Twenty, Panel One
        Cut over to this newly arrived time machine for a three-quarter SPLASH. Standing in the middle of this steamy contraption is a SUPER-HEROINE. She's about 35 years old, five-foot-six, raven-haired, busty, thin, and very, very attractive.

She's wearing a long cape, skirt, boots, and a tight corset-type top (her costume is torn and dirty in places, like she's just survived a terrible fight). As she steps into the low-hanging fog surrounding the bottom of this machine, she's clutching her stomach, which appears to be bleeding. (Though we need to be very subtle with this...maybe it blends in with her dark-colored outfit?)

1) <u>Heroine</u>: Please...please tell me what year this is...

Page Twenty, Panel Two
　　　　We're looking over the Heroine's shoulder in the foreground of this shot, over at an angry Gert and a confused Old Lace in the background.

2) <u>Heroine</u>: Oh...Karolina's still here...

3) <u>Heroine</u>: Must be *2005*...

4) <u>Gert</u>: Lady, you take another step, and my dinosaur will *end* you.

Page Twenty, Panel Three
　　　　This is just an extreme close-up of the Heroine, as she drops this bombshell:

5) <u>Heroine</u>: I seriously doubt that, Gertrude.

6) <u>Heroine</u>: Seeing how I'm *you*...

PAGE TWENTY-ONE

Page Twenty-one, Panel One
　　　　Pull out to the largest panel of the page for a big group shot, as the Heroine (still clutching her stomach) limps towards the stunned kids. The Heroine kindly strokes a friendly Old Lace's head, as the dino brushes up against her.

1) <u>Nico</u>: *What?*

2) <u>Gert</u>: She's *lying*. I wouldn't be caught *dead* in that get-up.

3) <u>Heroine</u>: Funny choice of words, kid...and you'll realize how much things can *change*...in about twenty years...when you start leading the *Avengers*...

Page Twenty-one, Panel Two
　　　　Change angles for this shot of Heroine and a wide-eyed Molly.

4) <u>Molly</u>: Gert's gonna be a *superhero?*

5) <u>Heroine</u>: It's not as fun as it sounds, Mol...

6) <u>Heroine</u>: She's going to be betrayed...by someone she's *stupid* enough to put on her team...

Page Twenty-one, Panel Three
　　　　Change angles for this shot of Heroine and Chase, as Chase rushes over to help hold up the injured woman.

7) <u>Heroine</u>: I barely escaped...with my life. He just *slaughtered* my Avengers...used my *files* to kill the others...

8) <u>Heroine</u>: Hisako and her X-Men, Daredevil, the Fantastic Fourteen...he murdered *all* of them...every hero on the planet...

9) <u>Chase</u>: *Who* did?

Page Twenty-one, Panel Four
　　　　This is just a close-up of Heroine, as she looks at the off-panel Chase and says:

10) <u>Heroine</u>: A supposed "champion" named *Victorious.* He's the most powerful man...on the *planet*...

11) <u>Heroine</u>: Please...you're the future's only *hope*...Iron Woman sacrificed her *life* to help power my one last trip...because I need you children...to *stop* him...

PAGE TWENTY-TWO

Page Twenty-two, Panel One
　　　　Change angles for this shot of Karolina and the Heroine, who's still being held up by Chase. Heroine is reaching for something in her belt here.

1) <u>Karolina</u>: Us?

2) <u>Karolina</u>: Ma'am, how are we supposed to stop something if the *grown-up* us's can't?

3) <u>Heroine</u>: You have to find Victorious when he was just a boy...before he becomes too strong...

Page Twenty-two, Panel Two
　　　　Push in on Heroine, as she holds up a torn-at-the-edges, slightly faded photo of VICTOR MANCHA, who looks exactly like he did at the beginning of this issue!

4) Heroine: His real name is *Victor Mancha.*

5) Heroine: He grew up...in Pasadena...

Page Twenty-two, Panel Three
        Pull out to a shot of Chase and the Heroine, as she begins to slump to the floor. Chase kneels with her, gently easing her to the ground in his arms.
6) Heroine: Don't trust him. He's not who he says he is...I knew only you guys would understand...

7) Heroine: His father...is a villain from your time..the greatest evil...in the *universe...*

8) Chase: What's that mean? Who's this guy the son of?

Page Twenty-two, Panel Four
        Push in closer on the two. Chase is cradling Older Gert much like Younger Gert cradled him when he "died" back in Issue #15. The Heroine lovingly looks up at Chase through half-shut eyes and breathes her last breath here.

9) Heroine (small, groggy): Sweet Chase...

10) Heroine (small, trailing off): In all those years… I never told you...how much I loved...*

PAGE TWENTY-THREE

Page Twenty-three, Panel One
        Pull out to a larger shot of Chase and the now-lifeless Heroine. He's still looking down at her.

        No Copy

Page Twenty-three, Panel Two
        Cut over to the other Runaways (and Old Lace). Karolina covers her mouth in horror. The others don't know what to say.

1) Chase (from off): She's dead.

Page Twenty-three, Panel Three
        Pull out to the largest panel of the page, as the girls begin to argue.

2) Molly: I'm...I'm really sorry, Gert.

3) Gert: That was *not* me! This is probably just another...another *lie* from our parents, one last *mind-freak* from the grave!

4) Karolina: But Old Lace seemed pretty sure--

Page Twenty-three, Panel Four
        Cut over to Nico, as she tries to take control of the situation.

5) Nico: *Quiet.* Let's think about this for a second.

6) Nico: What if this woman *was* telling the truth? Even if there really *is* someone out there who's gonna kill every hero on earth someday, what do we do about it *now?*

PAGE TWENTY-FOUR

Page Twenty-four, SPLASH
        Finally, we close on this dramatic SPLASH (with room at the *bottom* of this page for title and closing credits, please!). This is a somewhat high-angle downshot on Chase, still cradling the Heroine's lifeless body (she still has Victor's photo in her hands). We can now see that Chase has TEARS streaming down his face, as he looks up at us, and through angrily gritted teeth, says:

1) Chase: We find him...and we rip his damn heart out.

2) Title:
TRUE BELIEVERS

chapter one